CLOSER TO THE WIL. _____
ESSAYS ON CLARICE LISPECTOR

THE EUROPEAN HUMANITIES RESEARCH CENTRE

UNIVERSITY OF OXFORD

The European Humanities Research Centre of the University of Oxford organizes a range of academic activities, including conferences and workshops, and publishes scholarly works under its own imprint, LEGENDA. Within Oxford, the EHRC bridges, at the research level, the main Humanities faculties: Modern Languages, English, Modern History, Classics and Philosophy, Music and Theology. The Centre stimulates interdisciplinary research collaboration throughout these subject areas and provides an Oxford base for advanced researchers in the humanities.

The Centre's publications programme focuses on making available the results of advanced research in medieval and modern languages and related interdisciplinary areas. An Editorial Board, whose members are drawn from across the British university system, covers the principal European languages. Titles currently include works on Arabic, Catalan, Chinese, English, French, German, Italian, Portuguese, Russian, Spanish and Yiddish literature. In addition, the EHRC co-publishes with the Society for French Studies, the Modern Humanities Research Association and the British Comparative Literature Association. The Centre also publishes a Special Lecture Series under the LEGENDA imprint, and a journal, *Oxford German Studies*.

Enquiries about the Centre's publishing activities should be addressed to:
Professor Ritchie Robertson, Co-Director (Publications)

Further information:
Kareni Bannister, Senior Publications Officer
European Humanities Research Centre
University of Oxford
47 Wellington Square, Oxford OX1 2JF
enquiries@ehrc.ox.ac.uk
www.ehrc.ox.ac.uk

LEGENDA

<small>European Humanities Research Centre</small>

University of Oxford

Clarice Lispector in the 1970s
Photograph © Olga Borelli

Closer to the Wild Heart
Essays on Clarice Lispector

EDITED BY

CLÁUDIA PAZOS ALONSO AND CLAIRE WILLIAMS

LEGENDA

European Humanities Research Centre
University of Oxford
2002

Published by the
European Humanities Research Centre
of the University of Oxford
47 Wellington Square
Oxford OX1 2JF

LEGENDA is the publications imprint of the
European Humanities Research Centre

ISBN 1 900755 62 9

First published 2002

British Library Cataloguing in Publication Data
A CIP catalogue record for this book is available from the British Library

LEGENDA series designed by Cox Design Partnership, Witney, Oxon
Printed in Great Britain by
Information Press
Eynsham
Oxford OX8 1JJ

Copy-editor: Dr Jeffrey Dean

CONTENTS

ACKNOWLEDGEMENTS

In the process of putting this volume together, we have become indebted to many institutions, colleagues, family and friends. First and foremost, we wish to signal our debt of gratitude to Professor T. F. Earle. As one of the organizers of a one-day conference on Clarice Lispector held at the University of Oxford in November 2000 he accompanied this project from the beginning, and was most generous with his advice concerning matters of scholarly presentation while the volume came into being. We are most grateful to all our contributors for their collaboration and sharing of ideas, especially to those whose articles we commissioned from further afield.

We should like to acknowledge the valuable financial support of the Centre for Brazilian Studies at Oxford, as well as the constant encouragement that its director, Professor Leslie Bethell, gave to the project from the outset. The Faculty of Modern Languages and Wadham College both granted Cláudia permission to take a term's sabbatical leave. In addition, the Faculty's financial support enabled us to enlist the help of a research assistant, Sara Brandellero, in the final stages of preparation. Our special thanks go to her.

In Brazil, we wish to express our gratitude to Paulo Gurgel Valente for facilitating copyright permission, to Cecília and Patrícia Oliveira, to Denise Parana and the Silveira da Silva family. Closer to home, we should like to convey our heartfelt thanks to our respective families, who have given us so much over the years. To the memory of Q. V. Williams, Claire's late grandmother, who died in the same year as Clarice Lispector, and to Cláudia's sons, Alexander and Miguel, who have greatly helped to keep everything in perspective, we dedicate this volume.

NOTES ON CONTRIBUTORS

Nádia Battella Gotlib is Professor of Comparative Literature at the University of São Paulo (Brazil). Her single-authored books include *O estrangeiro definitivo* (Lisbon: Imprensa Nacional; Casa da Moeda, 1985), *Teoria do conto* (São Paulo: Ática, 1985), *Clarice: Uma vida que se conta* (São Paulo: Ática, 1995), *Tarsila do Amaral, a modernista* (São Paulo: Editora SENAC São Paulo, 1998). She is co-editor, with Walnice Nogueira Galvão, of *Prezado Senhor, Prezada Senhora: Estudos sobre cartas* (São Paulo: Companhia das Letras, 2000).

Anna Klobucka is Associate Professor of Portuguese at the University of Massachusetts, Dartmouth. She received an MA in Iberian Studies from the University of Warsaw and a Ph.D. in Romance Languages and Literatures from Harvard. She is co-editor of *After the Revolution: Twenty Years of Portuguese Literature, 1974–94* (Lewisburg, PA: Bucknell University Press, 1997) and author of *The Portuguese Nun: Formation of a National Myth* (Lewisburg: Bucknell, 2000). She has also published articles on twentieth-century Portuguese and Brazilian women writers and on the theory and practice of feminist criticism in the context of Luso-Brazilian literature and culture.

Luiza Lobo is Professor of Comparative Literature and Theory of Literature at the Federal University of Rio de Janeiro. Her critical works include *Teorias poéticas do Romantismo* (1987), *O haikai e a crise da metafísica* (Rio de Janeiro: Numen, 1992) and *Crítica sem juízo* (Rio de Janeiro: Francisco Alves, 1993). Her latest collections of short stories are *Sexameron* (Rio de Janeiro: Relume Dumará, 1997) and *Estranha aparição* (Rio de Janeiro: Rocco, 2000), and she has translated Virginia Woolf, Katherine Mansfield, Robert Burns and Edgar Allan Poe. Her integrated project on literature and culture (www.letras.ufrj.br/litcult) has the support of Brazil's National Council for Research.

Paulo de Medeiros studied Law at the University of Lisbon and went on to read for a BA in Political Science at the University of Massachusetts,

Boston, where he also took an MA in English. He was awarded a Ph.D. in Comparative Literature from the University of Massachusetts, Amherst. Since 1998 he has held the Chair of Portuguese Studies at the University of Utrecht in the Netherlands. He has published on literary theory, comparative literature and contemporary Portuguese authors. In 1996 he edited a special issue of the Portuguese journal *Discursos* on the subject of literature and nationalism and is currently working on a book provisonally entitled 'Haunting the Nation'.

Teresa Montero was recently awarded the doctorate in Literary Studies from the Pontifícia Universidade Católica in Rio de Janeiro. Her doctoral thesis, 'Yes, nós temos Clarice: A divulgação da obra de Clarice Lispector nos Estados Unidos', of which the article included in this volume is a part, deals with the dissemination and reception of Lispector's work in the United States. Her Master's thesis from the same university is a biography of Lispector, published as *Eu sou uma pergunta: Uma biografia de Clarice Lispector* (Rio de Janeiro: Rocco, 1999). An actress and writer, she is currently writing a play based on the world of Gil Vicente, 'Entre o céu e o inferno', in collaboration with the actress and director Cristina Pereira.

William Paulson is Professor of French at the University of Michigan, Ann Arbor. He has published extensively on eighteenth- and nine-teenth-century French literature, but his recent work focuses on the connections between literary studies and science, technology, and media. His current interests also include comparative Romance Studies and the contemporary novel. He is the author of *The Noise of Culture: Literary Texts in a World of Information* (Ithaca, NY: Cornell University Press, 1988) and *Literary Culture in a World Transformed: A Future for the Humanities* (Ithaca: Cornell, 2001).

Cláudia Pazos Alonso is a Senior Research Fellow in Portuguese and Brazilian Studies at Wadham College, University of Oxford. She is the author of *Imagens do eu na poesia de Florbela Espanca* (Lisbon: Imprensa Nacional Casa da Moeda, 1997). She has published in the area of Portuguese and Brazilian women's writing and images of women, and is the editor of *Women and Culture in the Portuguese-Speaking World* (Lampeter: Edwin Mellen, 1996) and *In Other Words/ Por outras palavras*, a special issue of the journal *Portuguese Literary and Cultural Studies*, devoted to Lídia Jorge (1999).

Marta Peixoto is Associate Professor of Brazilian Literature at New York University. She has published two books, *Poesia com coisas: Uma leitura de João Cabral de Melo Neto* (São Paulo: Perspectiva, 1983) and *Passionate Fictions: Gender, Narrative, and Violence in Clarice Lispector* (Minneapolis: University of Minnesota Press, 1994), as well as several essays on twentieth-century writers. She is now writing a book on the urban spaces of Rio de Janeiro in Brazilian literature at different historical times.

Carlos Mendes de Sousa is Professor of Brazilian Literature at the University of Minho. He has published many essays, especially in the area of contemporary poetry and is the author of *O nascimento da música: a metáfora em Eugénio de Andrade* (Coimbra: Livraria Almedina, 1992) and *Clarice Lispector. Figuras da Escrita* (Braga: Universidade do Minho, Centro de Estudos Humanísticos, 2001). He is joint editor of *Relâmpago,* a Portuguese journal devoted to poetry.

Lúcia Villares is a writer, translator and researcher. She has published poetry, children's fiction and critical reviews in Brazil. Her article 'Ana Cristina Cesar and Adélia Prado, Two Women Poets of the 1970s Brazil' was published in the journal *Portuguese Studies* in 1997. The Lispector essay featured in this volume constitutes the initial part of her Ph.D. research, which aims to study gender, ethnicity and national identities by comparing Clarice Lispector with two women writers from different national and ethnic backgrounds: the African-American Toni Morrison and the South African Bessie Head.

Claire Williams lectures in Portuguese Language, Literature, History and Culture at the University of Liverpool, where she is assistant editor of the *Bulletin of Hispanic Studies.* Her doctoral research at the University of Cambridge focused on the figure of the encounter in the works of Clarice Lispector (*Coming to Terms with the Other: The Encounter Between Opposites in the Work of Clarice Lispector,* Bristol: HiPLAM, forthcoming in 2002). Among her publications are articles on virtual orality, avant-garde narrative and women's writing in Portuguese and Brazilian literature.

Patricia Zecevic is a Lecturer in the University of Glasgow's School of Modern Languages where, as a member of the Centre for Inter-cultural Studies, she teaches German, Spanish and Portuguese. She is author of *The Speaking Divine Woman* (Oxford and New York: Peter

Lang, 2000), a comparative study of the kabbalistic–hermetic tradition, analysed in terms of modern feminist thought, in two major works of the German and Golden-Age Spanish novelistic tradition. Her work is focused mainly in the area of German–Spanish and German–Brazilian cultural relations, and she has a particular interest in the work of Clarice Lispector.

INTRODUCTION

Getting to the Heart of the Matter

Clarice Lispector is undoubtedly one of Latin America's most celebrated writers, as an ever increasing number of readers, drawn from academic circles and everyday contexts alike, can enthusiastically attest. Although only twenty-five years have elapsed since her death, she is studied across several continents, not only by scholars of literature, who have compared her to an impressive list of other fellow writers ranging from James Joyce to the more contemporary Toni Morrison, but also by philosophers, psychologists, social scientists and feminist theorists. As the present collection of essays bears witness, her dense texts certainly lend themselves to approaches from many different angles. Indeed, Lispector's kaleidoscopic inventiveness, which questions what is frequently taken for granted by deliberately privileging events, thoughts and reactions that are usually unnoticed or apparently innocuous, enables readers to experience life in a radical new way as she persuades them to actively participate in the text. For instance, in *A hora da estrela* (1977), the last novel published during her lifetime and arguably her best known work, Lispector offers her readers the choice of thirteen alternative titles including her own reproduced signature. Needless to say, each potential title casts a slightly different light and encourages a slightly different reading of the text in question.

Lispector changed the course of Brazilian literature forever. Her enigmatic texts stood out amidst those of her contemporaries, fore-grounding a previously unknown kind of subjectivity, pulsing with impressions: a female consciousness, sensitive to ambiguities and fluctuations in the feelings of others, to beauty and cruelty in the most unexpected places, to poverty and injustice. She wrote Portuguese as if it were a different language, leading many critics to the unfounded assumption that she did so because of her foreign roots. Quite aside from breaking with conventional syntactical and grammatical norms, she eschewed a linear chronological time-structure, right from her remarkable début novel *Perto do coração selvagem* (1944). She opted instead to sail closer to a stream-of-consciousness technique, as she instinctively sought to unveil new modes of apprehending language and reality.

During the author's own lifetime, the most popular critical interpretations included the philosophical (as her work seemingly invited superficial comparisons with French Existentialist philosophy), the comparative (especially with English Modernism and Hispanic South American writers) and the lyrical (focusing on her subjective, almost poetic use of language and stream of consciousness). Following her death from cancer in 1977, not only was Lispector's work intro-duced to a much wider audience throughout the 1980s and '90s (primarily owing to the influence of French feminist theorist Hélène Cixous) when nearly all her works were translated into major European languages such as French and English, but also fresh critical approaches emerged as feminist and post-structuralist readings afforded illuminating new perspectives on her writings. The most recent trends in Lispector criticism have shown a tendency to diversify away from her outstanding fictional production, to discussions of her journalism, Lispector as reader (including her translations into Portuguese), her paintings and portraits of her, film and stage adaptations of her works, and the complex relationships between the writer and her readers. Several of these trends are represented in the current volume.

Brazilian readers have marked the years since Lispector's death with special commemorative editions of journals and newspapers. Further-more, during the 1990s, two biographies penned by the Brazilian scholars Nádia Battella Gotlib and Teresa Montero were published. The interest that Lispector has elicited in Brazil over the years culminated when, under the auspices of the eminent critic and novelist Silviano Santiago, all her works were re-edited in 1997–8 by the Rocco publishing house, who had acquired the rights from another Rio-based publisher, Francisco Alves. In contrast, scanda-lously few book-length studies of the author and her works exist so far in English, restricting the access of the overwhelming majority of research articles and monographs to scholars with a reading knowledge of Portuguese. The exceptions to this rule are Earl Fitz's thorough introduction to the writer, *Clarice Lispector* (Boston: Twayne, 1985), as well as his latest work about her, *Sexuality and Being in the Poststructuralist Universe of Clarice Lispector* (Austin: University of Texas

Press, 2001); Marta Peixoto, *Passionate Fictions* (Minneapolis: Minnesota University Press, 1994), focusing on aspects of gender and violence and questioning Hélène Cixous's rhapsodic appreciation and appropriation of Lispector; and Maria José Barbosa, *Spinning the Webs of Passion* (New Orleans: University Press of the South, 1997), which examines feminist and post-structuralist elements of the Brazilian writer's oeuvre. One of the main aims of the present collection of essays, therefore, was to redress this glaring imbalance, by offering a wide range of challenging, up-to-date readings of this celebrated Brazilian writer to an English-reading public.

The present volume is divided into three parts in an attempt to bring out the thematic links that connect several of the essays together, although, needless to say, further thematic affinities between essays placed in separate sections here might also be pursued fruitfully. The opening section includes four pieces primarily concerned with the notion of identity formation, focusing on the autobiographical writing self, before moving on to consider the impact of 'identity markers' such as names, gender, social class and relationships on the process of self-discovery, enabling the imagining of a potentially less conventionally predicated self.

Lispector herself provocatively stated 'Vai ser muito difícil escrever a minha biografia. [...] Depois que eu morrer, pouco me interesserão as opiniões que tiveram a meu respeito: morrerei livre' [It is going to be exceedingly difficult to write my biography. After I die, I shall take precious little interest in the opinions people might have about me: I shall die free].[1] Her first biographer, Nádia Gotlib, has spoken of the feeling that the writer intentionally impeded the discovery of anything too close to the bone. Likewise, the title of Teresa Montero's biography, *Eu sou uma pergunta* (Rio de Janeiro: Rocco, 1999), vividly captures Lispector's deliberate construction of a sphinx-like persona. The sense of Lispector being (a) strange(r) is one of the aspects dealt with by Carlos Mendes de Sousa in his penetrating study of three of the milestones that marked Lispector's life and work: her 'foreign' status, the early death of her mother and her scarred right hand. Anna Klobucka explores the autobiographical nature of Lispector's pieces written for a newspaper column and the way in which she skilfully constructed a writing self, who simultaneously revealed herself and hid behind her writing mask. Later essays in the collection (particularly Lobo's and Gotlib's) take up this issue again, questioning the extent to which Lispector's newspaper columns, insofar as they

expose her intense emotions and feelings of pain, rejection, self-consciousness and loneliness, might give us access to the writer's un-
mediated self.

Yet, in the same way that attempts to pigeon-hole this elusive
writer into fixed categories are bound to fail, Claire Williams discusses
how Lispector throughout her works uses names and naming—and,
most tellingly, anonymity too—as a means to alert us to convergences
and divergences between the socially-assigned identity of various
characters on the one hand and the potential intrinsic freedom of their
inner self on the other. Following on from this, Patricia Zecevic draws
our attention to the discrepancies between the socially stable position
of Lóri, the perturbed protagonist of *Uma aprendizagem ou o livro dos
prazeres* (1969), and her transforming spiritual inner quest. Indeed, the
urge felt by many characters to go beyond their conventional social
(and gendered) roles is a thread that equally runs through the second
part of the volume in connection with two of Lispector's most famous
texts, *Laços de família* (1960) and *A paixão segundo G.H.* (1964), as well
as the newspaper chronicles.

Simultaneously, however, the five pieces included in the middle
section more clearly 'home in' on some of the social issues that
Lispector addressed explicitly or implicitly within her works. The
author has been criticized in the past for her extensive focus on
middle-class city-dwelling women. As these five essays show, however,
her awareness of the struggles faced by Brazilian women in search of
self-assertion was matched by an unusually acute sensitivity to the
plight of the urban and rural poor and marginalized. Cláudia Pazos
Alonso reflects on the structural patterns and recurrent images and
motifs in the short story collection *Laços de família* to suggest that
patriarchal modes of apprehending reality are perceived as inadequate
by the majority of the protagonists within the stories. Instead,
alternative, usually female subjectivities, not least of all that of the
black 'smallest woman in the world', are provocatively foregrounded
and revalued. In a similar vein, Luiza Lobo's detailed discussion of
Lispector's *crônicas* relates their unique innovative style specifically to
the adoption of a female gaze and consciousness, signalling their deconstructive significance in relation to the more traditional chronicle
genre as practised by Machado de Assis (and, one might add, José de
Alencar, as Klobucka's earlier essay makes clear).

Marta Peixoto's article, also partly dealing with the chronicles,
complements Lobo's contribution by broadening the social focus. As

Peixoto incisively points out, given the grave social inequalities that have been a distinctive feature of the Brazilian nation, it would have been almost impossible for Lispector to ignore the tensions, the ambiguities and the destabilizing power inherent to one of the most complex relationships routinely experienced between Brazilian women of differing social classes, that between mistress and maid. Lúcia Villares's essay then adds a further dimension to Lispector's interrogations of social and gendered identities by dwelling on the importance of race, as she explores the symbolic functions of the black maid and the 'mulatta' cockroach as figures that 'haunt' the white middle-class protagonist of the seminal *A paixão segundo G.H.* (1964). In articulation with Villares's essay, Paulo de Medeiros's study examines Lispector's deconstructive approach to gender and genre, as he considers 'foundational fictions' and symbols of the Brazilian nation to provide a daring, yet compelling rereading of *A hora da estrela*, as Lispector's response to (and obliteration of) José de Alencar's master-narrative *Iracema* (1865).

In the final part of this collection, the focus shifts away from the texts and their creator to explore the multiplicity of critical receptions that Lispector's works have elicited. Teresa Montero charts Lispector's critical fortune in North America in a closely-researched article that accounts for the growing awareness of her work in the States in the 1960s and '70s. Nádia Gotlib's essay then discusses the intricate relationship between the writer and her fascinated reading public, suggesting that Lispector's texts, be they journalistic or fictional, hinge on a highly seductive but manipulative relationship, which constantly re-enacts the cannibalistic ritual experienced in *A paixão segundo G.H.* with the aim of undoing readers' previously secure sense of identity. In that connection, Gotlib analyses the haunting TV interview that Lispector gave months before her death. Lispector's parting words are worth quoting here: 'Por enquanto eu estou morta. Estou falando de meu túmulo' [For the moment, I am dead. I am speaking from my grave],[2] words that imply her own awareness of her power to throw off balance and 'upset' her readers, not unlike the black maid in *A paixão* according to Lúcia Villares' reading of that novel. Following on from this, William Paulson, in the final essay of the collection, speculates on the fate of a text once it leaves the mind of the author and becomes a public artefact, as he considers the emphasis on the 'non-modern' that recurs in Lispector's works, with particular reference to *A paixão segundo G.H.* in the light of 'science studies'— a fascinating and unusual perspective on her works.

There is no doubt that Lispector enjoyed cultivating an esoteric aura, while she simultaneously sought to project a more reassuringly 'familiar' image in her journalistic works. Her varied output and eclectic interests, combined with her repeated blurring of the frontiers between life and fiction and her stretching of the boundaries of genre and gender will ensure that for years to come she and her texts will remain 'a question', and almost certainly one without an answer. This notwithstanding, we hope to have done justice to her memory, by offering fresh critical perspectives on some of her most well-known texts, while also drawing attention to little-known or even un-published material. In the process, we hope to have come a little closer to the wild heart of Clarice.

Last but not least, since one of the main aims of this volume was to make Lispector's works more accessible to an English-speaking audience, an English translation follows all quotations in Portuguese, or is given in the notes. English renditions of Lispector's works are based on published translations (listed in the Bibliography), but these were modified by the contributors and editors whenever necessary (most notably in the chapters providing close textual analyses). Where no English version was available (for Lispector's novels *Um sopro de vida* and *O lustre*, unpublished fragments from the Lispector archives, or works by other authors), the translations are by the contributors and editors. Claire Williams translated the chapters by Carlos Mendes de Sousa, Nádia Battella Gotlib and Teresa Montero with assistance from the authors.

Notes to the Introduction

1. Unpublished text, in the archives at the Fundação Casa de Rui Barbosa in Rio de Janeiro, catalogued as CL/pi 13.
2. These are the last words uttered by Clarice during her interview with Júlio Lerner for the TV programme 'Panorama Especial', recorded in the studios of TV Cultura, São Paulo, in February 1977. A transcript was published with an introductory text by Lerner as 'A última entrevista de Clarice Lispector', *Shalom* 296 (1992), 62–9. The interview also appears (in French) in Claire Varin, *Clarice Lispector: Rencontres Brésiliennes* (Québec: Trois, 1987).

PART I

Autobiography and Identity

CHAPTER 1

Mother, Body, Writing:
The Origins and Identity of
Literature in Clarice Lispector

Carlos Mendes de Sousa

During a visit to Belo Horizonte in 1941, the young Clarice wrote a letter to her friend, the writer Lúcio Cardoso. At the time, she had not yet made her debut on the literary stage as such, despite having published some of her short stories in a few newspapers. But her letter already hints at an overwhelming, if faintly perceptible and still barely expressed desire (the 'estado potencial' [potential state] it mentions), which allows us to glimpse her burning quest for literature:

Encontrei uma turma de colegas da Faculdade em excursão universitária. Meu exílio se tornará mais suave, espero. Sabe, Lúcio, toda a efervescência que eu causei só veio me dar uma vontade enorme de provar a mim e aos outros que eu sou mais do que uma mulher. Eu sei que você não o crê. Mas eu também não o acreditava, julgando o q. tenho feito até hoje. É que eu não sou senão em estado potencial, sentindo que há em mim água fresca, mas sem descobrir onde é a sua fonte.
O.K. Basta de tolices. Tudo isso é muito engraçado. Só que eu não esperava rir da vida. Como boa eslava, eu era uma jovem séria, disposta a chorar pela humanidade... (Estou rindo).[1]

Particularly revealing in this context is the reference to exile, fleeting because reduced to its figurative sense, but which will come to play a determining role in any reading of the writer's career. Equally noteworthy is the self-denomination which harks back to her origins ('Como boa eslava, eu [...]' [Like a good Slav, I ...]) and which, even with the irony intended here, cannot help but point towards literary models (one thinks immediately of Dostoevsky, a decisive literary reference for the young Lispector). It will not be easy to find a reference to the self of this kind again in her work.

Clarice had just reached the age of legal majority when, in early 1942, she put in a claim for naturalization, a drawn-out process that caused her great anxiety about the outcome of the President of the Republic's decision. In her first letter to Getúlio Vargas requesting the reduction of the waiting period under a legal technicality, she asserted that she was 'casualmente, russa também' [Russian too, by chance] and concluded by stating: 'um dia saberei provar que não a usei [a nacionalidade] inutilmente' [one day I will be able to prove that I did not use my nationality in vain].[2] In fact, from the moment that she became aware of her participation in the literary world, she was to defend her sense of belonging to the Brazilian nation, in spite of asserting herself in contrast to the dominant nationalist tendencies. Leaving the country at a time crucial to the construction of her name as a writer—straight after the publication of her first book—had serious repercussions for someone who for many years was only able to receive echoes of the critics' impressions of her work from a distance and with a time lag. We must not forget that the writing of her third book, *A cidade sitiada* [The Beseiged City] (1949), in Berne seems to a large extent to have been motivated by the silence that had greeted her second novel, *O lustre* [The Chandelier] (1946).

But the most important thing is to show that this feeling of exile was, came to be or always had been, above all, interior and not determined by any kind of geographical dislocation. The unknown land lies within ourselves. From Belém do Pará, where Lispector lived for a few months before going abroad, she wrote to her sisters: 'Que contar a vocês, quando o que eu desejo é ouvir? A vida é igual em toda a parte e o que é necessário é a gente ser gente' [What can I tell you, when what I want to do is listen? Life is the same everywhere and what matters is for us to be who we are] (18 March 1944).[3]

And at the beginning of the journey which was to take her to Europe, accompanying her diplomat husband, she sent these words (dated 19 August 1944) from Algeria:

Na verdade eu não sei escrever cartas sobre viagens, na verdade nem sei mesmo viajar. É engraçado como, ficando pouco em lugares, eu mal vejo. Acho a natureza toda mais ou menos parecida, as coisas quase iguais. Eu conhecia melhor um árabe com véu no rosto quando estava no Rio. Enfim, eu espero nunca exigir de mim nenhuma atitude. Isso me cansaria.[4]

When she returned to Brazil in the early 1960s after separating from her husband, she continued to pursue her voyage of self-discovery through a scrutiny of her inner self. The best example of this can be found in the way Clarice foregrounds the theme of exile precisely in the period that began with her settling back in Rio. This coincided with the maturation of her prose in the novel *A paixão segundo G.H.* (1964), but the text which best reflects this transitional phase is *Uma aprendizagem ou o livro dos prazeres* (1969).

The appearance of the later novel is intimately associated with an event that took place in the biographical sphere, which it is crucial to introduce here: an accident. On 14 September 1966, around half past three in the morning, a fire broke out in her apartment. Lispector fell asleep with a lighted cigarette and woke up amid flames.[5] The consequences of this incident were to be far-reaching, as can be seen from the fact that it even occasioned the need for a literal relearning to write, given that the part of her body that was most affected was her right hand, which suffered third-degree burns.[6] In Diane Marting's bio-bibliography of Lispector, the text that introduces the section dealing with *Uma aprendizagem* (written by Marting herself) starts by pointing out, right at the beginning, that the novel was written straight after the accident in which the novelist's arms and legs were seriously burned. Marting suggests that maybe the idea of a love story had occurred to Lispector because her body had, in a sense, 'betrayed' her, and had forced her to endure a long period of convalescence, 'during which she may have longed for dialogue'.[7] Nevertheless, another extremely important fact to note is that in August 1967, almost a year after the fire, Clarice began writing a column in the pages of the *Jornal do Brasil*, a practice that was to influence the composition of the 1969 book as well as those which followed it. Indeed, from then on, we can identify, to some degree, superficially at least, some relaxing of thematic and stylistic tensions, underscoring a new attitude towards the act of writing. In other words, we cannot help but associate the accident with a complex process of change in writing direction.

Scarcely had *Uma aprendizagem ou o livro dos prazeres* been published than a trend became apparent among its first critics, that of identifying the characters with the author herself. In an article in the *Correio do Povo* on 27 July 1969, Paulo Hecker Filho presented the novel in the following terms: 'Uma mulher [...] chamada Lóri mas que é a própria Clarice, namora um Ulisses que continua a própria Clarice travestida em professor universitário. Lóri–Clarice descreve o que sente durante o que seria essa aprendizagem do amor, embora desde o início ela seja magistral no assunto' [A woman, called Lóri but who is actually Clarice, falls in love with Ulysses, who is also a continuation of Clarice but this time in drag, in the character of a university professor. Lóri–Clarice describes what she feels during what could be called this apprenticeship in love, although from the outset she is already a specialist in the field].

Because the novel came out when it did, it was inevitably a target for certain queries based on games of identification, which, when read in the light of the real-life incident, the text encouraged. A question arises here: can we detect in Clarice's writing a deliberate intention to distract the reader, to divert her/him away from interpretations that are overreliant on the biographical facts, which would enable her/him to read the text as a reflection of that painful time? Yet, on the other hand (and most probably the author did exploit this effect), how can we help but read the novel through the biographical lens, considering the euphoric vision that convalescence brings about? The book would then act as the result (and the banner) of overcoming a crisis.

The importance of the accident should therefore be stressed because of the extremely violent impact it had on Clarice's life and because of the way that its consequences left a mark on her work. This impact can be seen through the prism of identification between and inter-changeability of body and writing. Through metonymic contiguity, from the image of the wounded hand and body, we are led to the metaphor of the writing-body in its infinite capacity for regeneration.

One year later, the author began to verbalize what had happened to her in interviews or in her usual column in the *Jornal do Brasil*, which continued to appear throughout the time of the accident and recuperation. For example, in the *crônica* published on 13 July 1968, entitled 'A opinião de um analista sobre mim' [A psychoanalyst's opinion of me],[8] she related the following story: several of her friends happened to be seeing the same analyst, to whom they spoke about Clarice. To compensate for the 'desgaste dos ouvidos do analista' [wear and tear on the analyst's ears] caused by hearing her name repeated over and over, Clarice sent him a book: 'Na dedicatória pedi desculpas pela minha letra que não está boa desde que minha mão direita sofreu o incêndio' [In the dedication I apologized for my handwriting, which isn't very clear ever since I burned my right hand in a fire]. The analyst commented that Clarice gave so much to others and yet begs to be allowed to exist. The short text ends with a declaration that is a prayer, an act of grace and a way of life: 'Peço humildemente para existir, imploro humildemente uma alegria, uma ação de graça, peço que me permitam viver com menos sofrimento, peço para não ser experimentada pelas experiências ásperas, peço a homens e mulheres que me considerem um ser humano digno de algum amor e de algum respeito. Peço a bênção da vida.' [I humbly ask to be allowed to exist, I humbly implore happiness, an act of grace; I ask to be allowed to live with less suffering, I ask not to have so many cruel experiences tested on me, I ask both men and women to think of me as a human being worthy of some love and respect. I ask for life's blessing.]

Such a discourse replete with anaphoras leads us close to the register used in many of the fragments incorporated in *Uma aprendizagem*, which reflect this attitude of gratitude:

Ajoelhou-se trêmula junto da cama pois era assim que se rezava e disse baixo, severo, triste, gaguejando sua prece com um pouco de pudor: alivia a minha alma, faze com que eu sinta que Tua mão está dada à minha, faze com que eu sinta que a morte não existe porque na verdade já estamos na eternidade, faze com que eu sinta que amar não é morrer, [...] faze com que eu tenha caridade por mim mesma pois senão não poderei sentir que Deus me amou, faze com que eu perca o pudor de desejar que na hora de minha morte haja uma mão amada para apertar a minha, amém.[9]

At other times the tone is sharper, as happens in the interviews, when it is the interviewee herself who interrupts the interviewer in an atmosphere of embarrassment about the wounded body.

Most revealing of a mood similar to that which runs through the passages quoted above, however, is a fascinating passage from the unpublished manuscript 'Objeto gritante' [Screaming Object].[10] On page 143 we come across a long fragment, a kind of prayer: 'Vou fazer um esforço sobrehumano e dizer profundamente a frase mais difícil de um homem dizer na terra: que seja feita a Vossa vontade, e não a minha, assim na terra como no céu' [I am going to make a superhuman effort and say profoundly the most difficult sentence for a man to say on earth: Thy will be done, and not mine, on earth as it is in heaven]. In this unpublished text, there are traces recognizable from the published texts—from its rhetorical-stylistic formulation, including the visible impact of the short sentences, to the dominant recurrence of themes and motifs, including, let us stress it here, the dialectic of amplification/reduction:

Meu senhor, eu às vezes sinto uma amplidão dentro de mim: mas eu tenho medo. Quero tanto Deus. Mas não consigo senti-lo. [...] Eu assim entrego as rédeas de meu destino a uma força maior que eu. Porque eu, meu senhor, não posso nada. Vejo-me pequena, fraca e desamparada na enorme casa de minha infância, sem ter a quem me dirigir e me sentindo abandonada por Deus.[11]

The feeling of smallness and loneliness is intensified by the writer's condition as creator, but this condition (of 'artistic maturity') is also the place from whence she draws enough strength to help her 'carregar as dores do mundo' [carry the pains of the world]. The topic of solace spreads throughout the whole fragment, in which the enunciating subject addresses an indeterminate interlocutor ('meu senhor' [my lord]) who can easily be identified as the divine entity, despite the ambiguity of the use of lower-case letters. Help is being asked for some sort of crossing over, and the image of the hand is decisive ('pela sua mão irei sem muito medo ao desconhecido' [with your hand I will go without too much fear into the unknown]). It is precisely the hand that will arise as a central figure in Clarician imagery and rhetoric: from the outstretched hand ('dar a mão a alguém sempre foi o que esperei da alegria' [giving someone a hand has been what I have always expected from happiness]), to the hand eagerly sought in an hour of need (conjuring up the idea of the hour of death).

However, right at the beginning of the fragment, the appeal to the anonymous entity allows us to glimpse the fact that at the origin of all her troubles there is something which seems to be writing, the activity of the writer: 'Não se canse de mim. Não quero o papel heróico de mártir. No entanto vivo em martírio. Digo para mim mesma: não há motivo de sofrer tanto. Meu senhor, o senhor tem razão: mas eu sinto às vezes, quando tenho sucesso, medo que exijam o impossível de mim.' [Don't tire of me. I don't want the heroic role of the martyr. Although I live in martyrdom. I tell myself: there is no reason to suffer so much. My lord, you are right: but sometimes, when I am successful, I feel afraid that the impossible will be demanded from me.]

The 'romantic' concept of the creator, which subconsciously corresponds to Clarice's way of situating herself in the literary sphere, manifests itself above all in the way that the religious dimension is presented in her texts. The relationship with the divine is, just as it was for the Romantics, 'preponderantemente de natureza sentimental e intuitiva' [preponderantly of a sentimental and intuitive nature],[12] and insofar as it is a recurrent motif in the work of the author of *A paixão segundo G.H.* it could be said to reflect her attitude towards what she repeatedly called the 'mistério da criação' [the mystery of creation].

This text, with its confessional tone, insisting on the feeling of vulnerability and pain, develops into the explicit representation of the unspoken motif that can be considered implicit in the whole confession, the 'predestined' existence of the writer: 'Meu mal é fazer perguntas, desde pequena eu era toda uma pergunta. Vou deixar de perguntar, vou deixar de esperar respostas. Ser escritor é não ter pudor na alma.' [My problem is that I keep asking questions, since I was little I have been nothing but questions. I am going to stop asking, I am going to stop expecting answers. Being a writer means there is no shame in your soul.]

Returning to 'Objeto gritante': in the fragment we have been analysing, we can see how the confession moves towards a meta-linguistic thematization of writing. Indeed, a cyclical method of structuring the discourse operates a return to the personal by way of the confessional register once again, and finally, to impose a reflection on the act of writing. Following on from the sentence 'ser escritor é não ter pudor na alma' [being a writer means there is no shame in your soul] comes a digression: 'Eu quero me cobrir toda. Quero me enrolar no cobertor quente e dormir.' [I want to cover myself up completely. I want to wrap myself in the warm blanket and go to sleep.] Significantly, a handwritten sentence, crossed out, would have functioned as the link between the two. Behind the crossing out, the following words can be deciphered: 'Esquecendo inclusive a minha mão enxertada por causa do incêndio' [Even forgetting my hand with its skin-graft caused by the fire]. This deviation in discourse which draws the line which links together suffering/being a writer/skin-graft/writing contributes towards a blurring of boundaries (a way of skirting round the difficulty), while the use of a cyclical structure imposes an intense vision: from the disembodied 'I' to poetics everything becomes co(n)-fused.

From naming the graft (a gift from/of self, to self) to the explicit metaphor of writing, the person experiencing these meandering, wandering reflections points to and exposes it at the same time:

Tendo lidado com problemas de enxerto de pele, fiquei sabendo que um banco de doação de pele não é viável, pois esta, sendo alheia não adere por muito tempo à mão do enxertado. É necessário que a mão do paciente seja tirada de outra parte de seu corpo, e em seguida enxertada no lugar necessário. Isto quer dizer que no enxerto há uma doação de si para si mesmo.

Esse caso me fez devanear um pouco sobre o número de outros em que a própria pessoa tem que doar a si própria. O que traz solidão e riqueza e luta. Cheguei a pensar-sentir na bondade que é tipicamente o que se quer receber dos outros e no entanto às vezes só a bondade que demos a nós mesmos nos livra da culpa e nos perdoa. E é também, por exemplo, inútil receber a aceitação dos outros, enquanto nós mesmos não nos doarmos a auto-aceitação do que somos. Quanto à nossa fraqueza, a parte mais forte nossa é que tem que nos doar ânimo e complacência. E há certas dores que só a nossa própria dor, se for aprofundada, paradoxalmente chega a amenizar. [...]
    Lembrei-me de outra doação a si mesmo: a da criação artística. Pois em primeiro lugar por assim dizer tenta-se tirar a própria pele para enxertá-la onde é necessário. Só depois de pegado o enxerto é que vem a doação aos outros. Ou é tudo misturado, não sei bem, a criação artística é um mistério que me escapa, felizmente. Não quero saber muito.[13]

The distant yet present wound (excessive, obstinate, nightmarish) is the crossing of the dark desert where the self devours itself, consumes itself in its quest; it is a surrender to the realm of writing that is powerfully unleashed in an intense concentration of both the limited and the infinite. The overwhelming centrifugal violence that drags everything along with it, the ripping, the abysmal damage that attacked the physical body during the fire and submitted it to the full fury of the horrific, is equivalent to the painful labour that had always lingered within Lispector's literary body, where invisible scars generated words.

Clarice can be situated alongside those authors who live their writing in an immersion that allows no interval and turns them into their writing. Literature is set in motion in a process whereby life participates in the gestation of one territory among many. The intensity of the surrender presupposes the inclusion of the self (working on itself) in the process of investigation that writing constitutes. This very idea was developed in the lecture on avant-garde literature that Lispector was to deliver in several venues: 'É maravilhosamente difícil escrever em língua que ainda borbulha, que precisa mais do presente do que mesmo de uma tradição. Em língua que para ser trabalhada, exige que o escritor se trabalhe a si próprio como pessoa.' [It is marvellously difficult to write in a language which is still bubbling, which needs the present more even than it needs a tradition. In a language which, in order to be fashioned, demands that the writer works on herself as a person.][14] Lispector's refined self-awareness of the craft of writing enables her to highlight insistently the notion that the chosen path is not tantamount to skill but is rather a conscious passage through passion. The degree of difficulty is a self-imposed order that begs for surprise. When asked in an interview in the magazine *Veja* about whether the idea of abandoning literature had been well thought-out or was more of a spontaneous decision, she replied:

Foi uma coisa muito pensada. Eu tinha medo de que escrever se tornasse um hábito e não uma surpresa. Eu só gosto de escrever quando me surpreendo. Além disso, eu temia que, se continuasse produzindo livros, adquirisse uma habilidade detestável. Um pintor célebre — não me lembro quem — disse, certa vez: 'Quando tua mão direita for hábil, pinte com a esquerda; quando a esquerda tornar-se hábil também, pinte com os pés'. Eu sigo este preceito.[15]

The vague memory of a name in the reply she gave only serves to accentuate the exemplary nature of the episode described. In other contexts, however, the name of the painter is identified. For instance, João Cabral de Melo Neto, in a poem in *Serial*, introduces the name of the artist Joan Miró ('Quis então que desaprendesse / o muito que aprendera, / a fim de reencontrar / a linha ainda fresca da esquerda' [He wanted it [his right hand] to unlearn / all it had learned / so as to recover / his left hand's still fresh curve]).[16] In an essay from *Discours/Figure*, François Lyotard quotes the example of Paul Klee, who said to his students: 'Exercise your hand, or even better, both hands, because your left hand writes differently from your right, *it is less skilful and therefore more manageable*. The right hand flows more naturally, the left writes better hieroglyphics. Writing is not about being clear, but about expression—think of the Chinese—and the exercise becomes ever more sensitive, intuitive, spiritual.'[17]

In a footnote, Lyotard explains that the emphasis is his and adds that Klee used to draw with his left hand and write with his right. The idea set out using the example of Klee as a starting point touches deep within the dark areas of the nature of the creative act. In contrast to the hand that shows, that displays itself in the sense of foreseeable and controllable clarity, and operates in the 'register of the visible' and the easily recognizable ('the hand that sketches for the eye that "sees"'), the left hand symbolizes the nocturnal side of the unforeseeable, which opens up difficulties in productivity. Lyotard associates the left hand with the 'feeling eye'—an association that allows for an opening-up and for the eruption of madness. One could say, then, that such an appropriation is apt to represent the practice of Clarician writing. The accident makes more visible the work of the Clarician 'left hand', which had always been active.

In the readings of certain scholars, Lispector created a literature that gave away the fact that she was actually born into a different language, that she had in her childhood lived with another language. Grace Paley asks the question: 'At what age did she enter the Portuguese language? And how much Russian did she bring with her? Any Yiddish? Sometimes I think that this is what her work is about [...] one language trying to make itself at home in another. Sometimes there's hospitality, sometimes a quarrel.'[18] One cannot help but recognize a certain empathy (akin to psychological transferral) on the part of the person pondering these questions, in that Paley recognizes herself in a similar situation to the daughter of Russian emigrants. This is in part how we should understand the interpretation that she projects intuitively: 'it must have been that meeting of Russian and Portuguese that produced the tone, the rhythms that, even in translation (probably difficult) are so surprising and right'.[19]

If the essence of the problem does not lie in this way of putting the question, it does, however, open the way for some crucial questions to be asked. Is the language the host, or is the author the host of the language she works with? If there a language to be forgotten, how can one forget the language heard in one's childhood home? What might remain as an example, as a mark of this enclosed space of difference?

In her critical study *Langues de feu*, Claire Varin puts particular emphasis on something she considered a decisive revelation in her research into the works of the Brazilian writer: she had learnt from Clarice's eldest sister Elisa that their parents had spoken Yiddish at home and that Clarice understood the language despite not being able to speak it.[20] Varin goes on to insist on the fact of Yiddish being spoken up until the death of the writer's mother.[21] We also know that Clarice went to a Jewish school in Recife (the Collegio Hebreo-Idische-Brasileiro) where she took Yiddish, Hebrew and Religious Studies classes.[22] This leads us to a vital insight: that it is around the maternal figure that the origin of Clarice's literature revolves.

Regarding this question of origins, we might look at an episode that has to do with the figure of the mother and implications of guilt. The deep-rootedness of the feelings of guilt assume such a weight that it is projected widely onto all aspects of life. The confessional tone of the *crônica* from the *Jornal do Brasil* on 28 June 1969 highlights this most clearly: 'Ah quisera eu ser dos que entram numa igreja, aceitam a penitência e saem mais livres. Mas não sou dos que se libertam. A culpa em mim é algo tão vasto e tão enraizado que o melhor ainda é aprender a viver com ela, mesmo que tire o sabor do menor alimento: tudo sabe mesmo de longe a cinzas.' [Ah, how I should like to be one of those who can go to church, accept penance and come away feeling liberated. But I find it difficult to liberate myself. The guilt I feel is so vast and deeply rooted that I might as well learn how to live with it, even if it takes away the taste of the tiniest morsel of food: everything tastes of ashes even from a distance.]

Without going into the field of 'psychobiography', which throws light on the development of the 'repercussions of the infantile trauma' in certain areas of a writer's works,[23] we must be aware of a key moment which emerges phantasmatically, obscure and unfathomable. In another *crônica* Clarice says:

Fui preparada para ser dada à luz de um modo tão bonito. Minha mãe já estava doente, e, por uma superstição bastante espalhada, acreditava-se que ter um filho curava uma mulher de uma doença. Então fui deliberadamente criada: com amor e esperança. Só que não curei minha mãe. E sinto até hoje essa carga de culpa: fizeram-me para uma missão determinada e eu falhei. Como se contassem comigo nas trincheiras de uma guerra e eu tivesse desertado. Sei que meus pais me perdoaram eu ter nascido em vão e tê-los traído na grande esperança. Mas eu, eu não me perdoo.[24]

Like a strange, invisible cloud, the failed mission (the lost mother) sets the stage for the 'scene'—something that hides in an underground realm and escapes, to emerge like a nocturnal ghostly intrusion. The wound is permanently reopened in the guilt and anguish reinscribed in the literary experiences. The original scene creates the enigma that falls back onto itself. The uncertainty that leads to the enigma stems from the overlapping versions and the hesitant enunciations of the story.[25] And it is also through this enigma that the image of the exile (orphan) will gain meaning. Some basic accounts show the significant ambivalence: 'mas eu era uma criança alegre' [but I was a happy child], the author repeats when she refers to the shadowy setting of her childhood, marked by poverty and the pain of a sick mother. In the same way, the image of the mother, which she will try to reproduce, will be marked by a fundamental ambivalence, oscillating between the failed mission and the projection onto the impossible figure of the total mother, the protector of the world:

Embora eu saiba que, mesmo em segredo, a liberdade não resolve a culpa. Mas é preciso ser maior que a culpa. A minha ínfima parte divina é maior que a minha culpa humana. O Deus é maior que minha culpa essencial. Então prefiro o Deus, à minha culpa. Não para me desculpar e para fugir mas porque a culpa me amesquinha.[26]

Could it be that the persistent image of Clarice is, indeed, that of the writer–mother? Despite what she asserts in some interviews, despite having tried at times to establish such an image, what prevails is an intensely dramatic and lonely face. She and the text, she and the writing for which she had once (before the birth of her own children) sworn to fight: 'Não escrevi uma linha, o que me perturba o repouso. Eu vivo à espera de inspiração com uma avidez que não dá descanso. Cheguei mesmo à conclusão de que escrever é a coisa que mais desejo no mundo, mesmo mais que amor' [I didn't write a line, which disturbs my repose. I live in hope of inspiration with an eagerness that gives me no rest. I have even reached the conclusion that writing is the thing I desire most in this world, more than love even] (letter to her sisters, 8 May 1946).[27] The corrosive tone and the embracing the awareness of an unforgiving reality—that is, of death—spring forth from guilt. It is fundamental to consider the scene in the light of textuality; we can read the body written into it. We could say that writing is a manifestation of desire to the same degree that it is a remission of guilt.

The need for her father to adapt—even in terms of his profession as a salesman—following the death of her mother, opened up opportunities for acculturation. Symbolically the paternal figure emerges as representative of this assimilation. It is thus that we see the father move away from Recife and head towards Rio de Janeiro with his three daughters. Claire Varin's reading relies on the importance that she attributes to the relationship with the mother's tongue and the consequences arising from that relationship. These 'expériences auditives' [aural experiences], the clandestine circulation of this 'langue errante' [wandering language] immersed the future writer 'dès sa plus tendre enfance dans un état de destabilisation d'une langue unique "pure"' [from her earliest childhood in a state of destabilization of a unique 'pure' language].[28] It is the body that reveals this tension precisely in one of the symbolic places that allow difference to be upheld:

Elle cache sous sa langue liée un conflit psychique converti en symptôme corporel. Faute d'assumer la langue de sa mère, elle se charge partiellement de sa paralysie. La langue yiddish, sème le désordre dans sa langue parlée d'autant plus secrètement que son [r] style français nous conduit sur une fausse piste. Le langage du corps maternel résonne dans la bouche de la fille.[29]

In interviews, Lispector had no problem in deconstructing the situation, by referring to the physical reason for her accent—a 'trapped tongue'—always in order to emphasize that she belonged to Brazil; but at the same time she continued to give contradictory information that caused confusion. According to one of the author's friends, the playwright and phonetic speech doctor Pedro Bloch (who was also born in the Ukraine and arrived in Brazil at the age of three), her defect in diction was not due to a 'trapped tongue' but could have been caused by the fact that Clarice, when she was little, imitated the way her parents spoke.[30] Pedro Bloch even seems to have managed to correct the impediment but 'ao reencontrá-la meses depois o médico notou que ela tinha voltado a usar os "erres". A razão desta atitude, segundo Clarice, devia-se a seu receio de perder suas características, pois sua maneira de falar era um traço da personalidade.' [When he met her months later the doctor noticed that she had started pronouncing her 'r's again. The reason for this attitude, according to Clarice, was due to a fear of losing her characteristics, since her way of speaking was a personality trait.][31]

For Lispector, the literary terrain became a quest born of the tension between an effect of deterritorialization and her insertion into a space at the very limits of the language to which she actually desired to belong. In the tension between the clear boundaries of a geo-graphically referentialized space and the search for a potentially unlimited space that could subsume all creative energy lay the fact that she was a foreigner, trying not to be one yet being one at the same time. Her nomadic transit originates, then, in the inhabitable zone of conflict that language constitutes. One could go so far as to say that it is in the very work on language that her transit is based.

Clarice wrote a short but significant text with the title 'Declaração de amor' [A declaration of love] (*Jornal do Brasil*, 11 May 1968), where she shows that she is aware of the task that she faces. She declares that the Portuguese language, 'como não foi profundamente trabalhada pelo pensamento, a sua tendência é a de não ter sutilezas e de reagir às vezes com um verdadeiro pontapé contra os que temerariamente ousam transformá-la numa linguagem de sentimento e de alerteza. E de amor' [not having been fashioned painstakingly and thoughtfully, tends to lack subtlety. It can also hit out at anyone foolish enough to try and transform it into a language of emotion and awareness. Or a language of love]. Her thoughts imply a non-peaceful confrontation—language itself will have to learn to react. Out of the conflict there emerges a desire to elaborate, a listening to one's internal voice, a dealing with subtleties that resembles the way thoughts are formed. Being inside the language as a foreigner presupposes a jolting of genealogies in such a way as to inscribe oneself in a place that, at the same time, you also aim to make your own:

O que eu recebi de herança não me chega. Se eu fosse muda, e também não pudesse escrever, e me perguntassem a que língua eu queria pertencer, eu diria: inglês, que é preciso e belo. Mas como não nasci muda e pude escrever, tornou-se absolutamente claro para mim que eu queria escrever em português. Eu até queria não ter aprendido outras línguas: só para que minha abordagem do português fosse virgem e límpida.[32]

The proclamation of a desire for a flat place—a language like a territory—does not presuppose an ideal of purity or crystallizing untouchability. The Clarician steppes are created in the search for this utopian space but also emerge, above all, in the extent to which the combat within it makes it possible to bring to the arena of language the madness of what is going on inside. To make it sing or whisper on the plains of an aggressively differentiating exteriority. José Gil asserts that when one discovers that one's homeland is one's mother tongue (in an allusion to a famous quotation by Portuguese poet Fernando Pessoa), one also realises that the 'visão da pátria' [vision of the homeland] is transformed by language:

que o país real é atravessado e transfigurado por múltiplos outros, feitos do 'tecido de que são feitos os sonhos'. Abriu-se um espaço diferente: o país natal da língua é uma estepe ilimitada que leva a regiões desconhecidas, onde o leitor reconhece em si rostos anónimos, por vezes excessivamente estranhos. Aí ele descobre-se estrangeiro, negro, índio, branco, barata, baleia, árvore, pedra. Homossexual, transexual, ímpio e piedoso, blasfemador. O país natal compõe-se de infinitos territórios estrangeiros; a língua materna de inúmeras línguas outras, línguas mestiças e crioulos, calões, falares idiolectais, murmúrios inaudíveis, sons elementares.[33]

Here we hear echoes of Deleuze: the repercussions throughout literature of the multiplicity and heterogeneity of the infinite fabrics that make up the territory of the language. Hence, in Lispector's writing, Deleuze's thoughts are repeated countless times: the art of literature is that of being a stranger in your own language. Literature is a kind of foreign language which is not another language 'mais un devenir-autre de la langue' [but a becoming-other of language].[34] Situating itself in a border zone, Clarice's literature implies the exclusion of any type of hierarchalization and proposes the establishment of a nomadic space: a being not from any one place, but rather existing in an infinite gravitation which is all places. Frontiers, which serve territories, impose categorizations, genre or conceptual distinctions. In the Lispectorian universe, heterogeneity, discontinuity and instability lead us to the space *in-between*. In terms of genre, her oeuvre can be categorized somewhere between fiction, essay and poem. We might say that, paradoxically, this is a kind of immobility in transit. The permanent autognosis of the side of immobility associates itself with the fleeing being, with problematization. The founding of the name (of literature) is thus sought on the horizon of the *non-place*.

We could say that Clarice Lispector is the first, most radical affirmation of a *non-place* in Brazilian literature. All great literature is marked by a principle of deterritorialization, although this does not necessarily imply a strategy that annuls geographical reference (in this context one only has to recall the skill of Guimarães Rosa). It is precisely the dereferentializing mode of Clarice's writing, the greatest proof of its difference, that will earn her a canonical place in the literature of her country. This is especially important because of the fact of her appearing in a period when literary affirmation was achieved through strategies of regionalism, which, even when articulated in dialectic with universalism, made it necessary to locate the specific region. And the true scope of this assertion of the reality of the non-place that Clarice's work presents can only be perceived when one keeps in mind the imposed obsession with territory within a vast cultural space with a very wide variety of implications and motivations, where literature is by and large a literature of place.

Last but not least, it is important to stress that the need to put in practice an experimentalism obsessed with difference underlies Clarice's writing, marked by a dense reflexive range. Such a need reflects on one hand a deliberate desire to innovate, to break with tradition, and on the other the creativity of an inner spirit that is permanently on the boil in its endless search for an original means of expression. Nevertheless, it does not seem possible to completely dissociate this constant effervescence from the deep-rooted disquiet that permeates nearly all her texts, a disquiet surely not divorced from a vision of a world faced through the pain of estrangement. This brings to mind the memory of the lost mother. Even the ludic nature of a writing that thrives on successive fictional experiments does no more than accentuate by contrast the disquiet that radiates from each and every text where the *wounded body* is, in the final analysis, intensely reflected.

Notes to Chapter 1

1. 'I met a group of classmates from the Faculty on an excursion. My exile will become a little easier, I hope. You know, Lúcio, all the fuss I caused has only served to make me feel an enormous urge to prove to myself and to others that I am more than just a woman. I know that you don't think so. But I didn't believe it either, considering what I have done up to now. It's just that I am still existing in a potential state, I can feel that there is fresh water inside me, but I cannot find the source. / O.K. That's enough silliness. All this is very amusing. But I didn't expect to laugh at life. Like a good Slav, I was a serious young girl, prepared to sob for humanity ... (I'm laughing).' Lúcio Cardoso Archive, Fundação Casa de Rui Barbosa, Rio de Janeiro.
2. Teresa Cristina Montero Ferreira, *Eu sou uma pergunta: Uma biografia de Clarice Lispector* (Rio de Janeiro: Rocco, 1999), 89–90.
3. Quoted in Olga Borelli, *Clarice Lispector: Esboço para um possível retrato* (Rio de Janeiro: Nova Fronteira, 1981), 106.
4. 'In fact I don't know how to write letters about travel, in fact I don't even know how to travel. It's funny how, because I don't stay very long in places, I don't see them. I find Nature more or less the same, things are almost identical. I was more familiar with Arabs wearing veils when I was in Rio. Anyway, I hope never to demand any attitude from myself. It would be tiring.' Ibid.
5. Ferreira, *Eu sou uma pergunta*, 224.
6. Ibid., 225.
7. Diane E. Marting (ed.), *Clarice Lispector: A Bio-bibliography* (Westport, CT; London: Greenwood Press, 1993), 15–18 at 15.
8. This *crônica* appears in the collection *A descoberta do mundo* (Rio de Janeiro: Nova Fronteira, 1984).
9. *Uma aprendizagem ou o livro dos prazeres*, 16th edn. (Rio de Janeiro: Nova Fronteira, 1989), 58–9: 'Shaking, she knelt next to her bed for that was the way one prayed and said in a low, serious, sad voice, stammering her prayer with slight embarrassment: "unburden my soul, make me feel that Your hand is in mine, make me feel that death doesn't exist because in reality we're already in eternity, make me feel that to love is not to die [...] make me be charitable toward myself or else I won't be able to feel that God has loved me, make me not feel ashamed to want the hand of a loved one to clasp mine at the hour of my death, Amen.' *An Apprenticeship, or The Book of Delights*, trans. Richard Mazzara and Lorri A. Parris (Austin: University of Texas Press, 1986), 34. Note the insistence with which this topic will occur, as for example in the following passage from 'Objeto gritante', an unpublished typescript that developed, in a

much condensed form, into the novel *Água viva* [Living water] (Clarice Lispector Archive, Fundação Casa de Rui Barbosa, Rio de Janeiro), fos. 154–5: 'Vou escrevendo o que vier aos dedos. Por falar em dedos, fico tão agradecida com o fato de eu não ter perdido a mão direita no incêndio: iam amputá-la com medo de gangrena. Mas uma de minhas devotadas irmãs, preciosas que elas são, pediu ao médico encarecidamente que esperasse. Ele esperou. {escrito à mão: 'Mas o médico esperou'}. E não foi preciso cortá-la. Posso pegar em qualquer coisa. Sabem mesmo o que é isto: pegar? É privilégio.' [I'm going to write whatever comes to my fingertips. And speaking of fingers, I'm so grateful for the fact that I didn't lose my right hand in the fire: they were going to amputate it because they were worried it would become gangrenous. But one of my devoted sisters, who are so precious, earnestly asked the doctor to wait. He waited {handwritten: 'But the doctor waited'}. And it wasn't necessary to cut it off. I can pick up anything. Do you know what it means: to be able to pick something up? It is a privilege.] See Alexandrino E. Severino, 'As duas versões de *Água viva*', *Remate de males* 9 (1989), 115–18.
10. Document from the Clarice Lispector Archive.
11. 'My lord, I sometimes feel an amplification inside me: but I'm scared. I want God so much. But I can't manage to feel him. Therefore I hand over the reins of my destiny to a force greater than myself. Because I, my lord, can't do anything. I see myself as small, weak and without shelter in the huge house of my childhood, without anyone to look towards and feeling abandoned by God.'
12. Vítor Aguiar e Silva, *Teoria da literatura* (Coimbra: Almedina, 1983), 559.
13. 'Having had to deal with problems with the skin graft, I found out that a bank for skin donors isn't a viable project since the skin, because it is foreign, doesn't adhere for very long to the hand receiving the graft. The skin has to be taken from another part of the patient's body and immediately grafted onto the relevant place. That means that the graft is a gift from oneself to oneself. This case started me wondering a bit about the number of other times that people have to give things to themselves. Which brings loneliness and enrichment and struggle. I started to think-feel about kindness which is typically something one wants to receive from others and nevertheless sometimes it is only the kindness we show ourselves that frees us from guilt and forgives us. And it is also, for example, useless to receive the acceptance of others, when we ourselves do not give ourselves the self-acceptance of who we are. As for our frankness, the strongest part of ourselves is the part which has to give us cheer and goodwill. And there are certain pains which only our own pain, if truly deep, paradoxically, manages to alleviate. I remembered another kind of gift we give ourselves: that of artistic creation. For in the first place, you could say that we try to tear away our own skin to graft it on where necessary. Only after the graft has taken can we start to think about giving to others. Or it's all mixed together, I don't really know, artistic creation is a mystery that escapes me, thankfully. I don't want to know much.'
14. Clarice Lispector, 'Literatura de vanguarda no Brasil', *Movimientos literarios de vanguardia en Iberoamérica: Memoria del 11.° Congreso* (Mexico City: University of Texas, Instituto Internacional de Literatura Iberoamericana, 1965).
15. 'It was something I thought about a lot. I was scared that writing would become a habit and not a surprise. I only like to write when I surprise myself.

Furthermore, I was afraid that if I continued to produce books I would pick up a detestable skill. A famous artist—I don't remember who—once said: "When your right hand is skilful, paint with your left, when the left becomes skilful too, paint with your feet." I follow that rule.' 'Escritora mágica', *Veja* 30 July 1975, 88.

16. João Cabral de Melo Neto, 'O Sim contra o Sim', *Obra completa* (Rio de Janeiro: Nova Aguilar, 1995), 297–301 at 298; trans. Richard Zenith as 'Yes Against Yes', *Selected Poetry, 1937–1990*, ed. Djelal Kadir (Hanover, NH, and London: University Press of New England, 1995), 123–7 at 125.

17. Jean-François Lyotard, *Discurso, figura* (Barcelona: Gustavo Gili, 1979), 231.

18. Grace Paley, Introduction to *Soulstorm: Stories by Clarice Lispector*, trans. Alexis Levitin (New York: New Directions, 1989), pp. ix–xi at ix.

19. Ibid.

20. Claire Varin, *Langues de feu: Essai sur Clarice Lispector* (Laval: Éditions Trois, 1990), 25.

21. Ibid., 58.

22. Ferreira, *Eu sou uma pergunta*, 43.

23. Dominique Fernandez, *L'arbre jusqu'aux racines: Psychanalyse et création* (Paris: Grasset, 1992), 40.

24. 'My birth was planned in such a lovely way. My mother was in poor health and there was a well-known superstition which claimed having a child could cure a woman who was ill. So I was deliberately conceived: with love and hope. Only I did not cure my mother. And to this day I carry this burden of guilt: my parents conceived me for a specific mission and I failed them. As if they had been relying on me to defend the trenches in time of war and I had deserted my post. I know my parents forgave me for being born in vain and having frustrated their great hopes. But I cannot forgive myself.'

25. See Nádia Gotlib, *Clarice: Uma vida que se conta* (São Paulo: Ática, 1995), 68, on these different versions about the mother's illness: 'E a mãe, Marieta, fica sempre em casa, paralisada por causa da doença. Segundo Clarice, a doença aconteceu "por causa de meu nascimento" [...]. Há outra versão, que passam para a menina Clarice. "Eu morri de sentimento de culpa quando eu pensava que eu tinha feito isso quando eu nasci, mas me disseram que eu já tinha nascido. Não: que ela já [...] era paralítica.' [And her mother, Marieta, did not leave the house, paralysed because of the illness. According to Clarice, the illness came about 'because of my birth'. There is another version which was passed down to Clarice as a child. 'I suffered from feelings of guilt when I thought that it was me who had done that when I was born, but they told me I was already born. No: that she was already paralytic.']

26. 'Although I know that, even in secret, freedom does not absolve guilt. But one must be greater than guilt. My least divine part is greater than my human guilt. God is greater than my essential guilt. I therefore prefer God to my guilt. Not to excuse myself and get away but because guilt lessens me.' *A paixão segundo G.H.*, 15th edn. (Rio de Janeiro: Francisco Alves, 1991), 91; *The Passion according to G.H.*, trans. Ronald W. Sousa (Minneapolis: University of Minnesota Press, 1988), 79.

27. Quoted in Borelli, *Clarice Lispector*, 114.

28. Varin, *Langues de feu*, 26.
29. 'Behind her speech impediment she hides a psychic conflict that has become a physical symptom. Because she does not adopt the language of the mother, she becomes partly to blame for her paralysis. The Yiddish language spreads disorder in her spoken language just as secretly as her French [r] which leads us down the wrong track. The language of the body of the mother sings out of the mouth of the daughter.' Ibid., 64.
30. Ferreira, *Eu sou uma pergunta*, 229.
31. Ibid.
32. 'What I have inherited from others is not enough. If I were mute and unable to write and people were to ask me which language I should like to belong to, I would say English, for its precision and beauty. But since I was not born mute and could write, it became absolutely clear to me that I what I wanted was to write in Portuguese. I should even have preferred not to have learnt other languages just in order to keep my command of Portuguese virginal and limpid.'
33. 'that the real country is crossed and transfigured by multiple others, fashioned from "such stuff as dreams are made on". A different space has opened up: the native country of one's language is an endless steppe that leads to unknown regions, where the reader recognizes in her/himself anonymous faces, sometimes excessively strange. There s/he discovers that s/he is foreign, black, native, white, a cockroach, a whale, a tree, a stone. Homosexual, transsexual, impious and pitying, a blasphemer. The native country is composed of infinite foreign territories; the mother tongue of numerous other languages, mestizos and Creoles, slang, ideolect speech, inaudible murmurs, elemental sounds.' José Gil, 'A invenção das estepes', *Público* (24 Sept. 1994).
34. Gilles Deleuze, *Critique et clinique* (Paris: Minuit, 1993), 15.

CHAPTER 2

Clarice Lispector by Clarice Lispector

Anna Klobucka

The existence of complicated, multi-level intersections between fiction
and autobiography in Clarice Lispector's writing has been noted and
discussed by many critics; to quote just one representative comment,
Earl E. Fitz has referred to the 'intensely private' and 'seemingly even
autobiographical' tonality of her novels.[1] Particularly in the last ten years
of her life and work, Lispector developed a practice of recirculating her
texts among, on the one hand, her works of fiction (whether already
published, such as *A legião estrangeira* [The Foreign Legion] (1964), or
still in progress, such as *Água viva* [The Stream of Life] (1973), and, on
the other hand, the weekly *crônicas*—a genre that requires explicit
deployment of an autobiographical persona—which she wrote from
1967 to 1973 for the *Jornal do Brasil*. These *crônicas* are now conveniently
available—with some omissions—in a single-volume collection
assembled by the writer's son, Paulo Gurgel Valente, under the title *A
descoberta do mundo* (*Discovering the World* in Giovanni Pontiero's English
translation; cited hereafter as DM).[2]
  The exchange process worked in a truly reciprocal manner. On the
one hand, fragments of writing that were, at their point of origin,
unambiguously autoreferential made their way into Lispector's novels,
there to attach themselves to fictional characters such as Lóri in *Uma
aprendizagem ou o livro dos prazeres* [An Apprenticeship, or The Book
of Delights] (1969) or Ângela in *Um sopro de vida* [A Breath of Life]
(1978). At the same time, however, snippets of seemingly fictional
material would appear in the personal space of the *crônica* without
being explicitly qualified as samples of 'literary' creation external to
the author's real-life persona. Needless to say, the hermeneutic effects
of such wilful blurring of the boundaries between fact and fiction
prove to be highly complex. As Marta Peixoto notes, tracing the trail

of 'textual reappearances' in *Água viva*, rewritten by Lispector so as to strip them of overt autobiographic reference, '[for] the reader familiar with Lispector's work, the effect of this textual *déjà vu* works against the grain of Lispector's revisions, endowing the nonautobiographical protagonist with an equivocal autobiographic resonance'.[3]

These patterns of solipsistic allusion may be traced in all of Lispector's later works, coalescing into a slippery dialectic of disguise and disclosure that is perhaps nowhere as prominently on display as in the notorious opening passages of her penultimate novel (and the last work she published before she died), *A hora da estrela*. There, the parenthetical qualifier of its 'dedicatória do autor' [author's dedication]—'Na verdade Clarice Lispector' [In truth, Clarice Lispector]—is followed by the confessional outpouring of the fictional author's 'sangue de homem em plena idade' [blood of a man in his prime].[4] This equivocally-gendered identification of narrative authority is then further complicated by the inclusion of Lispector's own handwritten signature among the novel's thirteen alternative titles. *A hora da estrela*'s prefatory manoeuvres establish thus a pendular vacillation of the writing subject between the affirmation of self-sameness and the overt practice of narrative *fingimento*, accentuated by the emphasis on the distribution of discursive agency across the dividing line of sexual difference. The latter is of course an important aspect of Lispector's late works, particularly salient in *A hora da estrela* and *Um sopro de vida*: they are explicitly metafictional texts that emphasize gender as a crucial formative aspect of human identity and linguistic expression. In both novels, the relationship between the representing and represented subjects, as well as the mechanism of literary production itself, are modelled according to the structure of sexual difference.[5]

Lispector's construction of the preamble to *A hora da estrela* invites an interesting parallel with another remarkable book published in France just two short years before her novel appeared in Brazil. *Roland Barthes by Roland Barthes* is the distinguished critic's meditative self-portrait, composed in discontinuous fragments and written largely in the third person, which opens with the following words of caution to the reader, reproduced in the author's own handwriting: 'It must all be considered as if spoken by a character in a novel.'[6] Barthes's perverse *avis au lecteur* may be viewed, in a very literal sense, as the counterpart of Lispector's prefatory intervention in *A hora da estrela*. However, the handwritten intrusion, the sign of the body writing and the ultimate proof of authorial authenticity, is used by Barthes to directly undermine its own reliability, while the Brazilian writer's more ambiguously positioned signature opens itself to a variety of potentially discordant interpretations, not the least convincing of which insists on the *cinéma-vérité* quality of the author's presence in her text.[7]

Although the nameless narrator of another of Lispector's later novels, *Água viva*, explicitly rejects autobiography as a generic framework for her monologue ('Não vou ser autobiográfica. Quero ser "bio".'[8] [I'm not going to be autobiographical. I want to be 'bio'.]), the autographic project—the writing of the self—figures prominently in Lispector's fictional works produced in the seventies. Peixoto has related this insistent emphasis to the writer's activity as the *Jornal do Brasil*'s weekly supplier of *crônicas*, where, in part by the dictates of the genre and in part, one imagines, by her own inclination, she was led to perform the role of herself—Clarice Lispector the woman and the writer—in front of the wide audience of newspaper readers. The dialogic dimension of her later work, particularly marked in *A hora da estrela* and *Um sopro de vida*, may also be hypothetically attributed to the writer's increased awareness of the circuit of communication generated by her readers' reactions to and interpretations of her weekly dispatches. I will therefore focus my following discussion precisely on the ways in which Lispector staged her own 'auto-graphic' presence in her newspaper columns, and on the sense in which her 'descoberta do mundo' [discovery of the world] becomes also a 'descoberta ao mundo' [discovery to the world], a textual two-way street, or a transitive act of reciprocal uncovering acted out between self and other.

The end result of that process, as demonstrated in *A descoberta do mundo*, is neither an autobiography nor a diary, although it has many points in common with both genres: it may be more productively described and analysed as the writer's 'self-portrait', a formula theorized by Michel Beaujour in his *Poetics of the Literary Self-Portrait* (*Miroirs d'encre* in the original French).[9] The textual 'mirrors of ink' Beaujour describes are distinct from autobiographies in that they lack a continuous narrative, opting instead for a loose 'collation or patching together' of thematic elements, and in that they fit no pre-existing generic moulds: 'Each self-portrait is written as though it were the only text of its kind.' Furthermore, such texts tend to function at a high level of representational abstraction, their operational formula being 'I won't tell you what I've done, but I shall tell you *who I am*' (original emphasis), a statement Beaujour adapts from a declaration in St Augustine's *Confessions*, 'where the author contrasts the confession of what he has perpetrated to the disclosure of "what I am at the very time that I am writing these *Confessions*".[10] Lispector's auto-graphic presence in *A descoberta do mundo* is precisely that: a complex interplay of self-referential elusiveness ('I will not tell you what I have done') with an ardently confessional emphasis on a complete revelation of the writing subject's most intimate sense of selfhood in the process of being spelt out in language ('I shall tell you *who I am*').

The theme of self-disclosure, which becomes one of the dominant motifs in *A descoberta do mundo*, manifested itself in Lispector's work as early as 1964, with the publication of *A legião estrangeira*. This volume of short stories contained a second part called 'Do fundo da gaveta' [From the Bottom of the Drawer], consisting of a varied mix of shorter and longer, mostly nonfiction pieces, ranging from brief philosophical aphorisms to personal anecdotes and comments on Lispector's own process of writing. Their heterogeneity supports the claim implicit in the collection's title: they do appear as if the writer had swept them out of her drawer more or less straight into the published form, with a minimal amount of self-censorship and editorial control. In the texts themselves, on the other hand, the revelation of private truth is discussed in much more ambiguous terms. The brief fragment '"Acabou de sair"' ['She has just gone out'] vacillates syntactically between the first and the third persons in what could be described as a portrait of self as the other, playing hide-and-seek with itself and, in particular, with the surrounding world: 'Sua enorme inteligência compreensiva, aquele seu coração vazio de mim que precisa que eu seja admirável para poder me admirar. Minha grande altivez: prefiro ser achada na rua. Do que neste fictício palácio onde não me acharão porque — porque mando dizer que não estou, "ela acabou de sair."' [Her immense, understanding intelligence; that heart of hers which is void of me and demands that I should be admirable in order to be able to admire me. My enormous pride: I prefer to be found in the street. Rather than in this imaginary palace where no one will find me because—because I have given instructions that I'm not at home: 'She has just gone out.']]11

It may be worth recalling here parenthetically that one of Lispector's several translations from English into Portuguese was Oscar Wilde's *Picture of Dorian Gray* and that it was published with the translator's name on the cover instead of the author's, perhaps, as Diane Marting suggests, 'to emphasize the freedom from the original

with which the work is presented in Portuguese'.[12] It is more significant to note that the fragment quoted above is followed immediately
by a short narrative, in which a male writer declares his intention to
become possessed by the identity of his female narratee (a missionary's
wife) and literally performs this changeover in the text, by switching
from the third-person, past-tense report to a present-tense, first-
person testimonial and from the masculine grammatical gender to the
feminine. While Giovanni Pontiero's English translation does not preserve the Portuguese grammatical markers of the gender change, it
does accentuate the parallel between this text and the much later
novel *A hora da estrela* by translating the story's original Portuguese
title, 'A vez de missionária', as 'The Hour of the Missionary'. Here
and elsewhere in 'Do fundo da gaveta', the writer engages in the
textual games with the notions of the authorial self-in-discourse
which will later become one of the central aspects of her fiction and
non-fictional work alike.

In *A descoberta do mundo*, this tendency is at the same time emphasized
and complicated by the heightened awareness of the text's intended
audience and by the specific generic framework of the *crônica*. Throughout her interventions, Lispector provides a running commentary on
the genre question, defining herself in relation to the established figure
of the *cronista*; one installment, entitled precisely 'Ser cronista' [Writing
crônicas] begins in the following way (DM 112): 'Sei que não sou, mas
tenho meditado ligeiramente no assunto. Na verdade eu deveria
conversar a respeito com Rubem Braga, que foi o inventor da *crônica*.
Mas quero ver se consigo tatear sozinha no assunto e ver se chego a
entender.' [I know I am not a columnist, but I have been giving some
thought to this matter. I really ought to consult Rubem Braga who
invented the *crônica*. But let me see if I can probe and understand this
matter on my own.]

The characteristically Lispectorian tone of this passage, humbly
unassuming and artfully mocking all at once, highlights also another
common feature that the *crônicas* share with the writer's late fictional
works: a sense of immediacy being conveyed to the readers, an
impression of the scene of writing that appears to be broadcast live
from the author's typewriter. This of course is one of the most
prevalent generic traits of the *crônica*, always ostensibly composed 'ao
correr da pena' [following the course of the pen] (to cite the title of
a collection by the first prominent Brazilian practitioner of the genre,
José de Alencar), or as Lispector rephrases it, 'Ao correr da máquina'

[following the course of the typewriter]. The *crônica* thus entitled, dated 20 September 1969, begins with a sudden, intimate outburst (DM 232): 'Meu Deus, como o mundo sempre foi vasto e como eu vou morrer um dia.' [The world has always been so enormous, dear God, and one day I shall die.] This exclamation neatly illustrates the writer's highly original approach to the genre's usual objective of providing spontaneous commentary on current events and social mores. The 'current events' glossed here are of a profoundly personal nature. The reader is left with an impression of having glimpsed a moment of wrenchingly truthful intimacy that is reinforced further on in the fragment, as the confessional outpour continues to spill from Lispector's typewriter (DM 232): '— Eu vou te dar o meu segredo mortal: viver não é uma arte. Mentiram os que disseram isso. Ah! Existem feriados em que tudo se torna tão perigoso. Mas a máquina corre antes que meus dedos corram. A máquina escreve em mim. E eu não tenho segredos, senão exactamente os mortais.' [I shall tell you my mortal secret: living is not an art. Those who said so were lying. Ah! There are certain holidays when everything becomes so dangerous. But the typewriter goes faster than my fingers. The typewriter writes on me. And I have no secrets, apart from, precisely, the mortal ones.]

The direct address to the reader and the intimation that he or she is being drawn into the writer's most private sphere recur at regular intervals in *A descoberta do mundo*. The writing appears to happen *ad hoc*, like a jazz improvisation in front of an audience (to borrow an expression from the narrator of *Água viva*) (DM 196): 'Vocês vêem como estou escrevendo à vontade? Sem muito sentido, mas à vontade. Que importa o sentido? O sentido sou eu.' [Can you see how I am writing at my ease? Without much sense, but at my ease. What does sense matter? I am the sense.] In this spectacle, however, audience participation is actively sought in order to stave off the possibility of the performer's becoming excessively self-absorbed (DM 194): 'Avisem-me se eu começar a me tornar eu mesma demais. É minha tendência.' [Warn me if I start becoming too personal. I do tend to do that.] These two remarks at the same time illustrate and subvert what Beaujour calls the literary self-portrait's 'original sin': 'it perverts exchange, communication and persuasion itself, while denouncing this perversion. Its discourse addresses the putative reader only insofar as he is placed in the position of an overhearing third person'.[13] Lispector's involvement with her addressees is, however, at the same

time intensely solipsistic and insistently dialogic: her text makes clear
her desire to captivate its readers in its own self-referential orbit, while
at the same time declaring that it remains humbly subservient to their
reactions and mandates.

Here and elsewhere, Lispector's confessional self on the stage of
writing promises and performs a ritual of complete and definitive
revelation, while at the same time covertly striving toward disguise and
concealment, as Nádia Battella Gotlib has observed in the section 'A
luta pelo não-autobiográfico' [The struggle for the non-autobio-
graphical] of her biography of Lispector.[14] The author and protagonist
of *A descoberta do mundo* is said there to share with Shakespeare's Hamlet
'a habilidade de "fingir que desempenha um papel no momento exato
em que está prestes a ser o personagem que representa"' [the ability to
'feign that s/he plays a role at the precise moment when s/he is about
to become the character s/he is playing'].[15] And, we might add, vice
versa: Clarice's persona in the *crônicas* engages in a textual game whose
results are not unlike the solution of Edgar Allan Poe's classic detective
story, 'The Purloined Letter', where careless disclosure is revealed as
the best form of disguise.[16] Interestingly, in one of the *crônicas*, Lispector
avails herself of an analogous prop—a misplaced document—in
commenting on the psychology of her self-consciousness:

Quando não sei onde guardei um papel importante e a procura se revela
inútil, pergunto-me: se eu fosse eu e tivesse um papel importante para
guardar, que lugar escolheria? Às vezes dá certo. Mas muitas vezes fico tão
pressionada pela frase 'se eu fosse eu', que a procura do papel se torna
secundária, e começo a pensar. Diria melhor, sentir. (DM 156)[17]

Let us recall that Auguste Dupin's method of detection in 'The
Purloined Letter' has two fundamental premises, and that the first of
them is an 'identification of the reasoner's intellect with that of his
opponent'.[18] Clarice's search for the misplaced document follows the
great detective's lead to the letter, so to speak, only to expose its
pitfalls when the projected identification of the concealer and the
searcher fails to produce the desired solution and instead opens up a
deeper mystery. That deeper mystery—the unbridgeable discontinuity
of the living and the writing self—is then presented to Lispector's
readers in the spirit of full disclosure, thus mimicking Dupin's second
premiss of detection: the recognition that the truth 'may escape
observation by dint of being excessively obvious'.[19]

Just like the hapless policemen in Poe's story, who fail to locate the concealed/revealed document they have been searching for, so too are the readers of Lispector's *crônicas* shown to be falling for the trick, as they implore the writer to continue to just '[ser] você mesma' [be yourself] (DM 180). In addition, they find her journalistic contributions easy to read and understandable, in contrast to her fictional works:

Um jornalista de Belo Horizonte disse-me que fizera uma constatação curiosa: certas pessoas achavam meus livros difíceis e no entanto achavam perfeitamente fácil entender-me no jornal, mesmo quando publico textos mais complicados. Há um texto meu sobre o estado de graça que, pelo próprio assunto, não seria tão comunicável e no entanto soube, para meu espanto, que foi parar até dentro de missal. Que coisa! (DM 421)[20]

The illusion of discursive simplicity, conveyed by the confessional immediacy of the *crônica*, is thus once again shown to be reinforced by the 'horizon of expectation' pertaining to the genre. At the same time, however, the *de facto* ambiguous textualization of the author's real-life identity is likewise encouraged by the ambiguity of the genre itself, an island of chattily subjective commentary in the journalistic sea of impersonal reporting and programmatically objective analysis. The description of the generic parameters of the *crônica* in the *Enciclopédia Verbo das literaturas de língua portuguesa* stresses precisely 'a ambiguidade do seu estatuto, oscilando entre o registo literário e o jornalístico' [the ambiguity of its status, which oscillates between literature and journalism], along with the resulting 'versatilidade enunciativa, temática e estilística' [enunciative, thematic and stylistic versatility] that allows its practitioners 'a livre expressão reflexiva, analítica, [ou] argumentativa [...] sem os constrangimentos dos géneros ficcionais' [free reflexive, analytic (or) argumentative expression free from the constraints operating in the fictional genres].[21]

The fact that so much of what is at stake in *A descoberta do mundo* pertains, on the one hand, to the discursive opportunities (as well as obstacles) presented by the genre of the *crônica* and, on the other hand, to the dialectic of revelation and concealment in the representation of the authorial self, finds its perhaps most concise expression in the fragment entitled 'Fernando Pessoa me ajudando' [Fernando Pessoa helping me out], dated 21 September 1968. Lispector begins it by restating her apparent discomfort with the generic framework of her writing and develops her complaint into a full-scale questioning of her personal investment in the *crônicas*. The paragraph is worth quoting in its entirety:

Noto uma coisa extremamente desagradável. Estas coisas que ando escrevendo aqui não são, creio, propriamente crônicas, mas agora entendo os nossos melhores cronistas. Porque eles assinam, não conseguem escapar de se revelar. Até certo ponto nós os conhecemos intimamente. E quanto a mim, isto me desagrada. Na literatura de livros permaneço anônima e discreta. Nesta coluna estou de algum modo me dando a conhecer. Perco minha intimidade secreta? Mas que fazer? É que escrevo ao correr da máquina e, quando vejo, revelei certa parte minha. Acho que se escrever sobre o problema da superprodução do café no Brasil terminarei sendo pessoal. Daqui em breve serei popular? Isso me assusta. Vou ver o que posso fazer, se é que posso. O que me consola é a frase de Fernando Pessoa, que li citada: 'Falar é o modo mais simples de nos tornarmos desconhecidos.' (DM 136–7)[22]

The apparent unpretentious simplicity and immediacy of this passage are of course highly deceptive, as indicated by the reference to the 'consolation' offered by, of all things, the example of Fernando Pessoa, a textual embodiment *par excellence* of occlusion and fragmentation of personal identity. Once again, in fact, the discursive mode of guileless self-revelation functions as a kind of mask that at the same time disguises and allows to glimpse the message repeated over and over by Lispector's self-portrait. This message is, in fact, a distinguishing mark of all literary self-portraits, according to Beaujour: they 'teach us through their topical dispersion, their restless metadiscourse, the splitting among the dislocated agencies of enunciation, that there is, in Foucault's words, "an incompatibility, perhaps without recourse, between the appearance of language in its being and the self's consciousness in its identity"'.[23] This distinctly poststructural lesson has often been derived by critics from Lispector's writing at large. In *A descoberta do mundo*, however, its function is particularly crucial: it is both the source of the text's constitutive anxiety and, ultimately, the reservoir of some of its most richly inspiring effects. The blank page that Clarice the *cronista* inserts into her wilful typewriter undergoes a transformation, while being filled with writing, into as much a 'mirror of ink', a space of self-involved reflection that purports to transcend the need to communicate ('What does sense matter? I am the sense.') as, more perversely and beguilingly, into a performative display-window through which the readers of Lispector's texts are beckoned at, provoked and ultimately seduced. The writing subject of her *crônicas* is thus not merely seen wandering in and out of autobiography and into fiction (and back again): it also engages with and intentionally dramatizes a vertiginous balancing act between the precarious mastery of self as (written by) self and the frightening vulnerability of self as (read by) the others.

Notes to Chapter 2

1. Earl E. Fitz, *Clarice Lispector* (Boston: Twayne, 1985), 60–1. The most comprehensive and rewarding discussion of Lispector's engagement with the 'mutual encroachments' between self and other, as they fluctuate in and out of the 'two permeable realms of autobiography and fiction' may be found in Marta Peixoto, 'A Woman Writing: Fiction and Autobiography in *The Stream of Life* and *The Stations of the Body*', a chapter of her book *Passionate Fictions: Gender, Narrative, and Violence in Clarice Lispector* (Minneapolis: University of Minnesota Press, 1994), 60–81. I wish to signal here my general indebtedness in considering these questions to Peixoto's insights.

2. Clarice Lispector, *A descoberta do mundo* (Rio de Janeiro: Rocco, 1999; orig. publ. 1984).

3. Peixoto, *Passionate Fictions*, 65.

4. Lispector, *A hora da estrela* (Rio de Janeiro: Francisco Alves, 1993).

5. I have discussed these issues in some detail in 'In Different Voices: Gender and Dialogue in Clarice Lispector's Metafiction', *Women, Literature and Culture in the Portuguese-Speaking World*, ed. Cláudia Pazos Alonso (Lampeter: Edwin Mellen, 1996), 155–72.

6. Barthes, *Roland Barthes by Roland Barthes*, trans. Richard Howard (Berkeley: University of California Press, 1977).

7. I am alluding here in particular to Hélène Cixous's extended commentary on *A hora da estrela* in her essay 'L'auteur en verité' [The author in truth], *L'heure de Clarice Lispector* (Paris: des femmes, 1989), 121–68. Although Cixous's reading of Lispector's writings is informed by poststructural notions of subjectivity and discursive authority that are anything but straightforward and naïve, her approach to the Brazilian writer remains predicated on a passionate recognition and subsequent conquest by assimilation of an object of desire, identifiable as 'Clarice herself', whose contours are revealed as imprinted throughout Lispector's texts. For further discussion of the Cixous/Lispector textual relationship, see Peixoto's chapter 'The Nurturing Text in Hélène Cixous and Clarice Lispector', *Passionate Fictions*, 39–59, and my article 'Hélène Cixous and the Hour of Clarice Lispector', *SubStance* 73 (1994), 41–62.

8. Lispector, *Água viva* (Rio de Janeiro: Francisco Alves, 1990; orig. publ. 1973), 40.

9. Michel Beaujour, *Poetics of the Literary Self-Portrait*, trans. Yara Milos (New York: New York University Press, 1991).

10. Ibid., 2–3.

11. Lispector, *Para não esquecer* [So As Not to Forget] (São Paulo: Siciliano, 1992; orig. publ. Ática, 1978), 22. The 'Bottom of the Drawer' section of *A legião estrangeira* was omitted in subsequent Brazilian editions of the collection, where only the thirteen short stories have been preserved. The 108 pieces constituting the section were first published separately after Lispector's death in *Para não esquecer*. The split between the two groups of texts has been preserved in all later

Portuguese-language editions, but the integrity of the original composition of *A legião estrangeira* was restored in Giovanni Pontiero's English translation. For further bibliographical details, see Diane E. Marting, *Clarice Lispector: A Bio-Bibliography* (Westport, CT: Greenwood Press, 1993), 79–80. Given the limited availability of the 1964 edition, I have quoted the Portuguese from the more recent edition of *Para não esquecer*.

12. Marting, *Clarice Lispector*, 175. Regarding Lispector's translation of Wilde's novel, see Severino J. Albuquerque, 'Reading Translation Queerly: Lispector's Translation of *The Picture of Dorian Gray*', *Bulletin of Hispanic Studies* 76 (1999), 691–702, where Albuquerque interprets the writer's translational endeavour in the context of her intense, 'never-resolved, ultimately frustrating relationship' with the gay writer Lúcio Cardoso.

13. Beaujour, *Poetics of the Literary Self-Portrait*, 9.

14. Nádia Battella Gotlib, *Clarice: Uma vida que se conta* (São Paulo: Ática, 1995).

15. Ibid., 113.

16. Incidentally, a volume of eleven short stories by Poe can be found among the books Lispector translated into Portuguese, or, more precisely, among her adaptations of literary classics for young adults, which she produced for Edições de Ouro (Marting, *Clarice Lispector*, 175–6). 'The Purloined Letter' does not, however, appear to have been one of the texts selected (presumably by Lispector herself) for the Poe volume. (I am grateful to Teresa Cristina Montero Ferreira and Claire Williams for their help in verifying the contents of this collection.) It should be noted, following Albuquerque, that it remains unclear which of the translations supposedly authored by Lispector were in fact her own, since the financial constraints she suffered from the time she separated from her husband until her death in 1977 apparently caused her to agree to lend 'her by-then famous name to a number of translations done by others' ('Reading Translation Queerly', 695).

17. 'Whenever I mislay an important document and cannot find it, I ask myself: If I were me and I wanted to keep a document in a safe place, where would I put it? Sometimes this works. But at other times, I am so harassed by the phrase "If I were me", that the search for the document becomes of secondary importance and I begin to think. Or rather, to feel.'

18. Edgar Allan Poe, *The Complete Stories* (New York: Alfred A. Knopf, 1992), 693.

19. Ibid., 697.

20. 'A journalist from Belo Horizonte told me that he had made a curious discovery: that some people found my novels and short stories difficult to read but had no problems in understanding what I write in the newspaper, even when I publish more complicated texts. I wrote an article once about the state of grace, a subject which, by its very nature, is not the most straightforward thing to get across, yet I later found out to my astonishment that it even ended up inside somebody's missal. Would you believe it!'

21. Maria Helena Santana, 'Crónica', *Biblos: Enciclopédia Verbo das literaturas de língua portuguesa* (Lisbon and São Paulo: Verbo, 1995), 1387–8.

22. 'I have noticed an extremely disagreeable thing. These things I am writing here are not exactly *crônicas*, I think, but I can now understand our best *cronistas*. They cannot avoid revealing their identity because they are obliged to sign their names

to their articles. Up to a point we come to know them intimately. And personally I do not like this. When I write my books, I remain anonymous and discreet. When I write this column I am in a certain way letting people get to know me. Am I losing my secret intimacy? But what can I do? As I type out my articles I follow the course of the typewriter, and when I look to see what I have written, I realize I have revealed something about myself. I even believe that if I were to write an article about the over-production of coffee in Brazil, I should end up sounding personal. Will I be popular soon? The thought scares me. I must see if I can do something about this, if there is anything I can do. What does console me is a verse by Fernando Pessoa which I read somewhere: "Speaking is the simplest way of becoming unknown."'

23. Beaujour, *Poetics of the Literary Self-Portrait*, 13.

CHAPTER 3

'Eu sou nome':
Clarice Lispector's *Dramatis Personae*

Claire Williams

> Conheces o nome que te deram, não conheces o nome que
> tens.
>
> José Saramago[1]

One of the longest-lasting debates in Western linguistic philosophy concerns the apparent disparity between an object, place or person and the word used to denote it. It dates right back to Plato, and continues up to Wittgenstein[2] and beyond, via considerations in the Old Testament Book of Samuel ('As his name is, so is he', I Samuel 25: 25), Shakespeare's Romeo, who asked wistfully 'What's in a name? That which we call a rose by any other word would smell as sweet' (*Romeo and Juliet* ii. ii. 85–6), and Alice's experiences in Wonderland, where she was asked who she was, what she was, and even whether her name meant what she looked like.

Proper names, or surnames, have developed as a way of distinguishing individuals and then classifying them in groups or families for legal, social, economic and religious purposes, and came into common use around the eleventh century.[3] People were named after the place where they lived, the master they served, their father or mother's first name, physical characteristics, profession, and so on. As new parts of the world, new species, new illnesses were discovered, humans set about mapping, classifying and naming, seeking to impose order and clarity on the chaos that they encountered. Written evidence, such as a name in a register or on a gravestone, may be the only remaining trace of a person's existence long after their body has turned to dust. The word thus comes to represent the person her/himself, a metonymic mark standing for physical presence and identity, as is obvious in the affirmative ritual of introducing oneself.

The dynastic implications of a name, either a surname or a Christian name passed down from father to son, mother to daughter, can be a burden on a child just as much as a matter of pride. The general conclusions reached in anthropology are that a name is a social classifying device that categorizes and differentiates the bearer. Anthropologists have discovered a huge variety of naming traditions, including the belief that knowing someone's name leaves them vulnerable to magic or sorcery. Significant moments in a person's life may be marked by the attribution of a new name. In Catholic cultures children are very often named after the saint on whose day they were born, or given a biblical name—and often two. In certain African tribes, people may have a whistled name or even a drummed name in addition to their spoken name.[4] And names change: with adoption, with marriage, with change of religion or by deed poll. People may have an official name for bureaucratic purposes and a family name or nickname that differs from it completely. The right to a name has been declared one of the basic human rights.[5]

Notions of names and naming are vitally important in the works of Clarice Lispector, whose fiction deals with a search for identity or a painful recognition of who and what a character is, or who or what they are not. A writer choosing names for her characters may do so arbitrarily, or with deliberate reference to other figures from literature, history or her own personal life. When the reader encounters an unusual name, it is impossible not to relate it to homonymous characters or figures, because names have inevitable associations. The plots of many narratives, including contemporary films and soap operas, revolve around protagonists' quests for their real name, their true identity, the discovery of their real parents, in order to receive their rightful inheritance. Even the titles of many classic novels are proper names, equating the name with the biography, or the accumulation of adventures and experiences that construct the hero's identity: Tom Jones, Dom Casmurro, Madame Bovary, Lolita, etc. This kind of narrative, known as the 'naming plot', thus contrives to fit an anonymous or wrongly-named character into a social and cultural system, neatly classifying them into a family, a class, a nation, and so on, explaining how they got their name, solving a conundrum and reaching 'the truth'.

While names can be used to reinforce nature (as they were deliberately by Shakespeare and Dickens), the critic must be careful not to be too reductive in turning the name into an explanation or allegory of the subject, or fatalistic proof that name equals destiny. Often personal pronouns or alternative ways of describing characters can be much more effective than a single name. In this light, the fact that many of Lispector's characters remain anonymous, although agents in the text, is telling; is she employing this technique as a way of generalizing and making one character represent humanity and its tribulations? Or suggesting that one's name does not really matter but one's own sense of self does? That names are arbitrary rather than influencing one's destiny? That it is not what others call you that is important, but who you know yourself to be? These are issues that will be addressed in the course of this chapter.

With a very distinctive name of her own, Clarice Lispector's Eastern-European roots were obvious among her contemporaries. Although they originally named her Haia, the Hebrew for 'life',[6] her parents changed her name to the less conspicuous, more Portuguese Clarice when they arrived in Brazil and started naturalization procedures, as many immigrants to a new country have done over the centuries, either to blend in more easily with their neighbours or because customs officials and other administrators could not spell their original names.[7] Her married name, which appears in some of the interviews she gave while accompanying her diplomat husband on postings abroad, was Senhora Maury Gurgel Valente,[8] a title that becomes a role she played on formal occasions. When earning her living from writing for the women's sections of newspapers, she used the pseudonyms 'Helen Palmer' and 'Teresa Quadros' and ghosted articles for the actress Ilka Soares. In the 'Explicação' [Explanation] that introduces *A via crucis do corpo* [The Via Crucis of the Body], signed ambivalently C.L., she claims that she had suggested using the pen-name 'Cláudio Lemos' to publish the risqué stories, but her editor refused, wanting to use her famous real name to sell the volume. Clarice Lispector was her professional name, her pen-name, the identity that she attached to her writing self and that occasionally overflowed into her texts.

Her name marked her out as different, exotic and mysterious among her peers, and later among her readers, and she used this tactic herself to make some of her characters stand out as being somehow 'outsiders' or 'misfits'. She commented on the origins of her own name thus: 'É um nome latino, né, eu perguntei para o meu pai desde quando havia Lispector na Ucrânia. Ele disse que há gerações e gerações anteriores. Eu suponho que o nome foi rolando, rolando, perdendo algumas sílabas e se transformando nessa coisa que parece "Lis no peito" em latim: flor de lis.' [It's a Latin name, isn't it; I asked my father how long there had been Lispectors in the Ukraine. He said for generations and generations before them. I suppose the name must have rolled on and on through time, losing some syllables and turning itself into this word that resembles 'lily on the chest': *fleur de lis* in Latin.]⁹

This chapter is a reflection on the fictional names that she chooses, changes, manipulates and invents. It analyses the resonances and connotations of the names, but also when and why she prefers some characters to be nameless. It is interesting to examine who calls who what, how the characters interrelate and their respect for social conventions and politeness. Tones of friendliness, intimacy and insult can all be detected from the way people address one another, particularly in Portuguese, which is a language highly sensitive to status and forms of address.

After a few general comments about different classes of names used by Lispector, I will focus on specific cases such as full names, nicknames, misnomers, the paring down to initials and anonymity. Lispector's nomenclature includes a vast selection of designations with different origins: biblically inspired or saints' names common in Catholic cultures, such as Francisco, Rute, José, Emmanuel, Jubileu and variations on Maria: Maria Angélica, Maria Aparecida, Maria das Dores. There are Brazilian names: Almira, Jandira, Jonga, Serjoca, Zilda, Janair; names with a foreign flavour: Arlete, Lisete, Marcel Pretre, Angela Pralini, Miss Algrave; and names with strong mythical, literary and historical connotations: Artur, Affonso, Cordélia, Eponina, Ofélia, Perseu, Ulisses. She also invented names in oneiric and surreal texts, such as Amptala, Simptar, Ele-ela, Psiu; aliens called Xext, Xexta, Ixtlan,¹⁰ and in her children's book *Quase de verdade* [Almost True] a community of chickens whose names all begin with O, 'em homenagem ao ovo' [in homage to the egg].

The majority of Lispector's characters are identified using their first name only, which at one level grants the reader an instant familiarity with them. In a similar retentive strategy, Lispector hardly ever gives physical descriptions of her creations: we are not told the colour of their hair or their eyes, their height and so on, as would be the case in a realist novel. The reader does, however, have access to the character's thought-processes and impressions, permitting a deeper empathy: getting to know them on the inside, as it were. When titles or nicknames are used to describe the characters, the reader sees how their relationships with the other characters work in a social context. For example, the short story 'Feliz aniversário' [Happy Birthday] (*Laços de família*) is told from the point of view of 'a aniversariante' [the woman celebrating her birthday], addressed as 'Mamãe' [Mum] by her children, obviously, and named 'Dona Anita' only once, by a neighbour. Her reduction to a depersonalizing descriptive term, 'a aniversariante', echoes her evaporated matriarchal power as the party, at which she is only really the pretext for a family reunion, goes on around her. The rest of her family is referred to according to their relationships with her, the daughters-in-law that she does not like being merely named by the neighbourhoods in Rio where they live: 'a nora de Ipanema' and 'a nora de Olária'.

Because the tendency is to describe a character using only the first name, when they are named in full including surname(s) it is for a significant reason. Social standing and pedigree can be guessed from one's name, as Carla, the bored bourgeois wife in the story 'A bela e a fera ou a ferida grande demais' [Beauty and the Beast or the Wound too Great] is very aware, enabling the narrator to satirize social convention: 'Ela tinha um nome a preservar: era Carla de Sousa e Santos. Eram importantes o "de" e o "e": marcavam classe e quatro-centos anos de carioca.' [She had a name to preserve: she was Carla de Sousa e Santos. The 'de' and the 'e' were important: they marked her class and four-hundred years of living in Rio.][11]

Another character, Dona Maria Rita Alvarenga Chagas Souza Melo in 'A partida do trem' [The Departure of the Train], is actually rather embarrassed by her ungainly name when she introduces herself: '"Alvarenga Chagas era o sobrenome do meu pai", acrescentou em pedido de desculpa por ter que falar tantas palavras só em dizer seu nome. "Chagas", acrescentou com modéstia, "eram as Chagas de Cristo. Mas pode me chamar de dona Maria Ritinha."' ['Alvarenga Chagas [wounds] was my father's surname', she added as a way of begging her pardon for having to use so many words just to say her name. 'Chagas', she added modestly, 'comes from the Wounds of Christ. But you can call me Dona Maria Ritinha.'][12] The pomposity of her full name is deflated by her invitation to address her in a much more informal way, using the diminutive Ritinha but maintaining the title which marks her age and the respect she expects. One of Lispector's most cocky and self-confident characters, Olímpico, the opportunist metalworker with pretensions to politics in *A hora da estrela*, introduces himself as Olímpico de Jesus Moreira Chaves, tagging on the final borrowed surnames to disguise his illegitimacy, betrayed by the 'de Jesus', which the narrator explains is the 'sobrenome dos que não têm pai' [the surname of those who have no father].[13]

The act of naming or baptism is recognized on several occasions as being significant in a child's future, either because their name suits them or because it is totally inappropriate. In a story about 'A menor mulher do mundo', a French explorer encounters a pygmy in the jungles of darkest Africa. He tries to colonize her with a gesture of discovery and naming, announcing solemnly: 'Você é Pequena Flor' [You are Little Flower].[14] This baptism categorizes her in a patronizing way, as if she were a botanical specimen, associated with the beauty and harmlessness of nature. The title of the story describes the pygmy, but only in terms of size, as 'the smallest woman in the world', and we never learn her 'real' name, the name she calls herself. Ironically, the explorer's name is Marcel Pretre, combining the roles of missionary ('prêtre' being French for priest) and colonizer, and alluding indirectly to Marcel Proust, the great literary cataloguer of people and their idiosyncrasies.[15]

Naming is a great responsibility, though, because a child becomes associated with the word chosen to represent them. A person may feel no identification with their name at all, like Lispector's Dona Frozina ('As manigâncias de Dona Frozina' [Dona Frozina's schemes]), who has to be consoled with the idea that things could be a lot worse: 'Olhe, d. Frozina, tem nomes piores do que o seu. Tem uma que se chama Flor de Lis — e como se acharam ruim o nome, deram-lhe apelido pior: Minhora. Quase Minhoca. E os pais que chamaram seus filhos de Brasil, Argentina, Colômbia, Bélgica e França? A senhora escapou de ser um país.' [Look, Dona Frozina, there are worse names than yours. There's a woman called Flor de Lis, and because they thought that name was awful she got an even worse nickname: Minhora. Which is almost Minhoca [worm]. And what about those parents who call their children Brazil, Argentina, Colombia, Belgium and France? You got away with not being a country.][16]

' The refusal to admit that a person is equal to or defined by their name is shown in 'A via crucis do corpo', where the story of the Nativity is retold with a pessimistic but realistic twist—the expectant mother is not called Maria Aparecida or Anunciada but Maria das

Dores, deriving from the Latin term *Mater Dolorosa* used to describe the Virgin Mary grieving for her son after the Crucifixion. Rather than calling him Jesus, she names her baby Emmanuel, meaning 'God with us', hoping to offer him magical protection against crucifixion. However, the last line of the text suggests that even so the child will not escape having to follow his own *Via Crucis* eventually, because 'Todos passam' [everyone has to go through it].[17] Lispector shows that the tactic of giving a positive name will inevitably fail as a talisman against fate.

Virgínia, the protagonist of Lispector's second novel *O lustre*, has an interesting view on the appropriateness of names in accompanying one's progress through life. She reflects:

Os meninos e as meninas deveriam tanto mudar de nome quando cresciam. Se alguém se chamava Daniel, agora, deveria ter sido Críl um dia. Virgínia [...] era um apelido cheio de paz atenta como de um recanto atrás do muro, lá onde cresciam finas ervas como cabelos e onde ninguém existia para ouvir o vento. Mas depois de perder aquela figura perfeita, magra, tão pequena e delicada como o maquinismo de um relógio, depois de perder a transparência e ganhar a cor, ela poderia se chamar Maria Madalena ou Hermínia ou mesmo qualquer outro nome menos Virgínia, de tão fresca e sombria antiguidade. Sim, e também poderia ter sido em pequena tranqüilamente Sibila, Sibila, Sibila.[18]

This character interprets her own name by linking it closely to her childhood and physical appearance, recognizing its Roman origins and literal etymological meaning and feeling that it no longer applies to her now that her body has matured, that she has embarked on a sexual relationship, and she therefore feels detached from it. Her choice of Maria Madalena as an alternative to her given name echoes clearly the virgin/whore contrast, which is explored in this novel through the figure of Virgínia herself, who is seen as representing various female archetypes: both virgin and whore, maternal at times but also unmaternal, and mysterious Sybil.[19]

The idea of one character having several names, either corresponding to the experience accumulated with age or to different facets of their personality, corroborates the idea that it is not possible to pin down identity in a word, a concept illustrated in the short story 'Praça Mauá' [Mauá Square]. Both protagonists have a real name and an assumed name, a *nom de guerre* that functions as a stage name, since both work in a nightclub, but the distinction between real and assumed becomes blurred. Luísa plays the role of Carla the stripper, in effect leading two lives: 'Carla era uma Luísa preguiçosa [...] uma Luísa tímida' [Carla was a lazy Luísa, a timid Luísa].[20] Carla seems to be playing Luísa, the names become confused, she does not know which is the real her. 'Luísa' is associated with home and husband (who refuses to call her Carla), 'Carla' with the nightclub and wild behaviour. At the end of the story, her femininity challenged, accused of not being a 'mulher de verdade' [a real woman], 'Carla virou Luísa. [...] Solitária. Sem remédio.' (85) [Carla turned into Luísa. Alone. No way back.] Stripped now of her gender she becomes definitively Luísa.

Luísa/Carla's best friend is Celsinho, a character composed of contrasts: he is a transvestite, neither man nor woman, born into a good family but working in the underworld, a man who is 'uma verdadeira mãe' [a real mother] to his adopted daughter, and whose *nome de guerra* is Moleirão. The names he uses contrast a diminutive with an augmentative: both are nicknames, but one is affectionate and infantilizing, and the other more of a joke-name that implies size and intensity. In the text, his names are used almost interchangeably, like his intermediate sexual state, indicating that he is the same person no matter how he is addressed, whereas the woman's alternating names emphasize the different roles she plays.

Other characters have no idea of what their name means, which also implies that they do not know their origins or, more importantly, who they are. This is the case with Macabéa, protagonist of *A hora da estrela*. Her unusual name associates her with the tribe of the Maccabees, eponymous heroes of the two books of Maccabees in the Old Testament.[21] The reader does not learn her name until half way through the text, when she introduces herself to Olímpico. Until this point she has been referred to as 'a nordestina' [the Northeasterner], 'a moça' [the girl], an anonymous immigrant among thousands of others who 'Não notam sequer que são facilmente substituíveis e que tanto existiriam como não existiriam' [don't even realize that they are easily replaceable and that nobody cares whether they exist or not] (28). From anonymity and disposability, she becomes now indelibly marked by her strange name. Indeed, at the end of the novel she becomes 'cada vez mais uma Macabéa' [more and more of a Macabéa] (101). When given access to speech for the first time in the text, she takes the opportunity to explain her name to Olímpico and the reader: 'E, se me permite, qual é mesmo a sua graça? /— Macabéa. /— Maca — o quê? /— Bea, foi ela obrigada a completar. /— Me desculpe mas até parece doença, doença de pele.' ['And, if I may ask,

what is your name?' 'Macabéa.' 'Maca—what?' 'Bea', she had to
complete it for him. 'Forgive me but it almost sounds like a disease, a
skin disease.'] (59)
    Olímpico is so thrown by this odd name that he cannot even
remember it completely and it is split in half. Macabéa is aware that it
provokes disgust in others and reveals that she was christened thus
because of a promise made to Nossa Senhora da Boa Morte: 'até um
ano de idade eu não era chamada porque não tinha nome, eu preferia
continuar a nunca ser chamada em vez de ter um nome que ninguém
tem' [Up until the age of one I wasn't called anything because I didn't
have a name; I would have preferred to never have been called anything
rather than having a name that no-one else has] (59–60). She would
much rather embrace anonymity than be made conspicuous with such
a distinctive and ugly name. When she asks Olímpico to reciprocate by
telling her what his name means, he panics and bluffs because he has
no idea, claiming: 'Eu sei mas não quero dizer!' [I know but I don't
want to tell you!] (61) He clearly associates name with identity, saying:
'de tanto me chamarem, eu virei eu. No sertão de Paraíba não há quem
não saiba quem é Olímpico. E um dia o mundo todo vai saber de mim.'
[I was called it so many times that I became me. In the backlands of
Paraíba everyone has heard of Olímpico. And one day the whole world
will know who I am.] (65) But this petty thief and callous opportunist
could not be more different from his name, which alludes to the home
of the gods and to sporting excellence.
    The rejection of name as predestination is implied in Lispector's
tactic of referring to her characters by initials, G.H., W... ('História
interrompida' [Story Interrupted], from the collection *A bela e a fera*
[Beauty and the Beast]), Rodrigo S.M.,[22] or alternative noun phrases
'a rapariga' [the girl], 'o autor' [the author], 'o homem' [the man], 'a
aniversariante', or of replacing the name with personal pronouns and
writing simply about 'ele' [he], 'ela' [she], or 'eu' [I]. For the reader,
it is tempting to see the initials as a puzzle and attempt to invest them
with meaning. It is also difficult to avoid identifying the narrators of
Lispector's first person narratives with the writer herself. Sometimes
she even introduces herself as Clarice or C.L. or gives clues in the
form of biographical details (Ângela Pralini, in *Um sopro de vida*, has a
dog named Ulisses and wrote a book entitled *A cidade sitiada*; the
narrator of *Água viva* suffers from insomnia and drinks endless cups of
coffee) which apply equally to the character and to Lispector, a
woman writer who really existed. Indeed, Carlos Mendes de Sousa

considers her inclusion of the representation of her own signature among the possible titles of *A hora da estrela* 'o culminar de um processo de auto-revelação que se entrevê ao longo do percurso literário de Clarice Lispector' [the culmination of a process of self-revelation which can be glimpsed along the course of Clarice Lispector's literary career].[23]

Many of her short stories and the novel *Água viva* are peopled with nameless characters. In 'Amor', only Ana is named, the other characters are shadows around her, 'o cego' [the blind man], 'os filhos' [her children], contradicting the thrust of the story where Ana seems only to have worth in relation to others. In 'Uma história de tanto amor' [A Story of such Love] (*Felicidade clandestina* [Clandestine Happiness]), the animals are named but the humans are not, and in 'O búfalo' [The Buffalo] (*Laços de família*) the designations 'a mulher' and 'o búfalo' work to dehumanize the woman and to put human and animal, male and female, on an equal footing in their shared pain. Martim's existential crisis in *A maçã no escuro* [The Apple in the Dark] is reflected in his loss of name—he is almost always referred to as 'o homem'—as well as his temporary lack of speech. He awaits the rebirth of his identity, which occurs when he is arrested, that is, recognized by and inscribed within the law. Joana, in *Perto do coração selvagem*, prefers not to know the name of her lover, denoted 'o homem' in the text: 'nem sabia o nome dele ... Não desejara sabê-lo, dissera-lhe: quero te conhecer por outras fontes [...] sou Joana, tu és um corpo vivendo, eu sou um corpo vivendo, nada mais.' [She didn't even know his name ... She didn't want to know it, she had told him: I want to know you from other sources. I am Joana, you are a living body, I am a living body, no more no less.] (209)

The ability to describe oneself in different terms, not just with the name that others use, can be seen as a step towards knowing oneself better. This is what Lóri learns from Ulisses in *Uma aprendizagem ou o livro dos prazeres*: 'ele dissera uma vez que queria que ela, ao lhe perguntarem seu nome, não respondesse "Lóri" mas que pudesse responder "meu nome é eu", pois teu nome, dissera ele, é um eu [...] não Lóri mas o seu nome secreto.' [He had once said that when she was asked her name, he wanted her not to reply 'Lóri' but be able to reply 'my name is I', because your name, he had said, is an I, not Lóri but her secret name.][24] By the end of the novel, after much meditation and soul-searching, she manages to break free of the social and personally imposed constraints on her self and is able to declaim to her lover: 'só agora eu me chamo "Eu". E digo: Eu está apaixonada pelo teu eu.' [Only now can I call myself 'I'. And say: I am in love with your I.] (173) According to this statement, she and Ulisses have reached total identification, both are 'eu', fully assumed subjects, equal. 'I' / 'eu' has become a name and a noun.[25]

G.H. reaches a similar kind of purification, stripping herself down to her essence by rejecting her name and the trappings of imposed identity. She had been dependent on others to tell her who she was, believing her reflection in them to be the real 'her': 'pouco a pouco eu havia me transformado na pessoa que tem o meu nome. E acabei sendo o meu nome. É suficiente ver no couro de minhas valises as iniciais G.H., e eis-me. Também dos outros eu não exigia mais do que a primeira cobertura das iniciais dos nomes.' [Little by little I had transformed myself into the person who bears my name. And I ended up being my name. All you need to do is see the initials G.H. in the leather of my suitcases and there you have me. And from others too I had demanded nothing more than knowing the bare cover up of the initials of their names.][26] Reduced to the monogram on her luggage, she feels as if she lives 'entre aspas' [in inverted commas] (35), like a remark 'aside', ironically detached from real life. From the outset, the use of initial letters abbreviates and condenses the name, short-circuiting language, fragmenting the word, returning to the initial, beginning, origin.[27] They are letters taken in sequence from the alphabet, which are followed, most appropriately by 'I', in English the letter and personal pronoun denoting self.

G.H. reflects long and hard about the relationship between language and reality:

Amor é quando não se dá nome à identidade das coisas? [...] De agora em diante eu poderia chamar qualquer coisa pelo nome que eu inventasse: no quarto seco se podia, pois qualquer nome serviria, já que nenhum serviria. [...] O nome é um acréscimo, e impede o contato com a coisa. O nome da coisa é um intervalo para a coisa. A vontade do acréscimo é grande — porque a coisa nua é tão tediosa. (91, 100, 143)[28]

In terms of a name, the reader only knows the character's initials, which could be interpreted as standing for Gênero Humano [Human-kind].[29] By the end of the novel, G.H. has completely embraced anonymity and submerged herself in subjectivity, assuming her 'nudity': 'não tenho nome, e este é o meu nome. E porque me des-personalizo a ponto de não ter o meu nome, respondo cada vez que alguém disser: eu.' [I don't have a name, and that is my name. And because I depersonalize myself to the point of not having a name, I reply every time someone says: I.] (179) The depersonalization of G.H. and Martim is echoed in the short story 'Desespero e desenlace às três da tarde'[30] where Senhor J.B.[31] is so nauseated by the physical proximity and unashamed sensuality of the people crushed against him on the bus that he has to endure an intense struggle not to vomit, his panic analogous to that of Ana in 'Amor' and also to Sartrean nausea. When he discharges the contents of his stomach it seems that his soul pours out with them, as well as the contents of his pockets, for all his personal documents fall into the mess. 'Espantou-se. Sabia que jamais teria a audacidade de sujar sua mão ao tocar na identidade imunda. Estava sem atestado de vida. Ele de repente não era mais. Simplesmente, sem documentos, não podia mais provar a sua vida.' [He was amazed. He knew that he would never have the audacity to dirty his hands by touching the filthy identity card. He had no documentary proof of his life. Suddenly he no longer existed. Without documents, he was simply unable to prove he was alive.] (53) But what at first feels like vulnerability is soon revealed as release:

Como é bom a vida sem eu [...]. E assim que nascera um homem comum. Quase alegremente tinha que começar tudo de novo e sobre outra base. [...] Acordou contente e pensou numa gargalhada muda contra o mundo: nada tenho a ver comigo mesmo. É como se eu fosse um búlgaro que acabasse de ter saltado no mundo de pára-quedas. E sem passaporte. Feliz estranheza, a desta inovação, um primeiro modo de existir. (53)[32]

Life without a name and a past becomes equated with the freedom to start from scratch and create himself anew. He has moved beyond legal and social classification, without an official identity, for he no longer has a bilhete de identidade.

Therefore it appears that the solution that Lispector's characters generally find to the problem of not identifying with one's name is to surpass it, embracing either the 'eu' or anonymity as the only satisfactory ways to refer to one's self. This is certainly the conclusion reached by Ângela Pralini (Um sopro de vida), who like G.H. sees the name as an artificial attachment: 'Me deram um nome e me alienaram de mim [...]. Fora de mim sou Ângela. Dentro de mim sou anônimo. [...] Eu sou nome.' [I was given a name and alienated from myself. Outside myself I am Ângela. Inside myself I am anonymous. I am name.][33] Ângela sums up a split in subjectivity, the chasm between how a person perceives herself and how others perceive her, the contrast between the view from inside and that from outside. While she does recognize the power of words to create by conferring identity—'O que não existe passa a existir ao receber um nome' [That which does not exist starts to exist when it receives a name] (100)—she cannot accept being encapsulated in language: 'Eu, reduzida a uma palavra? mas, que palavra me representa? De uma coisa sei: eu não sou o meu nome. O meu nome pertence aos que me chamam.' [I, reduced to a word? But what word represents me? I know one thing for sure: I am not my name. My name belongs to those who call me by it.] (133)

Ângela's dilemma sums up the essential problem of name and the fundamental contradiction between identification and rejection. She is torn between asserting her identity and declaring her freedom from categorization: between the ideas 'Eu sou nome' [I am name] and 'Eu não sou o meu nome' [I am not my name]. Like the other characters who find liberation through denying their name, Ângela embraces anonymity and eventually disappears, not adopting the private name 'eu', but instead embracing the infinite and fluctuating possibilities of nothing: 'meu nome íntimo é: zero. É um eterno começo permanentemente interrompido pela minha consciência de começo.' [My intimate name is: zero. It is an eternal beginning permanently interrupted by my awareness that it is a beginning.] (133)

Notes to Chapter 3

1. 'You know the name you were given, you do not know the name that you have.' This enigmatic phrase from 'The Book of Certainties' is the epigraph to Saramago's *Todos os nomes*, 7th edn. (Lisbon: Caminho, 1997); trans. Margaret Jull Costa as *All the Names* (London: Harvill, 1999). NB: all translations into English in this paper are mine unless otherwise indicated.
2. 'One could write the story of modern philosophy (and Wittgenstein's role in that story) as the attempt to dislodge philosophical thinking from [the] idea that naming (or language generally, or even philosophy itself) takes us to the center of being.' Michael Ragussis, *Acts of Naming: The Family Plot in Fiction* (Oxford and New York: Oxford University Press, 1986), 220.
3. See Peter Verstappen, *The Book of Surnames* (London: Sphere, 1982), 9.
4. See Tim Valentine, Tim Brennan and Sérge Brédart: 'Approaches to Proper Names', *The Cognitive Psychology of Proper Names: On the Importance of Being Ernest* (London and New York: Routledge, 1996), 1–19.
5. In e.g. Article 7-1 of the Convention of the Rights of the Child, which was adopted by the General Assembly of the United Nations on 20 Nov. 1989. See Valentine, Brennan and Brédart, 'Approaches to Proper Names', 6.

CLARICE LISPECTOR'S DRAMATIS PERSONAE 53

6. See Teresa Cristina Montero Ferreira, *Eu sou uma pergunta: Uma biografia de Clarice Lispector* (Rio de Janeiro: Rocco, 1999), 26.

7. Both Lispector's names were frequently misspelt by critics. Sérgio Milliet declared that her 'estranho e até desagradável' [strange and rather unpleasant] name could only be a pseudonym: *Diário crítico* (São Paulo: Brasiliense, 1945), ii. 27–32 at 27. Alvaro Lins wrote about the lyricism of 'Sra. Clarisse Lispector' in 'A experiência incompleta' (1944), *Os mortos de sobrecasaca* (Rio de Janeiro: Civilização Brasileira, 1963), 186–91. Carlos Mendes de Sousa mentions another review by Dirceu Quintanilha, 'Clarice Linspector [sic] e um monumento do passado', *Clarice Lispector: Figuras da escrita* (Braga: Universidade do Minho; Centro de Estudos Humanísticos, 2000), 66 n. 9.

8. In a letter to her sisters, she commented: 'Todo esse mês de viagem nada tenho feito, nem lido, nem nada — sou inteiramente Clarice Gurgel Valente.' Letter dated 19 Aug. 1944, Colecção Biblioteca Nacional, Rio de Janeiro.

9. Television interview with Júlio Lerner for TV Cultura, São Paulo, 1977. Claire Varin has commented on the symbolic resonances of the name in *Rencontres brésiliennes* (Quebec: Trois, 1987), and Hélène Cixous puns with it in several of her appreciations of Lispector's works, such as *Vivre l'orange* (Paris: des femmes, 1979).

10. Ixtlan is the name of a town in Mexico and also appears in the title of a book by Carlos Castañeda relating his experiences as the acolyte of a Yaqui Indian shaman who taught him the power of dreaming and the importance of accessing other worlds of perception—most appropriate for the Lispector story, in which Ixtlan the alien from Saturn arrives on earth to liberate Ruth Algrave from her inhibitions ('Miss Algrave', *A via crucis do corpo*). See *Journey to Ixtlan: The Lessons of Don Juan* (London: Arkana; Penguin, 1989; first publ. 1972).

11. *A bela e a fera*, 5th edn. (Rio de Janeiro: Francisco Alves, 1995), 106.

12. *Onde estivestes de noite*, 6th edn. (Rio de Janeiro: Francisco Alves, 1992), 24.

13. *A hora da estrela*, 19th edn. (Rio de Janeiro: Francisco Alves, 1992), 60.

14. *Laços de família* (Lisbon: Relógio d'Agua, 1989?), 63.

15. I have discussed this short story in greater detail in 'More Than Meets the Eye: A New Look at a Short Story by Clarice Lispector', *Portuguese Studies* 14 (1998), 170–80.

16. *Onde estivestes de noite*, 6th edn. (Rio de Janeiro: Francisco Alves, 1992), 88.

17. *A via crucis do corpo*, 4th edn. (Rio de Janeiro: Francisco Alves, 1991), 50.

18. 'Boys and girls really should have to change their names when they grow up. If someone's name was Daniel, now, it must have been Ciríl once. Virgínia was a name full of attentive peace like that of a nook behind the wall, there where grass as thin as hair grew and where no-one existed to hear the wind. But ever since she had lost that perfect, slim figure, as small and delicate as the mechanism of a watch, since she had lost transparency and gained colour, she could be called Maria Madalena or Hermínia or even any other name except Virgínia, which had the freshness and sombreness of antiquity. Yes, and she could have been, in her childhood, quite happily, Sibila, Sibila, Sibila.' *O lustre*, 8th edn. (Rio de Janeiro: Francisco Alves, 1992), 296.

19. Joana, in *Perto do coração selvagem*, is another figure constituted by the contrasting images of angel and devil: 'Joana, pensava o homem aguardando sua vinda. Joana, nome nu, santa Joana, tão virgem.' [Joana, thought the man, waiting for her to

arrive. Joana, a naked name, St Joan, so virginal.], in contrast to her rival, the ultra-feminine Lídia. *Perto do coração selvagem*, 16th edn. (Rio de Janeiro: Francisco Alves, 1994), 182. The novel narrates Joana's progress towards self-knowledge and independence, her quest to become a hero, like her namesake Joan of Arc.

20. *A via crucis do corpo*, 81.

21. Philip Swanson is one critic of many who have commented on the possible origins of the name: 'Clarice Lispector and *A hora da estrela*: *"Féminité"* or *"Réalité"'*, *Romance Quarterly* 42/3 (1995), 143–53 at 152 n. 5.

22. Marta Peixoto suggests that the initials point towards the narrator's sado-masochistic tendencies; see *Passionate Fictions* (Minneapolis: University of Minnesota Press, 1994), 91. They could also stand for 'Sua Majestade', ironically emphasizing his position as creator and his aspirations to be controller and ruler of his characters, or even 'sexo masculino'.

23. Carlos Mendes de Sousa, 'A assinatura, o nome, a coisa: Lispector', *Diacrítica* 11 (1996), 167–74 at 168–9.

24. *Uma aprendizagem ou o livro dos prazeres*, 18th edn. (Rio de Janeiro: Francisco Alves, 1991), 19–20, 21.

25. When asked who he is, Ixtlan, the alien from Saturn, replies 'em forma de vento: 'Eu sou um eu" [in the form of wind: 'I am an I']; *A via crucis do corpo*, 29.

26. *A paixão segundo G.H.*, 16th edn. (Rio de Janeiro: Francisco Alves, 1991), 29.

27. Américo Lindeza Diogo notes that 'a restituição à origem é rejeição da identidade clássica coberta pelo nome próprio (assim se pode ler as iniciais)' [the restitution to the origin is a rejection of the classical identity covered by the proper name (that is how we can read initials)]; *Da vida das baratas: Uma leitura d'"A paixão segundo G.H.' de Clarice Lispector* (Braga and Coimbra: Angelus Novus, 1993), 64.

28. 'Is love when you don't give a name to the identity of things? From now on I could call anything by the name I invented for it: one could, in the dry room, because any name would do, there since none would do. A name is an addition, and it impedes contact with the thing. The name of the thing is an interval for the thing. The wish for addition is great—because a bare thing is so tedious.'

29. Michel Peterson suggests that G.H. is the 'figuration du genre humain (gênero humano) dans sa totalité anonyme' [the figuration of humankind in its anonymous totality]; 'Les cafards de Clarice Lispector', *Études françaises* 25/1 (1989), 39–50. José Américo Motta Pessanha offers the alternative interpretation that G.H. stands for 'Gente Heróica' [heroic people]: 'Clarice Lispector: O itinerário da paixão', *Remate de males* 9 (1989), 181–98 at 198.

30. A rarely discussed text commissioned by the Portuguese journal *Colóquio-letras*, which appeared in number 25 (1975), 50–3.

31. Could they stand for *Jornal do Brasil*, meaning, by association, the man in the street? They are more likely to be the distant echo of a theatre review that Lispector sent home from the United States of Archibald MacLeish's play *J.B.*, an updated version of the book of Job, which became a Broadway hit: 'Deu-se em Washington a pré estreia da peça de Archibald MacLeish', *Diário carioca* (21 Dec. 1958), Clarice Lispector Archive, see Sousa, *Figuras da escrita*, 132–3 n. 6. Lispector comments that '"J.B." — homem de negócios em plena prosperidade

chamado ao jeito moderno pelas iniciais' ['J.B.', a successful business man, is referred to in the modern fashion by using his initials].

32. 'How good it is to live without an I. And that is how a common man was born. Almost joyfully, he would have to start everything from scratch and on a new basis. He woke up happy and thought with a silent guffaw at the world: I have nothing to do with myself. It's as if I were a Bulgarian who has just parachuted into the world. Without a passport. Lucky strangeness, that of this innovation, a primary mode of existence.'

33. *Um sopro de vida (Pulsações)*, 9th edn. (Rio de Janeiro: Francisco Alves, 1991), 21, 43, 47.

CHAPTER 4

Lóri's Journey:
The Quest for Identity in
Uma aprendizagem ou o livro dos prazeres

Patricia Zecevic

The main title of Clarice Lispector's novel *Uma aprendizagem*,[1] taken alone, is in a significant sense misleading, for it evokes the linear development of a person from early youth to maturity in the pattern of the *Bildungsroman*, leading to 'journeymanship' or even 'mastery'.[2] However, as the subtitle *O livro dos prazeres* suggests in its evocation of the long tradition of erotic pillow-books extolling the 'static' pleasures of the moment, what is presented here is a far more complex process, one in which the progress made is offset by repeated regressions and in which straightforward linear development is overcome by organic growth.

Indeed, the central character Lóri (like her worldly-wise mentor and partner, Ulisses), is already beyond 'apprenticeship' in any conventional sense of the word. She is fully developed in ordinary terms: 'uma mulher feita' [a mature woman] (96) in her late twenties, who is utterly conventionally comfortable in her socio-economic and gender identities. She 'gratefully' acknowledges the superiority of manly men; she is, indeed, 'uma adoradora dos homens' [a worshipper of men] (81), and sees Ulisses as 'o seu homem' [her man] (43). She in turn, as Ulisses says with approval, is 'uma mulher muito antiga' [a woman of antiquity] (68, 116), one who has not broken with 'a linhagem de mulheres através do tempo' [a female genealogy that is age-old] (116). For her, a woman's identity still means having children (51). And like the conventional 'man-made woman', Lóri consistently refuses to take the initiative in her relationship with Ulisses (126).[3]

Moreover, she fully accepts traditional male–female roles, such as the division of tasks: 'Ele, o homem, se ocupava atiçando o fogo. Ela nem se lembrava de fazer o mesmo: não era o seu papel, pois tinha o seu homem para isso.' [He, the man, took care of lighting the fire. She couldn't remember ever having done this: it was not her role, as she had her man to do it.] (122)

To the very end, for both of them, happiness equals conventional marriage.[4] In other words, she—like Ulisses—has a very strong sense of identity before the 'action' proper begins, one that both characters retain throughout. In addition, Lóri's class-identity is quite secure: 'De acordo como era feita [ser prostituta] parecia-lhe mais fácil e menos angustioso do que trabalhar atrás do balcão de uma loja' [Being the kind of person she was [a prostitute] seemed easier and less distressing to her than working behind the counter in some shop] (56). And although fearful of the socialist Ulisses' disapproval of her privileged family circumstances, she has no real regrets or guilt about her background as a rather spoilt rich girl whose father has always given her all she wants (59). She does not get on with her family: 'Tentaram me marcar mas sempre foram gente de segundo plano na minha vida' [They tried to leave their mark on me, but they were always of secondary importance in my life] (110); but this fact in no way disturbs the social identity she retains consistently throughout: her awareness of her marginal position as a woman of the Brazilian middle classes (179).

Lóri's problem is that she simply wishes to go beyond the boundaries of this social identity.[5] In this spirit, she accepts the challenge of her friend the fortune-teller: 'você é diferente dos outros — cosmicamente diferente [...] então aceite que você não pode ter a vida burguesa dos outros' [you are different from the others—cosmically different—so accept that you cannot have the bourgeois life that others lead] (97). While she is, like Ulisses, experienced in the ways of the world, and it is emphasized over and over again that she is no longer a virgin, she is, for most of the novel, a spiritual virgin: it is significantly not until the end of her journey that she declares 'mas esta noite é a minha primeira vez' [but tonight is my first time] (171). And it is precisely this lack of a sense of a spiritual dimension that drives her to transcend the identity she has inherited. Lóri does not want an identity-for-identity's-sake, but rather to find herself in relationship to the universe as a physical entity, even if that means regressing to the animal state: 'Não, eu não quero ser eu somente, por ter um eu próprio, quero é a ligação extrema entre mim e a terra friável e perfumada' [No, I don't want to be just

me, for the sake of having an identity of my own, rather I want the
ultimate bond between me and the fragile, perfumed earth] (51). She
is aware that her own path, 'o atalho onde ela fosse finalmente ela' [the
path where she might be herself at last] (67), is, as she herself underlines
in her use of the term 'atalho' [shortcut] rather than 'caminho'
[path/way], off the beaten track.

Lóri is deeply unhappy in her awareness that something fundamental is lacking in her life. Her past sexual experiences, for example,
have been merely physical and egotistical on her part: 'com os amantes
que tivera ela como que apenas emprestava o seu corpo a si própria
para o prazer, era só isso, e mais nada' [with past lovers she had given
her body for her own pleasure, nothing more nothing less] (127).
What she feels that Ulisses might be able to teach her is how one can,
in fact, learn to love and to be happy: 'pode-se aprender tudo,
inclusive a amar! E o mais estranho, Lóri, pode-se aprender a ter
alegria!' [One can learn everything, even to love. And curiously, Lóri,
one can learn to be joyful!] (61–2). Developed she may be, but Lóri's
anxiety derives from the terror she has of not growing. She claims,
disheartened, that her present identity is 'apenas uma pequena parte
de si mesma' [Just a small part of herself] (51). She feels she is stuck
at a primitive stage in her possible evolution comparable to the passage
'do homem-macaco ao pitecantropus erectus' [from early ape-man to
Pithecantropus erectus] (87).

Her very high, indeed 'Faustian' ambition (88) is, as Ulisses puts it,
to 'pedir o máximo a si mesma' [ask the maximum of herself] (64), an
ambition that certainly involves 'estágios necessários' [necessary
stages] (117), but entails too a cyclical process, full of regressions, in
which Lóri's fixed personality-structure is transposed from level to
(higher) level without ever losing its basic continuity. It involves, as
she puts it herself, the enormously difficult task of self-overcoming: 'É
com enorme esforço que consigo me sobrepor a mim mesma' [it is
with enormous effort that I manage to overcome myself] (64), in
which her given identity finds its place in a greater whole. The
Apprenticeship that Ulisses is in the middle of (49) and that she,
trembling with fear, embarks on is the eternal, everlasting path of the
human need to become human: 'A mais premente necessidade de um
ser humano era tornar-se um ser humano' [the most pressing need of
a human being was to become human] (39); a human necessity that,
we are assured, is also the highest of human aspirations (87).

In this essay, I hope to show that the nature of the growth process that Lóri experiences in her journey to a fuller sense of selfhood is an expansion of her personality, in which she is integrated in a higher, 'mais real' [more real] life (65). It is a growth and expansion of her personality that will incorporate the body *and* soul to love with that Ulisses is waiting for: 'Esperarei nem que sejam anos que você também tenha corpo-alma para amar' [I shall wait, years if need be, for you too to have a body-and-soul to love with] (57); which will embody the whole Lóri that he both loves and desires: 'é o corpo que eu quero. Mas quero inteira, com a alma também' [it is the body that I love, but I want it in its entirety, with the soul as well] (33), and which is symbolized in the novel by the allusive device of the expansion of her name from 'Lóri' to 'Loreley' (114).

Lóri's problem is summed up in the prologue, 'A origem da primavera ou a morte necessária em pleno dia' [The beginning of spring or a necessary death in broad daylight]. She is in anguish because she is caught in a web of (as yet) irreconcilable polarities: no matter how busy she keeps herself, whether embroidering or going to the cinema, this pain always returns (73). She is torn between physical experience—the haemorrhage, for instance, which may be menstruation (20, 22)—and psychological experience, the latter possibly a symptom of stress. She is torn between sexual desire (23, 26) and a desire to find herself in the divine, specifically in the lunar Goddess Diana (21), in whose rays she basks as others bask in the sun (41–2, 134). She is torn, too, between 'dry' desire (23, 30) and 'wet'— that is, fecund—love (25). Such contradictions and confusions accompany her on her journey. They are symptoms of the unbearable tensions that she feels between her everyday identity and another, greater self she dimly intuits within her—one that surfaces, occasionally and briefly, in her aesthetic identity as a 'pretty' object of desire (24, 27), but which remains for the most part, and certainly at the outset of her 'Apprenticeship', a mysterious occult absent presence: her hidden 'soul' (26–7).

As the title of the Prologue underlines, Lóri is being pulled apart, then, by an agonizing tension between a longing for Death as discontinuity (42–3) and Life as continuity (44). Her compassion for others attracts her to Life, but her fascination with her dormant inner self draws her to the silence of the Abyss within and without—the Nothingness that seems to promise everything: 'Viver na orla da morte e das estrelas é vibração mais tensa do que as veias podem suportar. O coração tem que se apresentar diante do Nada sozinho.'

[To live on the edge of death and the stars is a vibration so tense that the veins cannot sustain it. The heart has to appear before the Nothingness alone.] (46–7) In other words, paradoxically, it is the rhythm, the throbbing of life that Lóri feels in the silence. It is in the Nothingness that she feels her own pulse—her self. And in a real sense, 'nothing' happens to Lóri. Her whole way, her journey, is one of rediscovery (119); the elements that make up her life remain unchanged in themselves. What changes is the emergence of an ever clearer pattern holding them precariously and tenuously together, a pattern that can be identified as being made up of four distinct stages of a journey.

All that happens in the main body of the novel, 'Luminescência' [Luminescence], is in effect an unpacking of the 'prologue': we move from necessary confusion—'desarticulação' [disjointedness] (114)—to clarity and then to distinctness, with regular relapses into desperate confusion in between. It is a path with many detours, for which Lóri frequently prays (66, 67, 133). While her shame at having a body goes hand in hand with hiding her soul, she paradoxically longs to get physically very close to God: 'desejara colar o peito e os membros no Deus' [she had longed to join her limbs and breast with God] (79). This paradox contains both her anguish and her salvation, as I hope to show. So, too, her pain at not having a future (81) is alleviated by a feeling of being 'na sua primeira infância' [in her early infancy] (82) in her Apprenticeship. And it is '[n]o estranho e encantado momento em que estivera sendo' [in the strange and enchanted moment in which she was being] (83) that she begins to glimpse the necessary antithesis of Pain and Loss, and encounters 'si mesma' [herself] (84)— a deeper self that is a threat to her already-established self: 'o que ela fora até então' [what she had been up to then] (84).

At this first stage of her apprenticeship, Lóri, although frightened, experiences fleeting happiness at being a part of a whole: 'um dia será o mundo com sua impersonalidade soberba versus a minha extrema individualidade de pessoa mas seremos um só' [one day the world with its magnificent impersonality will be face-to-face with my extreme personal individuality but we shall be as one] (85). The 'grande passo dado na aprendizagem' [great step taken in the apprenticeship] (83) that both Lóri and Ulisses are aware of is that her former self is in some sense 'dying' and being born again in the peace of a larger, embracing identity (85). Lóri chooses to be her own guardian angel (88); in other words, her stable identity takes responsibility for, looks after and cherishes her emerging, greater identity—symbolized by water in the vast mysterious form of the ocean (89), which is both the World (90) and the Nothingness—for, unlike the swimming pool, the beach will be deserted (90)—of God: 'Aí estava o mar, a mais ininteligível das existências não-humanas' [Behold the sea, the most inapprehensible of all nonhuman entities] (91).

At this early stage, Lóri's lesser self struggles 'corpo a corpo' [in close combat] (90) with her inner self, but her courageous acceptance of being part of a larger whole gives her warmth and definition (91). The necessary death (17) and the rebirth (35) of the 'prologue' is re-enacted here at a higher, because more explicit and more complex, level of consciousness.

Now at the second stage of her journey, Lóri experiences the serious joy of awakening to a deep connection between sexual union (symbolized by her wading into the 'masculine' sea: 117, 129): 'E era isso o que estava lhe faltando: o mar por dentro como o líquido espesso de um homem' [And that was what she had been lacking: the sea inside her like the thick liquid of a man] (93), psychological integration, which is marked by the present tense: 'Agora ela está toda igual a si mesma' [Now she is wholly one with herself] (93), and the *unio mystica* with God that she dimly apprehends (92). In the sea (that is, symbolically in Nothing, the Abyss, God), Lóri possesses 'um ritmo de vida' [a rhythm of life] (93). For the first time, she feels something of the greatness of becoming part (albeit a tiny one) of God: 'podia-se era agregar-se a ele e ser grande também' [it was possible to become part of him and be great too] (95).

But this moment of illumination, of epiphany, soon passes, and Lóri returns to a state of desperate confusion (96), which she vainly seeks to disguise under a false mask that hides her soul (97–8). The result is a return of the bitter unhappiness (99) that we had witnessed in the 'prologue'. According to Ulisses, her transformation is short-lived because she has not yet learned how to live through pain's polar opposite, pleasure (105): 'quem é capaz de sofrer intensamente, também pode ser capaz de intensa alegria' [whoever is capable of intense suffering, is also capable of intense joy] (114–15). It emerges that the body-and-soul union (106) that Lóri seeks is impossible to sustain without love of other people, beginning with her pupils. Learning (and enabling learning through teaching) is once again brought to our attention by Ulisses as the *sine qua non* of successful becoming through loving human relations: 'Depois você aprenderá, Lóri, e então experimentará em cheio a grande alegria que é de se comunicar, de transmitir' [You'll learn, Lori, and then you'll fully experience the great joy of communicating and passing on your legacy] (108). Despite this temporary relapse to a self-defensive closing-down of her personality—'sentiu, já por defesa, um esvazia-mento de si própria' [she felt, as if in self-defence, an emptying of herself] (117)—Lóri has made some progress, as symbolized by the use of her full name (114). She loves communicating with others, especially in her teaching and takes loving care of her pupils by using her allowance to buy them suitable warm clothing and red umbrellas and red woollen socks for the winter (118, 119).

Indeed, her *joie de vivre* is almost irrepressible (120). Nevertheless, in another bout of regression—'entrou numa fase [...] em que regrediu como se tivesse perdido tudo o que ganhara' [she entered a phase in which she regressed as if she had lost all that she had gained] (128)—Lóri feels, again, that she has gained nothing: 'o que ganhara? Nada' [what had she gained? Nothing] (128)—a formulation that neatly encapsulates her position. From an ordinary, practical point of view, her gain is indeed negligible. But from the point of view of her spiritual growth, she has penetrated deeper into the silent Nothingness of being, of God. Significantly, she has not lost the happiness that regular bathing in the sea gives her (129).

Much of Lispector's realism lies in the depiction of the terrible and frequent regressions that afflict Lóri, and which precipitate a destructive aggression (132), which is, however, held in check by her equally strong compassion for others: 'E não havia perigo de realmente destruir ninguém ou nada porque a piedade era nela tão forte quanto a ira' [And there was no real danger of destroying anyone or anything, because compassion was as strong in her as anger] (132). This 'balance', this acceptance of the mysterious, contradictory, and (for the intellect) confusing polarity at the heart of life is, in fact, the emergence in Lóri of a self that is more in touch with the mystery of being alive: 'Então com ternura aceitou estar no mistério de ser viva' [Then with tenderness she accepted being in the mystery of being alive] (134). This expression of Lóri's, in its juxtaposing of but differentiation between the two (essential and existential) verbs 'to be'—*ser* and *estar*—elegantly articulates a harmonious resolution in Lóri, at this stage of her journey, to the problem of being, one that results in her falling into a calm and gentle sleep (134).

This acceptance marks the passage of a year since the 'Spring' of the opening 'prologue': Lóri has come full circle in her Apprenticeship (135) and to the end of the second phase of her journey. Now she has some sense of having a future (135), which will involve an integration, expressed longingly in terms of 'finas misturas' [subtle interminglings] (136) of the physical and the spiritual that, for her, go to make up the quintessence of life: 'a vida melhor e mais fina' [a better, finer life] (136). She feels that she appreciates, indeed shares the (terrible) beauty of the world (137), a beauty achieved through discipline (138). And she longs to be in possession of that inner growth that only a part of her—her inner self—understands: 'nem entendia aquilo que parte dela entendia' [yet she did not understand that which a part of her understood] (140).

Even so, Lóri frequently feels 'lost' and impelled to take a step beyond pleasure (142). She is now, in this third phase, in search of the beautiful external world (144–5), a search accompanied by her own sense of inner growth ('era um crescimento dentro dela' [it was a growing within her] (145)), which she compares to the fruits of the earth that she sees at the market (146). Indeed, Lóri's inner self is beginning to gain ascendancy over her outer identity: 'ela estava procurando sair da dor, como se procurasse sair de uma realidade outra que durara sua vida até então' [she was trying to emerge from the pain, as if trying to emerge from another reality which had lasted all her life until then] (146). This is a clear allusion to the fact that she is moving beyond rebirth into a New Life. The nevertheless difficult 'overcoming', that is, integration of her lesser self is signalled in her self-conscious use of the first person singular: 'se eu fosse eu' [if I were I] (147) in reference to herself, and in her allusion to biographies in which people 'de repente passavam a ser elas mesmas' [suddenly became themselves] (148).

This breakthrough to the dangerous stage of fully being one's self turns out to be overpowering and barely controllable: 'Ser-se o que se é era grande demais e incontrolável' [to be who one is was too big and uncontrollable] (148). But it is held (precariously) in check by making contact with the Other—here, a girl at the bus-stop, 'uma estranha' [a stranger] (149)—as a sign of Lóri's acceptance of love of the other and the happiness it brings, even though inextricably linked by Ulisses with the tragedy (111) and traumatic cruelty of Life: 'Nossa vida é truculenta, Loreley: nasce-se com sangue e com sangue corta-se para sempre a possibilidade de união perfeita: o cordão umbilical' [Human

life is cruel, Loreley: we are born with blood and with blood we sever
for ever the possibility of perfect union: the umbilical cord] (115).
Lóri is aware to some extent that this fuller identity can never be
known, in the sense of understood by the mind: 'um pouco de mim
eu sei [...] mas isso não responde quem sou eu' [I know a little of me,
but this does not answer who am I] (151). But while it cannot be
known, it can be felt, consciously by humans, unconsciously by
animals: 'ela continuava a não saber quem ela era [...] mas sabia que
era uma feroz entre os ferozes seres humanos' [she continued to not
know who she was, but she knew that she was a [female] wild animal
among wild human beings] (152).

Lóri's acceptance—the fourth and final stage of her journey—of the
inherently problematical and paradoxical nature of life, beyond Good
and Evil in its terrible beauty, brings in its wake 'o começo — de um
estado de graça' [the beginning of a state of grace] (154) when she bites
into the red apple on the table in her house on the very next day. This
marks Lóri's conscious enactment of her insight into and identification
with the 'fruits of the earth' on the previous day's visit to the market,
when her emerging sense of an inner self had begun to gain ascendancy
over her (merely) outward appearance. As a result, 'ela se comia
internamente, cheia de sumo vivo que era' [she consumed herself
internally, brimming with the juice of life as she was] (146). Unlike the
biblical Eve, eating the apple marks Lóri's symbolic entry into 'paradise':
a conscious beginning of self-possession in her new life. The feelings
of peaceful happiness, gentle lucidity and a kind of effortless knowing
are accompanied by an incomparable sense of bodily well-being: 'a
dádiva indubitável de existir materialmente' [the unquestionable gift of
physically existing] (155). The great happiness accompanying the state
of grace, however, is not severed from the pain born of compassion for
others (157), but rather as an all-too-transitory glimpse into paradise,
'uma pequena abertura para o mundo que era uma espécie de paraíso'
[a small opening into the world that was a kind of paradise] (157).

Lóri's subsequent regression to days of aridity, such that she longs
to give years of her life in exchange for minutes of the state of grace
(158), does not stop her being generous to others—having bought red
sweaters in the winter for her pupils, she now buys them blue outfits
for the spring (160)—or being ready to join Ulisses in sexual union
(160). In fact, it is precisely her acceptance of this negative–positive
rhythm of life, of the rhythmic cyclicality of Nature's ups and
downs—'a hora mais escura precedeu aquela coisa que ela não queria

sequer tentar definir [...] alegria, alegria mansa' [the darkest hour preceded that thing that she didn't even want to try to define: joy, sweet joy] (165)—that marks her growth proper: 'Fora, porém, germinada' [The seed had sprouted] (162).

This inner struggle and growing sense of self is symbolized by the phantasms in Lóri's mind: of the slow, gentle, and 'burdensome' tenderness of the Elephants (29), that is, of her feelings (31), on the one hand and on the other the wild energy of the black Horse that represents Lóri's inner self: 'Existe um ser que mora dentro de mim como se fosse casa dele, e é. Trata-se de um cavalo preto e lustroso que apesar de inteiramente selvagem [...] tem por isso mesmo uma doçura primeira de quem não tem medo.' [There exists a being that lives within me as if it were its house, and it is. It is a shiny black horse that, although completely wild, has the natural gentleness of someone who has no fear.] (36) This inner self needs restraint, 'como se retivesse as rédeas de um cavalo' [as if holding the reins of a horse] (50), if it is to achieve the harnessed strength that the Elephant embodies.

Acceptance turns out to be the key to Lóri's becoming herself. By accepting life for what it is, she discovers that the problem itself is the solution. There is no place for happiness or fulfilment beyond the painful struggle for meaningful existence. Rather, the struggle to accept life as painful brings, from time to time—in a rhythmic alternation—the happiness that she so craves. She has sought 'o atalho onde ela fosse finalmente ela' [the path that she might follow to be herself at last] (67), which turns out to be a never-ending march, a pilgrimage she shares with other human beings, towards Nothingness (77), but it is a Nothing that was in fact the Everything: 'O que era um Nada era exatamente o Tudo' [what was a Nothing was precisely the Everything] (77).

The pain is still there, but it is no longer the constant anguish that derives from trying to avoid pain for fear of feeling pain: 'Angústia também era o medo de sentir enfim a dor' [Anxiety too was the fear of at last feeling the pain] (77). Instead, it is the intermittent pain that is the necessary counterpart of joy. Such conscious acceptance is human, and 'ser humano parecia-lhe agora a mais acertada forma de ser um animal vivo' [to be human seemed to her now the best way of being a live animal] (174).

And it is a process in which Lispector involves her readers,[6] exposing them to the labyrinthine, 'irrational' workings of Lóri's psyche by means of her narrative techniques of stream of consciousness (Prologue) and interior monologue ('Luminescence'). Moreover, her very style, in its alternations between on the one hand a lack of syntax and grammar (*asyndeton/parataxis*) and on the other syntactical and grammatical structuring (*syndeton/hypotaxis*)—draws the reader into the search for meaning that is precisely the novel's concern.[7] The opening sentence's lack of syntactical articulation (it begins with a comma and takes up three pages, divided into five paragraphs without a single full stop in between) is expressive of Lóri's confused state of mind, of her stream of consciousness (19–21). This is further emphasized in the lack of certainty that characterizes her speech in this opening passage as she asks (indirectly addressing Ulisses) who she is, what she should know, wear and do, and even how she should live her life. Similar confusion is drawn to our attention in Lispector's violation of grammar, for instance, at the beginning of 'Luminescence': 'Antes ela evitara sentir. Agora ainda tinha porém já com leves incursões pela vida.' [Before she had avoided feeling. She still did now, but more and more she was making slight incursions into life.] (41)

To equally expressive effect, Lóri's lucidity and calm is expressed in appropriately syntactical form, in a statement that privileges the irrational, ineffable—a not-knowing—as a means of self-redemption: 'Agora lúcida e calma, Lóri lembrou-se de que lera que os movimentos históricos de um animal preso tinham como intenção libertar, por meio de um desses movimentos, a coisa ignorada que o estava prendendo' [Now lucid and calm, Lori remembered reading that the hysterical movements of a trapped animal were designed to free it, precisely through one of these movements, from the very thing it did not know that was holding it] (22). Similarly, a striking example of Lispector's manipulation of language to poetic effect comes at the beginning of 'Luminescence', when we are told by the narrator that 'A mais premente necessidade de um ser humano era tornar-se um ser humano' [A human being's most urgent necessity is to become a human being] (39). The attempt to give order to the irrational workings of Lóri's psyche is, then, mirrored in Lispector's mastery of highly rhetorical and quasi-poetic uses of language.

Despite critics' attempts to categorize Lispector's *Uma aprendizagem* as a textbook case of Existentialism blended with mysticism,[8] what we are concerned with here is far from conventional, either philosophically or religiously. Lispector's warning in her preliminary 'Nota' has a specific point to make: 'Este Livro se pediu uma liberdade maior que tive medo de dar. Ele está muito acima de mim. Humildemente tentei escrevê-lo. Eu sou mais forte do que eu.' [This Book required more freedom than I had the courage to give. It is far beyond me. With humility I tried to write it. The person in me is stronger than the author.] For the 'I' subject of the essential verb 'ser', that is, the *person*, is indeed far more powerful than the (implied) *author*, the second 'I'. Because, whereas the authorial narrator struggles to make sense of Lóri's journey to her self, the details of style (and *le style, c'est l'homme même*—that is, 'the person') indicate a process at work that cannot be captured by the rationalization of either the authorial narrator or the characters themselves. This is the point of their rather severe limitations.

Just as conventional images of God and worshipping God (75–6) have to give way to a most unorthodox 'erotico-physical relationship' with the Godhead, depicted for example in Lóri's desire to get physically close to God (79) or when she experiences a mystical-cum-sexual union with the (masculine) sea, 'O sal, o iodo, tudo líquido deixam-na por uns instantes cega, toda escorrendo — espantada de pé, fertilizada' [The salt, the iodine, all the liquids leave her, for some moments, blind, dripping, standing frightened, and impregnated] (92), so too the behaviour of the characters goes far beyond their attempts to capture their relationship in a conventional marriage. It is beyond, in the words of the author, 'a lógica romântica dos humanos' [the romantic logic of human beings] (75), beyond 'o pecado do romantismo' [the sin of romanticism] (103) that seeks a closure, a 'happy ending'.

For what the characters demonstrate is the 'divine' human greatness (66) that Lóri sees in Ulisses and fears initially (71); it is the 'feliz e terrível grandeza humana, grandeza dele e dela' [the joyous and terrible human greatness, the greatness of him and her] (102) that the sight of Ulisses unexpectedly provokes in her. And which is described in reference to Lóri's state of grace as beginning to feel the imperceptible energy emanating from things and people: 'uma espécie de finíssimo resplendor de energia. Esta energia é a maior verdade do mundo e é impalpável.' [a kind of pure radiant energy. This energy is the greatest truth in the world and it is intangible.] (155) It is that greatness that holds life to be as great as death in its endless immortality:

Lóri passara da religião de sua infância para uma não-religião e agora passara para algo mais amplo: chegara ao ponto de acreditar num Deus tão vasto que ele era o mundo com suas galáxias: isso ela vira no dia anterior ao entrar no mar deserto sozinha. E por causa da vastidão impessoal era um Deus para o qual não se podia implorar: podia-se era agregar-se a ele e ser grande também. (95)[9]

This is, after all, the object of Lóri's repeated prayer of supplication—to feel that death does not exist, because in reality we are already in eternity: 'Alivia a minha alma, faze com que eu sinta [...] que a morte não existe porque na verdade já estamos na eternidade, faze com que eu sinta que amar amar não é morrer, que a entrega de si mesmo não significa a morte' [unburden my soul, make me feel that death does not exist because in truth we are already in eternity, make me feel that to love is not to die, that to give one's self does not mean death] (133). It is human greatness that, according to Lóri, is measured in a person's capacity for inevitable suffering: 'Achava agora que a capacidade de sofrer era a medida de grandeza de uma pessoa e salvava a vida interior dessa pessoa' [She now thought that the capacity to suffer was a measure of the person's greatness and that it saved this person's inner life] (161).[10]

Lispector's *Uma aprendizagem* is, then, an investigation of the deepest level of identity—a 'cosmic' identity that transcends (while leaving intact) ego, national, class and gender identities. Let us remind ourselves of Lóri's express desire at the outset of her Apprenticeship to transcend her merely social identity, her identity-for-identity's-sake, and take on a greater identity, which she had described as 'a ligação extrema entre mim e a terra friável e perfumada' [the ultimate bond between me and the fragile perfumed earth] (51): the 'earth' that had already become for her synonymous with Ulisses: 'O que chamava de terra já se tornara o sinônimo de Ulisses' [What she called earth had already become synonymous with Ulisses] (51). At the end of her journey, Lóri has clearly reached this point: 'Nunca imaginara que uma vez o mundo e ela chegassem a esse ponto de trigo maduro. A chuva e Lóri estavam tão juntas como a água da chuva estava ligada à chuva.' [She had never imagined that she and the world, like ripe wheat, would reach this point together. The rain and Lóri were as at-one with one another, as the rainwater was with the rain.] (166) Such 'cosmic' identity is about the ultimate identification with Reality, traditionally called the spiritual *unio mystica*, but here presented as ineluctably erotic, necessarily involving the physical symbolism of sexual union in a relationship of loving reciprocity that brings about the birth of a 'new soul' for each partner: 'para Lóri foi muito bom. Sobretudo porque sabia que estava sendo bom para ele.' [For Lori it was very good, especially because she knew that it was good for him.] (168) And it is a quest without end and, therefore, inherently and everlastingly painful—'sua voz estava lenta e abafada porque ele estava sofrendo de vida e de amor' [his voice was slow and muffled for he was suffering from life and love] (182)—as well as full of delights.

Notes to Chapter 4

1. All references are to the 1993 Francisco Alves edition [Rio de Janeiro: Francisco Alves, 1993]. Translations into English are based on the excellent translation by Richard A. Mazzara and Lorri A. Parris, *An Apprenticeship, or The Book of Delights* (Austin: University of Texas Press, 1986), with changes made in order to bring out the meanings that my close reading of the text highlights.
2. Cf. Rita Terezinha Schmidt, 'Clarice Lispector: The Poetics of Transgression', *Luso-Brazilian Review* 26 (1989), 103–15 at 106, on Lispector's appropriation of a gendered *Bildungsroman* pattern in *Uma aprendizagem*.
3. See, too, '[Lóri] queria que as coisas "acontecessem" e não que ela as provocasse' [Lóri wanted things to 'happen' without her instigating them] (123).
4. Cf. Anna Klobucka, 'Quest and Romance in Lispector's *Uma aprendizagem ou o livro dos prazeres*', *Luso-Brazilian Review* 36/1 (1999), 123–30 at 126: 'there is nothing sexually or socially ambiguous about either the woman Lóri or the man Ulisses'.
5. Schmidt, 'Clarice Lispector', refers to Lóri's 'linear and vertical journey': her 'slow apprenticeship of differentiation' (108), the distinct stages of which 'give her access to a dimension of female identity that bypasses the laws of repression' (107). Cf. also Belmira Magalhães, 'Representação de gênero em *Uma aprendizagem ou o livro dos prazeres* de Clarice Lispector', *Seminário Nacional Mulher e Literatura: Anais 6* (Rio de Janeiro: NIELM, 1996), 226–51 at 243: 'Lóri não quer troca de papéis, mas encontro de diferentes.'
6. See Richard A. Mazzara and Lorri A. Parris, 'The Practical Mysticism of Clarice Lispector's *Uma aprendizagem ou o livro dos prazeres*', *Hispania* 68/1 (1985), 709–15 at 714, for a discussion of Lispector's intention to involve the reader in the search for meaning.
7. Cf. ibid. 712–14, on the duality of her style: simultaneously complex (symbolism) and simple (solecisms); and, citing Olga de Sá, *A escritura de Clarice Lispector* (Petropolis: Vozes, 1978), 115–16, the elliptical use of syntax and fractured punctuation to reflect 'the [fragmentary] inarticulateness that characterizes humanity's search for meaning' (714).
8. Ibid., 709, 710, 712.
9. 'Lóri had gone from the religion of her childhood to a non-religion and now on to something more boundless: she had reached the point of believing in a God so vast that he was the world with its galaxies: this she had seen on the previous day when she entered the deserted sea alone. And because of this impersonal vastness it was a God one could not plead with: one could only join with him and be great too.'
10. Cf. Nádia Batella Gotlib, 'Un apprentissage des *sens*', *Études françaises* 25/1 (1989), 69–80 at 77: 'En exposant de plus en plus le personnage féminin à la douleur et au plaisir, l'apprentissage [...] transforme la douleur en un amour plus

grand. Un réalisme nouveau apporte un amour nouveau.' [By progressively exposing the female character to more pain and pleasure, the apprenticeship transforms pain into a greater love. A new reality brings with it a new kind of love.]

PART II

❖

Gender, Class, Race
and the Nation

.

CHAPTER 5

Defamiliarization and Déjà Vu in *Laços de família*

Cláudia Pazos Alonso

Laços de família [Family Ties] (1960)[1] remains one of Lispector's most famous and enduringly popular works. Yet, as Marta Peixoto notes, the collection has seldom been read for what it is in essence: 'a set of interracting texts'.[2] Indeed, it is a feature of short-story compilations that 'As in a musical sequence, the short story repeats and progressively develops themes and motifs over the course of the work; its unity derives from a perception of both the successive ordering and recurrent patterns.'[3] In other words, such collections rely both on a linear or sequential reading, and on what might perhaps be best defined as a circular, 'cyclical' or 'organic' reading, where themes are taken up only to undergo various modulations.[4] Taking my cue from these observations, I should like to analyse *Laços de família* both structurally and thematically, in order to discuss the extent to which the overall bleak outlook that a sequential reading seems to promote is nevertheless called into question between the lines by a more 'circular' or circuitous reading, in which a succession of déjà vu functions as a defamiliarizing device.

In the light of its title, the theme of *Laços de família* can be defined as, broadly speaking, an enquiry into relationships within the sphere of the family. But the very ambiguity present in the wording chosen (*laços* can mean both an emotionally important link and an imprisoning restrictive bond) allows us a first glimpse into Lispector's attempt to shake the reader out of his/her comfortable assumptions with regard to the family unit. Of course, the family, undoubtedly one of the most important social institutions of modern times in Brazil as elsewhere, has been criticized from different points of view—be they

Marxist, psychoanalytical or indeed feminist—for its repressive or oppressive effect on the individual. Particularly pertinent to any reading of *Laços de família*, however, is Betty Friedan's *Feminine Mystique*, published in 1963.[5] This seminal American feminist text outlines the unacknowledged mutilation that confinement to unfulfilling domestic roles inflicts on middle-class women and displays several points of contact with the feelings experienced by many of Lispector's protagonists.[6] In fact, it can be argued that Lispector is tackling from a fictional point of view the phenomena that Friedan attempts to pin down from a sociological perspective. As a work fuelled by imaginative thinking, however, Lispector's fiction is able to capture and voice (or least murmur) a broader spectrum of issues than are discussed in Friedan's account. In so doing, Lispector can be said to be ahead of her time, foreshadowing many late-twentieth-century debates: for indeed her collection suggests that constrictive social expectations, enacted at a micro-level within the family unit, cause untold damage not only to women, but just as importantly to men, as well as to the older and younger generations.

It is of course not a coincidence that the opening story, 'Devaneio e embriaguez de uma rapariga' [A girl's daydreams and drunkenness] should feature a woman whose break from daily routine precipitates all kinds of revelations about her unspoken desires and potential. The story's *incipit* positions the protagonist looking out of her bedroom window, in other words, looking from indoors at the outside world, aptly reflecting the position that women over the centuries have been forced to adopt as passive spectators. The narrative goes on to show her looking at herself in the mirror, a situation equally endowed with symbolic meaning, and one that will be subsequently re-enacted by many other protagonists. Significantly, she sees herself reflected as an other, and it is only through this identity-split that we learn her name, Maria Quitéria.

But, as the thrust of the story foregrounds her temporarily eschewing the roles of responsible wife and mother, we witness a deeper scrutiny of her perceived identity, with her stepping into the prohibited realms of daydreaming—later defined in 'Preciosidade' [Preciousness] as 'agudo como um crime' [acute like a crime] (78)—and then socially unacceptable drunkenness. These enable Maria Quitéria to experience a profound sense of release and a glimpse into the nature of her (true?) self, not unlike Ana in the story that follows. Her magnified self, whose heightened sensory perceptions are akin that of a powerful pregnant female body—foreshadowing the 'monstrous' pregnancy of 'A menor mulher do mundo' [The smallest woman in the world]—is quite alien to the limited socially-imposed female role that patriarchal society had envisaged for her and which she has internalized. Furthermore, the temporary madness of her drunken state will soon be followed up in the altogether more disturbing breakdown of Laura in 'A imitação da rosa' [The imitation of the rose].

Similarly, in the following story, the well-known 'Amor' [Love], Ana experiences the confusing vastness of the Botanical Garden, a world again pregnant with possibilities, precisely at the moment when she momentarily forgets about her motherly and wifely duties. It is certainly fair to say that the first half of *Laços de família* dwells repeatedly on the imprisonment of middle-class married women and their (socially unacceptable) attempts to escape from it. However, the third story in the collection, 'Uma galinha' [A hen], questions the limitations of the maternal role on a metaphorical level, through the tragicomic image of a hen whose death sentence is deferred when it unexpectedly lays an egg. The implicit equation is that women, when exclusively valued by society for their reproductive capacities, become like so many animals, grotesquely but effectively reduced to a biological function. Confined to the 'ar impuro da cozinha' [the impure air of the kitchen] (29), women, like the anonymous hen, are made to lead a prolonged death-in-life, devoid of wider horizons and fulfilment, before eventually meeting their physical death when they become redundant in old age: 'Até que um dia mataram-na, comeram-na e passaram-se anos' [Until one day they killed her, ate her and years went by] (29).

The conflation of women into a mothering role has different, albeit equally damaging repercussions for those unable to bear children, since it deprives them of any sense of social purpose and, by extension, identity.[7] This is dramatically highlighted by the breakdown of Laura, the protagonist of 'A imitação da rosa', the tale that comes after 'Uma galinha'. Laura's childlessness is hauntingly thrown back at her when she stares at herself in the mirror, which again vividly echoes her (non)-identity: 'alguém veria nesse mínimo ponto ofendido a falta dos filhos que ela nunca tivera?' [Would anyone have seen in that ever so tiny hint of sorrow the lack of the children she had never had?] (31). Her struggle to be invisible leads her instead into self-absorption and heightened self-awareness. As a result, she becomes 'luminosa e inalcançável' [luminous and unreachable (49)], blossoming outside the stifling parameters of normality. At the end of this tale, it is implied that Laura reaches a point of no return, 'alerta e tranquila como num trem. Que já partira.' [alert and calm as if she were on a train. A train that had already departed.] (49) Indeed, unlike Maria Quitéria and Ana, the protagonists of the opening two tales, she does not have any maternal duties to anchor her in the social reality that she is expected to inhabit.

The next story, 'Feliz aniversário' [Happy birthday] expands on themes first tackled in 'Uma galinha', as it centres on the twilight of an ageing matriarch whose reproductive role has been completed and now has nothing to look forward to, even on her birthday. Through a scathing portrayal of the hypocrisy upon which family relationships are shown to be so frequently based, a topic developed here more fully for the first time, Lispector unmasks the lip-service paid to women as mothers and domestic angels. Silent throughout most of the narrative, like so many of the other characters in this collection, the old woman, who incidently shares the same name as the protagonist of 'Amor', Ana, eventually bursts out; her cursing and spitting constitute a graphic embodiment of her pent-up frustration. Simultaneously, Lispector reveals how the woman's daughter Zilda, with whom she lives, is completely taken for granted by her male siblings and other relatives. She is effectively shown to be serving everyone as 'uma escrava' [a slave] (54), leading her to feel as frustrated and embittered as the old woman. This subliminally sets up an illuminating contrast with the black pygmy woman of the story that follows, who contrary to readers' expectations, far from being enslaved, will in fact turn out to be freer than most of her white Brazilian counterparts.

It can thus be argued that, by the time the collection draws almost to its half-way point, Lispector has provided a fairly detailed indictment of the position of married women in Brazilian society in her own day and age, finding it to be depressingly wanting. The stories, like so many refracting mirrors, amplify the sombre message: childless women are relentlessly patronized by society and within their own families, while mothers are missing out on the wider world and the potential to develop their inner lives, only to be patronized too in due course once their child-rearing years are over. Women can certainly achieve a degree of autonomy through the power of their imaginations, which reconnect them to themselves, as is shown humorously in the opening tale that conveys the perspective of the

Portuguese 'rapariga'. But this comes at a heavy price, for, as shown in the later case of Laura, it is incompatible with social convention.

Given women's clouded horizons and wrecked lives, it is hardly surprising to find Lispector widening her focus, shifting her gaze to a wider cross section of society. As she does so, family settings become paradoxically but revealingly absent from the next two stories, 'A menor mulher do mundo' and 'O jantar' [The evening meal], the story that occupies the central position in the collection. Furthermore, although Lispector will return hereafter to more conventional family settings, it is telling that she will only stage once more a married woman as protagonist, in 'Os laços de família' [The family ties], a tale nevertheless invested with special significance, given its eponymity. Thus, in the second half of the collection, Lispector embarks on a close analysis of how social roles become internalized by society at large, not just by women. But before such examination is carried out, the 'central' two tales provide alternative perspectives and narrative outcomes, outside more familiar contexts.

'A menor mulher do mundo' and 'O jantar' warrant close examination, not least because they may seem at first sight thematically so unrelated to the rest of the collection, since neither deals with relationships within the family (a fact that to some degree also holds true for 'O búfalo' [The buffalo], as we shall see). Like the inner movements of a musical composition, however, they do have a central role to play, insofar as they actually provide a contrast to the stories that come both before and after them. Indeed, both tales unobtrusively but effectively debunk prevailing cultural stereotypes: firstly about 'femininity' and secondly about 'masculinity'. As they shatter our assumptions about the world as we know it, they force us to review the foundations upon which Brazilian and by extension Western culture is built. As such, they serve to underline the fact that the microcosm of the family, which not only constitutes the 'horizon of expectations' of many Brazilian women but crucially also has a central role to play in the shaping of the next generation of men and women alike, is in fact the site where gender stereotypes are all too often uncritically confirmed.[8]

'A menor mulher do mundo' offers a radical revision of the European civilizing mission responsible for the foundation of modern Brazil. By presenting its readers with an alternative (supposedly uncivilized) model of social organization, when a French explorer, Marcel Pretre, discovers 'the smallest woman in the world', the story implicitly challenges the sacredness of the European, man-made symbolic order that was unquestioningly adopted in the process of colonizing Brazil.[9] The encounter between the minute black pygmy and the white explorer is a heavily loaded one right from the outset, as in Portuguese 'explorador' means both explorer and exploiter. The explorer's nationality, French, makes him a representative of a former colonial power. Furthermore, his surname (*prêtre* means 'priest' in French) signals the key role played by the Church in the course of the overseas expansion of Europe, as does his mock baptism of his prized specimen, whom he daintily names Pequena Flor [Little Flower].

If Marcel Pretre is a caricature of the superior civilized white man, the pygmy woman, shown to be physically inferior and moreover heavily pregnant, similarly becomes a distortion of the stereotype of the uncivilized native woman. Perhaps unexpectedly, the reality of her pregnant body becomes of strategic importance in the process of questioning Marcel Pretre's supremacy. For one, her pregnancy throws his 'discovery' into doubt, since his finding might be invalidated by her unborn baby, whose gender is yet unknown. Secondly, her pregnant body reveals her resistance to Pretre's symbolic appropriation of her, since her reaction to the artificially feminine name that he bestows on her is to scratch herself 'onde uma pessoa não se coça' [where a person does not scratch herself] (66).

Pequena Flor's tribe lives under the constant threat of the cannibalistic activities of a neighbouring tribe, the *bantos*. Such a detail might in the first instance appear to play up to Western prejudices regarding uncivilized customs, but this is deftly undermined by Lispector, who hints a few lines later that the visual 'consumption' of Pequena Flor by the supremely civilized Marcel Pretre is equally cannibalistic in intent: 'Ali estava uma mulher que a *gulodice* do mais fino sonho jamais pudera imaginar' [There stood a woman whom the *greediness* of the most exquisite dream would never be able to imagine] (66; my italics). Such eager consumption is not circumscribed to the explorer: in fact it becomes re-enacted by the entire Western world when Pequena Flor's life-size replica in the form of a colour photograph is published in the Sunday papers and avidly consumed by Western readers.

At first sight Pequena Flor may seem, much like an animal in a cage, powerless and imprisoned by the gaze and fantasies of her Western readers, foreshadowing the closing story of *Laços de família*, where the nameless protagonist finds herself surrounded by cages in a zoo. But in fact her image as a freak of nature (at 45 cm she is smaller than a Western newborn) proves to be deeply unsettling to a range of predominantly female readers.[10] The sight of her forces her viewers to confront the precariousness of their own position in life, leading them to adopt strategies of denial or evasion. One woman is shown 'obstinadamente aperfeiçoando o lado cortês da beleza' [obstinately perfecting the courteous aspect of beauty] (68), precisely because the thought of any parallel between herself and Pequena Flor is too much too bear. Other readers immediately envisage various demeaning ways of dealing with the pygmy, in an unconscious gesture confirming their superiority in opposition to her otherness: one child imagines her as his plaything, while at the hands of another family she would become a servant, treated as a sub-human.

But Pequena Flor's disruptive potential cannot be ignored, as is graphically made clear in a subsequent close-up of Pretre and Pequena Flor's encounter: 'Metodicamente o explorador examinou com o olhar a barriguinha do menor ser humano maduro. Foi neste instante que o explorador, pela primeira vez desde que a conhecera, em vez de sentir curiosidade ou exaltação ou vitória ou espírito científico, o explorador sentiu mal-estar. É que a menor mulher do mundo estava rindo. Estava rindo quente quente.' [Methodically, the explorer examined with his gaze the little belly of the smallest mature human being. It was at that moment that the explorer, for the first time since he had known her, instead of experiencing curiosity or excitement or a sense of victory or scientific interest, felt ill at ease. Because the smallest woman in the world was laughing. She was laughing, hot, hot.] (69)

Far from adopting a submissive or demure position, she is laughing at him. Her laughter signals that she is oblivious to the proprietorial gaze of this civilized man, a man revealingly described from the outset as 'caçador e homem do mundo' [hunter and man of the world] (64), as well as his scientific project. Furthermore, not only is Pequena Flor subversively shown to be a desiring being in her own right, conversely the object of her affections is symbolically deflated, unsettling his authority: for she seems comically unable to distinguish between the man and his belongings, coveting his boots, his ring, and so on (all outward symbols of power) as much as his person. The process culminates in her mischievous wink, bursting with sexual innuendo: 'Pequena Flor piscava de amor, e riu quente, pequena, grávida, quente' [Little Flower blinked with love and laughed hot, small, pregnant, hot] (71).

As Hélène Cixous has argued, women have come to represent the dark continent of the Other, available to be colonized by men.[11] But through her uncompromising negation of the possibility of being sexually colonized and tamed, Pequena Flor succeeds in destabilizing the prevailing cultural assumptions and balance of power between male and female. Furthermore, in the specific case of Brazil, the image of the explorer as potential conqueror/founding-father of a nation, fictionally embodied in nineteenth-century Brazilian literature in the form of the love affair between the white colonizer Martim[12] and the 'virgem de lábios de mel' [honey-lipped virgin] Iracema in José de Alencar's novel *Iracema*, is emphatically shattered here. For, unlike Iracema, Pequena Flor is not a virgin. More to the point, the fact that she is *already* pregnant renders the explorer wholly redundant in his potential role as conqueror of new worlds, as Claire Williams has incisively pointed out.[13] Therefore, Pequena Flor unwittingly but radically undermines the explorer and the dominant order that he represents: Marcel Pretre 'então perturbou-se como só homem de tamanho grande se perturba' [then became disturbed as only a full-sized man can become disturbed] (71).

In contrast to Pequena Flor, who remains very much her own person, Pretre can only *pretend* that he is still in charge: 'Disfarçou ajeitando melhor o chapéu de explorador [...] Foi provavelmente ao ajeitar o capacete simbólico que o explorador se chamou à ordem, recuperou com severidade a disciplina de trabalho, e recomeçou a anotar.' [He disguised it by adjusting his explorer's helmet. It was probably when adjusting his symbolic helmet that the explorer called himself to order, and resumed his note-taking.] (71) His loss of control is on the surface temporarily remedied by the fact that he repositions his outward symbol of power, the 'capacete simbólico' [symbolic helmet], a symbol of power according to Chevalier and Gheerbrant.[14] Nevertheless this superficial façade of orderly behaviour is from the outset subtly but relentlessly undermined by Lispector herself, who chose to spell Pretre's surname without a circumflex, a symbol often referred to in Portuguese as a *chapeuzinho*, that is to say, a little hat.

Marcel Pretre pretends to remain in charge by taking notes, similarly to the earlier characters, who negated the potential disruption that Pequena Flor embodies by whatever means at their disposal. The story ends with the reaction of an elderly female reader, a mock closure encoded in the image of her closing the newspaper that she is reading. She, not a 'priest' like Pretre, has to revert to the idea of divine order to account for the inexplicable existence of the 'menor mulher do mundo': 'pois olhe, eu só lhe digo uma coisa: Deus sabe o que faz' [Well, look, I'll say just one thing—God knows what he's doing] (71). This grand statement restores the illusion of order to her life, which had been thrown into momentary disarray. But ultimately hers is an inadequate explanation and, as such, patently unable to erase the interrogations raised and the utopian space that Pequena Flor has opened up: a radically woman-centred space, simultaneously monstrous and attractive.

By dislodging Pretre's phallogocentric view of the world, Lispector is indicating that the foundations on which Brazilian society—and by extension Western society at large—have been based must undergo a complete revision. This explains why the tale that follows, 'O jantar', the central story within the collection, which takes as its point of departure the central tenets of masculinity as socially defined in 1950s Brazil, turns out to be as disruptive as 'A menor mulher do mundo', offering a radical questioning of prevailing double standards.

'O jantar' is the only story in the entire collection to employ a first-person narrator, unsurprisingly male, a fact that seemingly highlights men's unrestricted access to a subject position. It may moreover appear fitting that this tale, from which women are almost entirely absent, should take centre stage within the collection, denoting women's peripheral position in relation to men. The narrative is by and large taken up with the description of a powerful older man dining in a restaurant, but simultaneously foregrounds the reactions of the narrator, a younger man, to the spectacle that he is witnessing. The diner is described halfway through the story by the nameless narrator as 'um desses velhos que ainda estão no centro do mundo e da força' [one of those old gentlemen who are still at the centre of the world and of power] (74), in other words as someone occupying a powerful social position. But the 'ainda' [still] should alert us to a temporal shift being signalled. For what the story is about is in a sense a last supper, echoing in a different guise the religious parody of the preceding story. Tellingly, in this last supper, far from displaying an unconditional worship of masculine power, the narrator ultimately prefers to betray his own (man)kind.

Indeed, as the narrator watches with a mix of fascination and repugnance his older *alter ego*, who represents a projection of himself in a distant future, the potential identification between the two men is such that it forces him to confront his gender identity. By contrast to the older man, who, plagued by an unspecified sorrow, nevertheless refuses to give in to tears ('o patriarca estava chorando por dentro' [the patriarch was crying inside] (76)), the younger man gives free rein to his emotions, as evidenced by a text teeming with emotional outbursts. Like female characters such as the earlier Maria Quitéria and Ana, he even experiences nausea: 'Estou tomado pelo êxtase arfante da náusea' [I am overcome by the heaving ecstasy of nausea] (75).[15] This culminates in his articulation of resistance in the parting lines of the tale: 'Não sou ainda esta potência, esta construção, esta ruína. Empurro o prato, rejeito a carne e o seu sangue (74)' [I am not yet this power, this construction, this ruin. I push my plate away, I reject the meat and its blood.] (74) The text actually uses the word 'construção' to signal the artificial nature of the power held by the older man. Moreover, the asyndeton leaves no room for doubt about his ultimate collapse into a 'ruína'. The younger man therefore refuses to commune with the transfiguring body and blood of a warped ideology, defining himself instead through his adoption of a dissident position by not eating. By extension, his refusal to eat can also be read on a symbolic level as a refusal to adopt a predatory role, since in Portuguese the word 'comer' can also refer to sexual possession.

'O jantar' thus constitutes a central text, both structurally and on a symbolic level, because of the daring challenge that it presents to prevailing images of masculinity. In that sense, it paves the way for the second half of *Laços de família*, where Lispector returns to her underlying theme, the portrayal of family ties. Her portrayal is now increasingly modulated by the notion of all gendered roles being cultural constructs, which therefore, in theory at least, every person ought to be at liberty to adopt or reject. In practice, however, 'Preciosidade' and, after a pause, 'Começos de uma fortuna' [Beginnings of a fortune] followed by 'Mistério em São Cristóvão' [Mystery in São Cristóvão] pinpoint adolescence as a crucially formative time when conformist roles are dogmatically reinforced by and within the family and are subsequently internalized. Placed amidst these stories, 'Os laços de família' might be said to offer a corrective, disrupting the sequential reading as it articulates to some degree the possibility of an alternative outcome.

In 'Preciosidade', a fifteen-year-old girl's uniqueness is highlighted in the opening paragraphs: 'E dentro da nebulosidade algo precioso. Que não se espreguiçava, não se comprometia, não se contaminava. Que era intenso como uma jóia. Ela.' [And within the haze was something precious. Which did not stretch its arms, did not compromise itself, did not contaminate itself. Which was intense like a jewel. She.] (78) But her intense, undiluted, uncompromising, uncontaminated individuality, which can be condensed into the one-word sentence 'Ela' [She], has to give way to the more self-effacing role that society demands of women, if she is not to be violently assaulted on the streets again, as is indicated in the closing paragraph of the story: 'Até que, assim como uma pessoa engorda, ela deixou, sem saber por que processo, de ser preciosa' [Until, just as a person puts on weight, she stopped, without knowing by what process, being precious] (89). Quite aside from the reproductive function and the ageing process, both evoked implicitly through the reference to putting on weight, the structure of the sentence, beginning with 'Até que' [Until], functions as yet another déjà vu, linking it subliminally to the earlier 'Uma galinha', recalling the deferred death sentence hanging over the hen.

Simultaneously, however, the roles that the male protagonists act out as the girl's assailants are equally shown by Lispector to be *culturally* determined rather than being a *natural* vocation: 'o que se seguiu foram [...] quatro mãos de quem não tinha vocação [...] Eles, cujo papel predeterminado era apenas o de passar junto do escuro de seu medo.' [What followed were four hands belonging to someone without a vocation. They, whose predetermined role was merely that of passing close to the darkness of her fear.] (86)

The story that comes after 'Preciosidade' is the eponymous 'Os laços de família', interrupting the accounts of adolescent initiation into the gendered world of adults that, as in a musical composition, will be taken up again in the two pieces immediately following it. Occupying a symmetrical position to 'Feliz aniversário', 'Os laços de família' likewise examines the complex web of family dynamics through multiple, conflicting points of views. But it seems to imply, much more explicitly than the earlier tale did, that the 'papel predeterminado' [predetermined role] played out by each individual is in fact a cultural construct, and therefore not forever fixed. In so doing, it sets up a contrast between the perspective of Catarina and that of her husband António. Catarina is a woman who seems able to draw on her inner strength to rise above stifling relationships, be it with her own mother[16] or with her husband. Whether she might be able to build a less stifling relationship with her four-year-old son remains an open-ended question. Her choice to take the boy for a walk without her husband would seem to signal a widening of her horizons, beyond the confining 'normality' of house and home.

But when seen from the point of view of her momentarily excluded husband António, the image of the mother walking hand in hand with her child, far from embodying a journey towards freedom, in fact brings out an extremely negative image of the damaging potential of motherly love as 'a prisão de amor que se abateria para sempre sobre o futuro homem' [this prison of love that would be forever collapsing onto the future man] (97). António's perspective, of course, does not coincide with that of Catarina, who is cross-eyed and therefore forced to see the world in a different, 'abnormal' way: 'nunca precisara de rir de fato quando tinha vontade de rir: seus olhos [...] tornavam-se mais estrábicos — e o riso saía pelos olhos' [she had never needed to laugh out loud when she felt like laughing: her squint became more obvious and her laughter shone out through her eyes] (91). Therefore, while António thinks that he can tame and possess his wife (much like Pretre in connection to Pequena Flor), his struggle to remain in control is ultimately fruitless. Her leaving the flat (for the afternoon? for good?) is tantamount to inscribing her freedom of choice.

Unlike the adolescent girl in 'Preciosidade', who eventually becomes socially integrated after accepting the apparent inevitability of conforming symbolized by her acquisition of new tight-fitting, rubber-soled (i.e. silent) shoes, albeit with the ensuing loss of her inner 'preciosidade', Catarina in the later story remains very much her own person, as reflected in her name, which means 'the pure', as well as her freedom to walk unconstrained. To that extent, much like Pequena Flor, she can be said to question male hegemony and prevailing family structures, encoded in her gesture of leaving the family home behind. Such a gesture nevertheless signals a pattern of disjunction, where any meaningful communication with the 'opposite' sex seems to be deemed impossible, a fact that had already been hinted at in the opening short stories. In a new modulation of the conclusion to 'A imitação da rosa', where Armando was left behind, in 'Os laços de família' the husband is once more left empty-handed: António is pictured staring out of the window, while his self-assured wife has stepped into the wider world with their child. Unlike Armando, however, António refuses to acknowledge defeat, reassuring himself that a return to 'normality' will resume when the couple go to the cinema that evening.

Of course, the narratives shown on screen often reproduce asymmetrical gender roles and thus reinforce the *status quo*. As such, the cinema (in contrast to the Botanic Garden, the jungle or even the zoo) mostly represents a socially conformist space. In this connection, it is particularly striking that the next story, 'Começos de uma fortuna', during which we witness the progressive construction of masculinity in great and realistic detail, should also make reference to a cinema outing as a place of initiation, a site where socially-differentiated roles will be enacted, with the adolescent Artur expecting to be able to carve out a privileged position for himself once he becomes endowed with buying power.

Yet Lispector does not allows us to forget the constructed nature of social identities: the next story, 'Mistério em São Cristóvão', while dwelling once more on the traumatic initiation of an anonymous 'mocinha' [young girl], thereby echoing the theme of 'Preciosidade', describes the encounter between three young men wearing Carnival costumes that highlight their masculine role (a rooster, a bull and a knight) and a nameless adolescent girl whose role is defined as 'se equilibrando na delicadeza de sua idade' [getting used to the delicate nature of her age] (108). Significantly, this is viewed as an encounter between not three, but four masks: 'a simples aproximação de quatro máscaras' [the simple encounter of four masks] (103), echoing the earlier underlining in 'Preciosidade' of the cultural construction of social roles and behaviour in the case of both men and women.

Youngsters, male and female alike, are thus literally as well as metaphorically shown to be groping in the dark as they try to come to terms with their so-called socially 'pre-determined' gendered roles. Their identity crises in this latter half of *Laços de família* often reflect those of the adult population at large and tend to result in the reproduction of assymetrical gender roles, with the majority of young females passively conforming and the majority of young males displaying aggressive or acquisitive traits deemed necessary for survival.

For most of the collection, men are shown to cling on, against all odds, to the blind belief that they are or somehow must remain in control (the exception being the young, anonymous and almost 'hysterical' male narrator of 'O jantar'). In the earlier 'A menor mulher do mundo', the male protagonist was shown to retreat and hide behind his professional identity or mask, as a means of last resort to protect his integrity. A similar stance is re-enacted in the latter 'O crime do professor de matemática' [The crime of the Mathematics Teacher], when the Mathematics Teacher sets about discovering a mathematical 'solution' to an existential 'problem', that of having abandoned his dog José. The closing paragraph of the story, however, suggests the Mathematics Teacher's eventual tragic realization that no such 'solution' can ever be found (he has to live with his guilt). This is nevertheless a grim outcome, since the Teacher is left with the realization of the burden of occupying a privileged social position as a man but is ultimately unable to break free from the imprisoning circle of social conventions.

It is significant, however, that Lispector chose not to close her collection with 'O crime', preferring instead to conclude with the unsettling effect of a thirteenth text, 'O búfalo'. For the first time within *Laços de família*, almost as a postscript, the narrative stages as a protagonist an unmarried but sexually mature woman. It is therefore telling that what the story brings out is her complete lack of status. As a woman who has been abandoned by her lover, she only seems to exist in a limbo. In the society in which she lives, a woman is nothing without a man, a fact reflected in her lack of name. Indeed, she does not even feature in the title of the story, having being displaced by the male buffalo. Symbolically clothed in a dull 'casaco marrom' [brown coat] (122), brown being a colour also favoured earlier by the childless Laura, her plight becomes all but invisible to the outside world.

While, physically speaking, she is outwardly free to roam in the Jardim Zoológico, mentally she is in effect still trapped by her internalization of social conventions: thus she is repeatedly described as 'enjaulada pelas jaulas fechadas' [caged in by locked cages] (122). Having adopted a loving, self-abnegating female position in the past, she now feels that the only way to free herself from her socially-defined role is to learn to hate. But the tale culminates in her realization that hatred is an equally destructive feeling, as she succumbs to it under the implacable gaze of a black buffalo: 'presa ao mútuo assassinato. Presa [...] Em tão lenta vertigem que antes do corpo baquear macio a mulher viu o céu inteiro e um búfalo.' [Caught up in mutual assassination. Trapped in such a slow-moving dizzy fit that, before her body tumbled gently to the ground, the woman saw the entire sky and a buffalo.] (131) In other words, her horizon of expectations is both potentially limitless (the entire sky) and completely circumscribed, as the only presence to feature therein is the male buffalo. What the closing lines of this story and of *Laços de família* as a whole seem to tentatively articulate is that while women (but by extension presumably also men) remain locked into stifling binary oppositions, such as love and hatred, male and female, thereby confirming each other in their traditional asymmetrical social roles, they are in fact committing a destructive 'mútuo assassinato' [mutual assassination]. Is it surprising then, that the collection should close with the anonymous woman fainting under the weight of this insight?

Thus it is certainly not a coincidence that the collection opens with the image of Maria Quitéria, a female apparently re-enacting a traditional passive role, as she looks at the wider world outside from indoors. For the story then emphasizes that, despite her initial physical confinement, Maria Quitéria is in fact endowed with a great amount of inner freedom. By contrast, in the closing story, the anonymous woman is roaming free, but is still imprisoned in the mental structures of her time. In fact, her walking is constrained by her shoes, a telling detail that looks back to 'Preciosidade' with its outlining of the loss of adolescent individuality for the sake of conformity. In keeping with this, the images of pregnancy, which in 'Devaneio' were associated, albeit tentatively, with temporary escape and power, give way in 'O búfalo' to the metaphor of miscarriage, stripping the woman of all her (pro)creative potential: 'Mas dessa vez porque dentro dela escorria enfim um primeiro fio de sangue negro' [But this time it was because there flowed inside her at last the first trickle of black blood] (130).

Despite what appears to be a supremely pessimistic ending, which seems designed to mirror Brazilian women's invisibility and lack of choice in the 1950s both within and without family life, the collection as a whole works organically on the reader to invalidate a deterministic, linear (dare we say 'masculine'?) reading, thereby subliminally pointing to the possible ways out of the seeming impasse reached by the woman in 'O búfalo'. Through a combination of a complex web of déjà vu and other defamiliarizing devices, Clarice Lispector deftly turns the tables on Freud's infamous dictum that 'biology is destiny'. Mature women's blighted lives in the first half of the collection and in 'O búfalo' are the result of the conformist outcome of the adolescent tales, which are promoted by traditional family settings. But society's gender polarities and their reinforcement within oppressive family contexts need not remain forever fixed, as 'A menor mulher do mundo' and 'O jantar' in particular imply.

Indeed, a more 'cyclical' reading of the collection suggests that, irrespective of their assymetrical social positions and powerlessness, women are endowed with inner freedom and, as such, can take steps to acknowledge their existence as autonomous beings. Such is the message that emerges from 'Devaneio e embriaguez', 'A menor mulher do mundo' and 'Os laços de família'. Simultaneously, men must not remain complacently locked into conventional parameters of masculinity, all the more so since these are shown to be on the brink of collapse in 'O jantar'. If they do, they risk being left behind, in a truly undesirable reversal of subject positions. That Lispector should have been able to envision this conclusion on a fictional level, decades ahead of more systematic articulation of similar lines of thought by feminist thinkers, is a truly remarkable achievement.

Notes to Chapter 5

1. All references in Portuguese will be to *Laços de família,* 3rd edn. (Rio de Janeiro: Editora do Autor, 1965).
2. Marta Peixoto, *Gender, Narrative and Violence in Clarice Lispector* (Minneapolis, University of Minesota Press: 1994), 24.
3. Robert M. Luscher, 'The Short Story Sequence: An Open Book', in *Short Story Theory at a Crossroads,* ed. Susan Lohafer and Jo Ellyn Clarey (Baton Rouge: Louisiana State University Press, 1989),' 148–67.
4. There are many indications that the author wished her thirteen short stories to be read together. *Laços de família* is in fact a compilation that substantially reworks *Alguns contos,* published in 1952. The earlier collection featured six stories. These made a reappearance in *Laços de família,* but in a different order as the collection more than doubled in size, incorporating seven new stories. Both the opening tale and the closing one, crucially important insofar as they can be said to 'frame' the revised collection as a whole, were new additions. Likewise, the strikingly suggestive title, taken from one of the seven newly-added stories, unavoidably 'frames' our interpretation of *Laços de família.* The end product therefore conveys a very different overall impression.
5. Betty Friedan, *The Feminine Mystique* (Harmondsworth: Penguin, 1992).
6. It is pertinent to recall that Lispector lived in the States during the fifties. Her position as a diplomat's wife was similar in many respects to that of the middle-class urban American housewives depicted by Friedan: materially comfortable, but spiritually and intellectually frustrating.
7. The damaging conflation of women into wives and mothers will be explored in the closing tale of the collection, 'O búfalo', featuring the only other childless adult woman, significantly an unmarried one.
8. Needless to say, Lispector is playing with the difference of meaning between European Portuguese, where 'rapariga' means young woman, and Brazilian usage, where 'rapariga' means a prostitute.
9. Although the discovery takes place in Africa, the tale resonates with obvious echoes for Brazil, a country profoundly shaped by its African heritage stemming from centuries of slave-trading.

10. Lispector wryly shows us that Western female readers are in fact confined to their houses or apartments, in other words more imprisoned than the pygmy woman.
11. Hélène Cixous and Catherine Clément, *La jeune née* (Paris: Gallimard, 1976).
12. The warlike associations that this name conjures up are echoed in the name of the French explorer, Marcel.
13. Claire Williams, *Coming to Terms with the Other: The Encounter Between Opposites in the Work of Clarice Lispector*, Bristol: HiPLAM, forthcoming in 2002.
14. *Dictionnaire des symboles*, 2nd edn. (Paris: Robert Laffont, 1982), 176–67.
15. In fact, the first indication as to the gender of the narrator, deferred until the second page of the story, significantly comes in the form of the adjective 'nauseado' [nauseated] (70).
16. Her mother's waning power as an ageing matriarch is encoded in the loss of her hat. This unmasks the futility of attempting to conform to social norms, and obliquely echoes Marcel Pretre's vain attempt to retain control.

CHAPTER 6

Feminism or the
Ambiguities of the Feminine
in Clarice Lispector

Luiza Lobo

In this paper I shall attempt to establish whether there is a feminist
position (though not necessarily an overt one) in the works of Clarice
Lispector, with special reference to her *crônicas*. Written between 19
August 1967 and 29 December 1973, Lispector's *crônicas* were initially
published in a column in the Saturday issue of the newspaper *Jornal do
Brasil* [Rio de Janeiro] and subsequently collected in the volume *A
descoberta do mundo* (1984, hereafter DM).[1] Other *crônicas* or fragments
were reprinted in *Para não esquecer* (1979). Some of her texts may be
considered either *crônica*s or short stories, such as those published in
Onde estivestes de noite (1974), *A via crucis do corpo* (1974), *Água viva* (1973)
and *Um sopro de vida (Pulsações)* (1978).

Clarice Lispector seldom expressed an explicit political point of view,
either in her writings or in her interviews. For instance, she did not
write a word in her *crônica*s about the 'Institutional Act number 5',
signed by Marshal Costa e Silva on 13 December 1968, one of the most
repressive laws against intellectuals issued by the military dictatorship
(1964–84).[2]

As well as seldom disclosing her political opinions, one can furthermore notice that Lispector did not overtly defend a 'feminist' position.
According to Gayatry Spivak, feminism derives from the question 'Who
am I?', which becomes overwhelming in a Third-World country.[3]
Lispector quite often asked herself about her own being, but she did
not consciously or explicitly do so in the name of feminism. In keeping
with the mentality of her time, she seemed to assume that 'feminism'

was the antithesis of being 'feminine'. Lispector attaches an idea of essentialism to the term 'feminine', as if it were automatically associated with the female gender or with being a woman.[4] At the time she was writing, she did not yet interpret both these terms as cultural constructs. Therefore, the term 'feminine' has an ambiguous resonance in her prose, and she does not refer to 'feminism' directly.

Feminism in the 1970s meant the defence of civil rights: the right to abortion and divorce, sexual freedom and equal rights to work. Earlier women writers in Brazil, particularly Nísia Floresta Brasileira Augusta in the late nineteenth century and Carmen Dolores in the first decades of the twentieth, had openly defended feminism in their articles for the press. However, from the 1970s onwards, academic specialization led to a split between literature and the social and political sciences. Women writers began to shun political issues and to leave them to feminist activists. As writers, they focused instead on their own inner development and on existential choices. Maybe they took for granted that the law—in theory if not in practice—had already secured the most important social achievements for women in Brazilian society: the right to vote, to work and to separate from their husbands.

Lispector's lack of direct involvement with feminist movements was therefore something she shared with many intellectuals of the 1970s, who showed an ambivalent attitude towards issues of race and gender. Their reaction to such issues was often indirect and metaphorical. Lispector's position is concealed beneath a 'feminine' veneer, which nevertheless provides an implicit challenge to patriarchal society. Indeed, Clarice employs subjective and psychological images to describe feelings against male domination of women, and she often uses humour or irony as tools to criticize men. Given her creative genius, she encircled the term 'feminine' with 'undecidability'. She made it into an 'undecidable' sign, as in Derrida's notion of *différance*, and was thus able to destabilize its meaning.

In other words, Lispector felt free to launch a new form of writing, which being 'feminine' and woman-centred was also arguably 'feminist' by implication. Indeed, she renewed the *crônica* as a genre by revealing women's long-repressed feelings, and making society acknowledge them as valid experiences.

The modern Brazilian *crônica* was first born a century earlier, in the 1870s. It combined the form of the serial novels published in newspapers and magazines with that of the short story.[5] Machado de Assis was one of the first *cronistas* in Brazil, and probably the best. He intertwined descriptions of Rio de Janeiro with a highly inventive narration. He directed his gaze mainly at its monuments, its people and streets, whilst discussing everyday events and historical landmarks. He also dwelt on the administrative acts that ruled the city, as well as other political topics about which he disclosed his own feelings and opinions. Such comments were a cue for him to show his erudite cultural background. At the same time, he also kept his reader informed about current local politics, for the main aim of the *crônica* published in the press was to provide readers with information. Any trifle was a pretext for Machado to display his knowledge of politics, philosophy, several languages and literatures, mythology or the Bible. For example, he informs his readers about the new electric streetcars by engaging two donkeys in a philosophical discussion, which is followed by his own equally highbrow comments on the flux of history and on the passing of time.[6]

Although Machado's narrator is informative and develops an interaction with his reader, he always retains the upper hand. He employs a cynical, stoical or pessimistic viewpoint that balances opinions between politics, philosophy, literature and history. Machado's influence continues to be widely felt among Brazilian writers, with special reference to his humour, his taste for describing the city, and his interest in ordinary people.

Closer to Lispector's own time, in the 1960s and 1970s, the city of Rio de Janeiro became a popular theme among *cronistas*, who seemed to develop strong feelings for the so-called 'Marvellous City'. The Brazilian *crônica* became a phenomenon almost entirely linked to Rio. Authors of that period masterfully depicted its bohemian bars and beaches, among the other pleasures that Rio offered 'cariocas'. Some of these *cronistas* include Fernando Sabino, Rubem Braga, Stanislau Ponte Preta (Sérgio Porto's pen name), Paulo Mendes Campos, Carlos Drummond de Andrade and José Carlos de Oliveira. Like Clarice Lispector, the latter two had a column in *Jornal do Brasil*.

But while male writers identified with a phallic and vertical city created by male architects, albeit one impregnated by male urban violence, women writers felt excluded from this urban environment. As a collective reaction, from the 1970s onwards they systematically began to express their intimate feelings and to focus on the subjective. Their constant use of the imaginary helped to corrode old-fashioned values and thus became an indirect tool against patriarchy and the male-dominated literary canon.

The attempt to build an intimate relationship with women readers had of course already been pursued by Machado de Assis, especially in his novels *Memórias póstumas de Brás Cubas* (1881) and *Quincas Borba* (1891). However, his narrators were naturally *the other*, and stood for a *difference* in relation to their female readers. By contrast, identification allowed Lispector to abolish distance and attain a perfect association with her readers as if they were her persona. She established an original and successful two-way dialogue in which both the female narrator and the female reader could identify with one another.

Lispector's tone in her *crónicas* draws on the modernist short story. Not only does it break with the descriptive *crónica*, but also it introduces narration and subjectivity into its form. According to Jürgen Habermas, the transformation of the press into a medium that expresses public opinion and sells advertisements provokes both the subversion of the traditional role of publicity and the invasion of the public sphere by business. This brings together the circulation of merchandise and 'human interrelations' and blurs the frontier between the public and the private spheres.[7] Lispector's main contribution to the *crónica* genre, then, was to bring her personal experience into the public sphere. Hence she was able to display women's desires and feelings right inside the shop-windows of 1970s Brazilian capitalist society.

Lispector made the 'feminine' position more public and projected the 'history of private life' (to employ Georges Duby's terminology) onto a wider historical context. While male writers held a distant, realistic, denotative or 'masculine' attitude towards their public, Lispector's use of a personal narrator allows her to develop an intimate dialogue with her female readers. She identified with her anonymous female readers and let their voices be heard. She did not employ realist descriptions of the city, but saw it through the feelings of its female inhabitants and those of her female readers; they in turn identified with her problems and opinions on life. Her *crónicas* feature a constant dialogue with and observation of the everyday world of the female city-dweller. Her narrator develops a totally 'feminine' voice and persona, even to the point of parody. She shows her fragile feminine side and complains about her exhaustion and perplexity before a fragmented world that rejects any possibility of a utopian or holistic view. In her *crónicas*, Lispector identifies with her female domestic servants and with the female students and journalists who telephone her or even visit her to discuss issues pertaining to her work—but also her private life.

Lispector's involvement with the feminine makes her adopt an intimate, familiar tone in her writing for the press. Yet Lispector's attitude towards publishing in the media appears to be ambiguous. On the one hand, she despises the everyday language it employs because it does not allow for the versatility of her creative work. On the other hand, she derives unexpected pleasure from becoming 'famous' and from her intense rapport with her female readers, which she could hardly have attained through publishing a book. Obtaining such a widespread response from people of all classes and provenance therefore had some compensation.[8] She justifies writing for the media out of financial need, yet she criticizes the press for not paying her for her interviews. In 'Amor imorredouro' [Undying love], 9 September 1967 (DM 20–3 at 20), she confesses her inability to get paid for her work, as any male professional would expect:

Ainda continuo um pouco sem jeito na minha nova função daquilo que não se pode chamar propriamente de crônica. E, além de ser neófita no assunto, também o sou em matéria de ganhar dinheiro. Já trabalhei na imprensa como profissional, sem assinar. Assinando, porém, fico automaticamente mais pessoal. E sinto-me um pouco como se estivesse vendendo minha alma. Falei nisso com um amigo que me respondeu: mas escrever é um pouco vender a alma. É verdade. Mesmo quando não é por dinheiro, a gente se expõe muito.[9]

In her early crônicas Lispector shows her uneasiness and her fear of her lack of experience (though obviously not lack of ability) in the craft of crônica writing. She declares, rather ironically, that she will seek advice from more experienced writers than herself, such as Elsie Lessa, Dinah Silveira de Queiroz and Rachel de Queiroz, or even Carlos Drummond de Andrade (see e.g. 'Adeus, vou-me embora!' [Farewell, I am leaving!], 20 April 1968, DM 122–6 at 124). In 'Ser cronista' [Writing crônicas], 6 July 1968 (DM 155–6 at 155), she jokingly calls Rubem Braga 'o inventor da crônica' [the inventor of the crônica].

Lispector's feeling of self-consciousness in this form of writing is an excuse for her use of sentimentality. She introduces personal topics into her crônicas, approximating them to short stories or literary fragments more than to pieces for the press. For example, Machado, who may be considered the epitome of the genre in Brazil, begins his very first crônica for his column História de 15 dias [A story every fortnight] in Ilustração brasileira (1 July 1876) with a formal address to his readers: 'Dou começo à crônica no momento em que o Oriente se esboroa e a poesia parece expirar às mãos grossas do vulgacho. Pobre Oriente! Mísera poesia!' [I begin my *crônica* at the moment when the Near East collapses and poetry seems to expire at the coarse hands of the populace. Pitiful Orient! Miserable poetry!][10] In another *crônica* on 1 November 1877, he states that any trifle might be a possible subject for a *crônica*: 'Há um meio certo de começar a crônica: por uma trivialidade. É dizer: Que calor! Que desenfreado calor!' [There is one surefire way to begin a *crônica*: start with something trivial. State, 'How warm it is! How unbearably hot!'] From the weather, Machado recommends that one should generalize to the atmosphere, the sun and the moon or yellow fever.[11]

In relation to Machado's, Lispector's approach to the genre is disconcerting, if not deconstructive. Her first *crônica* for *Jornal do Brasil* is entitled 'As crianças chatas' [Annoying children], 19 August 1973 (DM 9). It begins on an utterly personal note and is therefore radically different from Machado:

Não posso. Não posso pensar na cena que visualizei e que é real. O filho está de noite com fome e diz para a mãe: estou com fome, mamãe. Ela responde com doçura: dorme. Ele diz: mas estou com fome. Ela repete exasperada: durma. Ele insiste. Ela grita com dor: durma, seu chato! Os dois ficam em silêncio, no escuro, imóveis. [...] Até que, de dor e cansaço, ambos cochilam, no ninho da resignação. E eu não agüento a resignação. Ah, como devoro com fome e prazer a revolta.[12]

Lispector's aim seems to be the deconstruction of the *crônica* as a genre, having in mind the introduction of a new voice that might express women's feelings. Writing in a confessional style and deploring her being too personal are obviously resources that enable her to evince a 'feminine' voice, something that would initiate a new canon or history of the *crônica*. Lispector was much more daring than her predecessors Rachel de Queiroz, Dinah Silveira de Queiroz or Cecília Meireles, who wrote their *crônica*s in straightforward, realist form. Lispector's tone was freer and more personal than Carmen Dolores's, too, who followed Machado de Assis's descriptive style in her column 'A semana' in *O paiz*.[13] For example, 'O grito' [The scream], 9 March 1968 (DM 102–3 at 102) is the outburst of Lispector's sentimentality and confessional tone: 'Sei que o que escrevo aqui não se pode chamar de crônica nem de coluna nem de artigo. Mas sei que hoje é um grito. Um grito! De cansaço. Estou cansada!' [I know that what I write here cannot be called a *crônica*, or a column, or an article. But I know that today it is a scream. A scream! Of exhaustion. I am exhausted!]

On 14 September 1966, Lispector suffered an accident in which her hands and legs were seriously burnt. Her taking sleeping pills and smoking in bed caused the fire. Her bedroom, books and even her papers were lost. She spent three months in hospital recovering. The accident did not destroy her beauty, but her right hand was seriously burnt, and the psychological scars remained forever. She mentions this accident in several of her *crônicas*, which testify to the enormous solidarity of her friends and fans.

Her 'scream' of suffering—for her separation from her husband and for having to write for the press or to publish books to earn enough to help her to support herself and her two sons—intermittently spreads to the point of her identification with the marginalized. Her text 'A bela e a fera ou a ferida grande demais' [Beauty and the Beast, or the Wound Too Great] (1979) opposes the female beauty of her elegant character to the horror she experiences at the grotesque figure of a beggar standing on the sidewalk in Copacabana,[14] in a case of *Unheimlichkeit* similar to that experienced by the bourgeois character Ana at the sight of a blind man staring blankly at her in 'Amor' [Love].[15] However, in her last novel published in her lifetime, *A hora da estrela*, Lispector shows authentic interest for the other in her portrayal of the lower social strata.

Lispector's interest for the less-privileged begins to transpire in some of her *crônicas* such as 'Escândalo inútil' [Useless scandal], 27 April 1968 (DM 127–30), in which she narrates her interview with a woman who ran a brothel in Catete, a neighbourhood of Rio de Janeiro. Lispector excuses herself for her 'obscene' intention as well as for failing in this achievement (130): 'E aqui termina a entrevista que falhou. Nós todos falhamos quase sempre.' [Here ends this failed interview. All of us fail almost always.] Although she does not make explicit political statements, it is possible to read between the lines her disapproval of this poor and unattractive figure, of her work as well as of the socio-economic condition of the country. Lispector conveys a feeling of frustration about meeting her in a bar in Catete where they drink fruit juice. Might this character be a first draft for the future portrayal of the emblematically poor migrant Macabéa or the fortune-teller Madame Carlota in *A hora da estrela* (1977)?

In 'Mulher demais' [Too womanly], 8 June 1968, Lispector rejoices when an invitation for her to write on 'feminine' subjects for a newspaper is not followed up. She states (DM 148) that 'na extensão em que *feminino* é geralmente tomado pelos homens e mesmo pelas próprias humildes mulheres: como se mulher fizesse parte de uma comunidade fechada, à parte, e de certo modo segregada' [the *feminine* is often interpreted by men and even by humble women themselves as a closed and segregated group consisting only of females]. In this *crônica*, both interviewer and interviewee were distracted from their aim (the journalistic interview) and lapsed into a discussion on makeup. Lispector concludes: 'E parece que a culpa foi minha. Maquilagem nos olhos também é importante, mas eu não pretendia invadir as seções especializadas, por melhor que seja conversar sobre modas e sobre a nossa preciosa beleza fugaz.' [Apparently it was my fault. Makeup and fashion, and our precious fleeting beauty are important subjects to talk about; but I didn't mean to interfere with the specialized sections of the newspapers.] Her opinion appears in the light of a self-excuse, as if she could only write about the 'feminine mystique' for monetary reasons, and even so in the special or 'half-private' sections of the papers. But it can also shed an ironic light on the fact that the 'public' sections of the printed media are male-dominated.

The 'feminine mystique' became for Lispector a kind of motto, which she defended as if it were women's civil rights. She wrote a column under the pen name of Helen Palmer in the *Correio da manhã* from August 1959 to October 1960. Before this, in 1952 and 1953, she had a column in the small newspaper *O comício* under the pen-name Teresa Quadros. In both she gave beauty advice to women. In 1959, she acted as a ghostwriter for the actress and fashion model Ilka Soares in the column 'Nossa conversa' [Our chats] in *Diário da noite*.[16] In *Jornal do Brasil*, a *crônica* such as 'O vestido branco' [The white dress], 9 March 1968 (DM 104), discusses the influence of a white or black dress on women's appearance of inner purity. *A paixão segundo G.H.* shows her female protagonist getting down to terms with everyday life towards the end, after a long epiphany of self-discovery, by the simple act of dressing fashionably and going out to dance. Beauty is thus shown to be a psychological release for women from the troubles of life that cannot be so easily solved in the long run.[17]

Her identification with the 'feminine' as an intrinsically beautiful or elegant characteristic essential to women helped her establish a dialogue with her female readers.[18] She projects herself as a lonely and victimized woman, who receives great psychological support from a stream of female visitors, letters and telephone calls.[19] Each of these visitors provides her with an opportunity to celebrate an epiphany in her existence. Their presence constitutes a soothing ointment for her bruised ego and compensates for her feeling as a victim.

Lispector's development of a female narrator is her greatest contribution to the *crônica* genre. Her utterly personal, autobiographical, confessional narrator establishes an emotional and dialogical relationship, especially with the female reader. Almost like a persona, her 'feminine' core expresses women's psychological worries and replaces everyday press news or political commentary with a focus on the self. The function of her *crônica*s shifts from the traditional role of the press, which is information, to psychology or self-help. In some of her *crônica*s for *Jornal do Brasil*, she reveals herself as an understanding mother of two children, who tries to unveil the meaning of their reactions and behaviour. Having undergone psychoanalysis with Dr Azulay and with Dr Hélio Pellegrino, and through her friendship with the psychoanalyst Inês Besouchet, she sometimes tries to analyse her sons' psyches, hinting in her writing at the serious psychological problems experienced by her older son Pedro.

While a selection of women friends kept her company, she seldom refers to male friends in her *crônica*s except in connection with professional work or reviews. She might have feared suffering prejudice for being separated from her husband, bearing in mind that these *crônica*s appeared during the dictatorship when there was still no divorce in Brazil, a strongly Catholic country.[20] In 'Amor imorredouro' [Undying love], 9 September 1967 (DM 20–3 at 21), she comments on her 'adoration' and 'infinite love' for men. She presents a list of their qualities and flaws, and combines seriousness with humour. She conveys her admiration for men in an ironic manner when she writes in 'Armando Nogueira, futebol e eu, coitada' [Armando Nogueira, soccer and poor me], 30 March 1968 (DM 115–18) about the football columnist and states (117): 'Eu, coitada, não entendo de futebol, ia preferir balé mesmo' [Poor me, I don't understand anything of soccer; I would rather have ballet instead]. However, this admiration for men hides a sense of ridicule that she attributes to the idea that gender might have a single and unambiguous definition. Thus, in 'A partida do trem', Angela Pralini's dog is named Ulysses,[21] but ironically Ulysses is also the name given to the professor of philosophy in *Uma aprendizagem ou o livro dos prazeres*.[22] And in *A paixão segundo G.H.*, when the maid Janair has drawn a man, a woman and a dog in charcoal on her bedroom wall, it is the dog rather than the humans in whom G.H. recognizes herself.

Furthermore, in her *crônica* 'Brasília', Lispector playfully states: 'Eu sou o meu cachorro. Eu me chamo Ulisses.' [I am my dog. I am called Ulysses.][23] And then she repeats, referring to herself and to her dog-companion: 'Estamos ambos cansados' [We are both tired]. Stating that she is her dog may stand as a parody of Flaubert's famous statement, 'Madame Bovary, *c'est moi*.'

One must remember that Machado de Assis used the dog as a parody for a human being. In *Quincas Borba*, Rubião's receiving the philosopher Quincas Borba's inheritance was conditional upon his treating the philosopher's dog, also called Quincas Borba, as well as if it were the man himself. Clarice Lispector's innovation in this topic in her identification with the dog is that her texts allow for several possible readings, in which one may contradict the other. If, on the one hand, she depreciates herself by saying she is a dog, on the other, to call man a dog, or to call a dog after a hero like Ulysses, also devalues man and levels them all.

It is this 'undecidability' accompanying Lispector's texts that abolishes the Aristotelian logic of the contrary. It represents her innovation in the *crônica* genre, although she may have remained oblivious to her achievement. Quite aside from her unconventional female narrator and her innovative relationship with her female public, her use of language succeeds in stretching the boundaries of the *crônica* to an unprecedented degree. She constitutes a unique example of a *cronista* who often employs personal narration and hardly ever any external description. Her language disrupts patriarchal order, represented by the city, its buildings, its economic order, its geometrical streets and avenues and its social order, at the time symbolically embodied by the dictatorship. The rejection of this order takes place metaphorically through language.

This 'revolution in writing' (to employ Julia Kristeva's expression), while it incorporates body into self, was possible because of Lispector's implicit use of Nietzsche, Kierkegaard and Heidegger and of Sartre's existentialism. These were authors she had read during the years she spent in Switzerland, England and the United States when married to a diplomat. Significantly, she often stated in *crônica*s as well as in interviews that, despite being a law graduate, she was an intuitive person, free from canonical affiliations and literary influences. Thus she denied being an 'intellectual'. Being sensitive and therefore 'feminine' represented for her a way of denying patriarchal society. (See 'Sensibilidade inteligente' [Clever sensitivity] and 'Intelectual?

Não.' [An intellectual? No.], both 2 November 1968 (DM 215–16).
See also 'O uso do intelecto' [The use of the intellect], 6 November
1971 (DM 604).)

Lispector made pioneering use of the 'stream-of-consciousness'
technique in Brazil. She specifically denies having received any influence from Virginia Woolf, in response to an article by Álvaro Lins on
Perto do coração selvagem.[24] Nevertheless, she acknowledges having read
Katherine Mansfield's short story 'Bliss' when she was 15 years old,
which gave her a taste of the use of epiphany and the 'stream of
consciousness' in Mansfield's work.[25] Her *crônicas* increasingly develop
the stream of consciousness, which she had first used extensively in
Perto do coração selvagem and subsequently in *Laços de família*, most
notably in the celebrated short story 'Amor'. She, and later on other
female writers in the 1970s, employed this technique mostly to
express suppressed feelings of the imagination, as in Molly Bloom's
monologue at the end of Joyce's *Ulysses*. As such, it features prominently in her final works.[26]

Besides the use of the stream of consciousness and the replacement
of description by narration, her *crônicas* break with the usual description
of the city inserted in the Euclidean-space and chronological-time
dimensions. History has always been the major source for the traditional
crônica, which latterly had always taken place in Rio. In Lispector's
crônicas, however, the reference is not the outward space and time of
Rio but the inward dimension of the self, particularly the female psyche.
Her self condenses external and internal facts in one sole unity. In *Narrar
ou descrever* [Narrating or describing], Gyorgy Lukacs opposes these two
approaches to literature, which occur in traditional writing.[27] However,
in contrast to canonical literature, here only the facts that matter for
the female narrator's existence, her experience and point of view,
constitute the subject matter for her stories or *crônicas*.

Lispector's use of space and time is therefore a virtual, psychological
or imaginary way of representing reality.[28] In one of her *crônicas*, 'A
irrealidade do realismo' [The unreality of realism], 20 January 1968
(DM 83), she comments on the translation that she is doing of an
article by Struthers Burt about the unreality of realism. She wonders
whether the word 'realism' is not a contradiction when applied to any
form of art, 'essa palavra está em contradição quando aplicada mesmo
na suposta descrição de fatos numa coluna de jornal ou numa
reportagem' [this word is in contradiction even when it is applied to
the supposed description of facts in a newspaper column or report].

The use of the stream of consciousness provokes a shift from the external to the internal point of view. The author abolishes the city's spatial-temporal dimension while internalizing it into a subjective, representational or imaginary dimension. She employs creative narration rather than the description of external details. She replaces information about political or historical facts with the confession of existential feelings or the expression of her personal thoughts about everyday life. Moreover, her *crônicas* function as test-runs for short stories or vice versa. This experimenting with language has seldom taken place in Brazilian fiction. As with Woolf, who elaborated her diaries into novels and stories, part of Lispector's fiction works as metafiction for her other work.[29]

The foundation of a new language by Lispector's female narrator implies that the 'I' expresses all its intimacy as representative of the whole female universe in a scandalously overt way. The feminine, which was previously shy, rejected or hidden from the public eye, is now exposed to the camera lucida (to employ Barthes's expression) and parades in the newspaper like an overexposed photograph. Lispector liked exotic or grotesque words that could unveil a new world. These veiled feelings reveal her states of mind, her frustrations or her fear of death. Her use of the stream of consciousness goes deeper and is more subjective than Joyce's. Katherine Mansfield often employed it in relation to a third-person character, which is also the case in Woolf, as when her character Mrs Ramsay broods over the sock she is knitting in *To the Lighthouse*. In Lispector, the stream of consciousness occurs almost invariably in the first-person narrator. It represents an epiphany in the form of confession, which makes it possible to enact women's feelings.

Lispector paved the way for the expression of women's imagination through self-questioning, self-pity and self-victimization. This was now offered to the public eye as an insight into what had been denied or rejected until then. She opened up a place of recognition and validation of women's existence in its own right. Women ceased to feel as though they were nothing but an object of desire for men. Lispector conveyed these possibilities not through theoretical discourse but through a dialogical confession that reveals women's desires and fears. She identified with her dog, or with an egg. She became language itself. The description of the city was subsumed into the description of the 'I'. Lispector's *crônicas*, which provoked a tremendous response from her readers, paradoxically contributed towards liberating Brazilian women from an aura of 'femininity', giving them a voice in the public sphere. Female students, older professional women and housewives alike understood her writing and appreciated her advice or the poetic prose of her texts. We should not look for information in her writing, or for external, realistic discussion about feminism. Instead we should look for the egg that inaugurates language.

When Lispector refused the role of inheritor of the traditional male *crônica*, the process culminated in the inauguration of a language derived from and directed towards women. This new genre, which ironically she was only able to develop because of her access and exposure to the media that she despised, contradicted the prevailing male-dominated sense of reality and founded a new meaning for the imaginary and for the self. In order to perform it, she employs the undecidable, the unnamable. This nameless and undecided signifier hides behind the feminine mask. In proportion to its exposure in the press, this 'feminine' bore fruit in a more positive feminist position, even if this was not explicit.

Ultimately, Lispector disrupts the logic of the master and the slave, of the male and the female, of canonical knowledge and common sense; she disorganizes syntax and distorts semantics. The logic of the great epic is twisted when Ulysses, a professor of philosophy, loses his grandiose role of seafarer and shares his name with a dog. The housemaid Janair helps her mistress G.H. to discover the world of *the other*, which she had disregarded: the maid's room and the slum that she can see from her window. Writing of this kind illuminates and challenges ideologies and mentalities. Hence, it disrupts patriarchal order and is worth hundreds of essays written in defence of women's rights.

Notes to Chapter 6

1. Clarice Lispector, *A descoberta do mundo* (Rio de Janeiro: Nova Fronteira, 1984). See also Richard A. Mazzara, 'A descoberta do mundo', in *Clarice Lispector: A Bio-Bibliography*, ed. Diane E. Marting (Westport, CT: Greenwood Press, 1993), 29–31.

2. However, on 22 June 1968 she took part in a political demonstration on behalf of a student killed by the police, during which she was photographed by the press.

3. See Mary Eagleton, Introduction to *Feminist Literary Theory: A Reader* (Oxford: Basil Blackwell, 1990), 5.

4. Marta Peixoto states, in *Passionate Fictions: Gender, Narrative, and Violence in Clarice Lispector* (Minneapolis: University of Minnesota Press, 1994), 101: 'It is important to remember, however, that what we may loosely call Lispector's

feminism—her concern with the predicaments of women's lives and the powers to which they have access—is never cast as a simple defence of women and the feminine, but rather as a keen awareness of the struggles in which they are active, and not necessarily morally superior, participants.'

5. See Afrânio Coutinho, *A Literatura no Brasil*, 2nd edn, 6 vols. (Niterói: Editora da Universidade Federal Fluminense, 1986), chap. 57, 'Ensaios e crônicas', vi. 117–43.

6. José Maria Machado de Assis, *História de 15 dias*, 3 vols. (Rio de Janeiro: Aguilar, 1973), 15 March 1877, iii. 363–4 at 364: 'Um deles [dos burros], humanitário, ambicioso, murmurava:—Dizem: *les dieux s'en vont*. Que ironia! Não; não são os deuses, somos nós. *Les ânes s'en vont*, meus colegas, *les ânes s'en vont*.' [One of them, a humanitarian and ambitious donkey, whispered:—People say: *The gods have gone away*. How ironic! No; it's not the gods, it is us. *The donkeys have gone away*, my friends, *the donkeys have gone away*.]

7. Jürgen Habermas, *L'espace public: Archéologie de la publicité comme dimension constitutive de la société bourgeoise* (Paris: Payot, 1978), 189.

8. In 'Ser cronista' [Writing *crônicas*], 26 June 1968 (DM, 155–6 at 156), she confesses: 'E também sem perceber, à medida que escrevia para aqui, ia me tornando pessoal demais, correndo o risco daqui em breve de publicar minha vida passada e presente, o que não pretendo.' [And also without noticing it, as I was writing for this paper [*Jornal do Brasil*], I became too personal, and I risked making public my whole life, past and present, which I didn't mean to.] Then, she guiltily admits that writing *crônicas* in the newspaper gives her pleasure because they please her readers, even if they do use a lighter style or subject matter. Unfortunately, this change makes her uneasy, because it results from the medium itself and not from a deeper or inner transformation in her own self.

9. 'I am still a little awkward in my new function of writing something that cannot be called a *crônica*. Besides being new to the subject, I am also new to being paid for my work. I have already worked for the press as a professional, but without signing my name to the articles. When I sign, however, I automatically become more personal. I feel a little as if I were selling my soul. I commented on this to a friend who said that writing is similar to selling our soul. It is true. Even when we do not do it for money, we are exposed to it.'

10. Machado de Assis, *História de 15 dias*, iii. 335–6 at 335.

11. See ibid., iii. 369–70 at 369.

12. 'I cannot. I cannot think of the scene I visualized and which is real. It is night-time and a child, hurting from the pain of hunger, says to his mother: I am hungry, Mummy. She answers sweetly: Go to sleep. He says, But I am hungry. She repeats, irritated: Go to sleep. He insists. Then she painfully screams: Go to sleep, you annoying child! They both stay quiet, mute, in the dark. Finally, from pain and tiredness, they both slumber, in their nest of resignation. I can't stand such resignation. Ah, how I devour revolt with hunger and pleasure.'

13. See Carmem Dolores, *Crônicas 1905–1910,* ed. Eliane Vasconcellos (Coleção fluminense, 3; Rio de Janeiro: Arquivo Público do Estado do Rio de Janeiro, 1998).

14. See 'A bela e a fera ou a ferida grande demais' [Beauty and the Beast, or the Wound Too Great], (Rio de Janeiro: Nova Fronteira, 1979). It was later included, with a facsimile of its manuscript, in the critical edition of *A paixão*

segundo G.H., ed. Benedito Nunes (Florianópolis: Universidade Federal de Santa Catarina; UNESCO, 1988), 151–7.

15. From *Laços de família* (Rio de Janeiro: Editora do Autor, 1960).

16. See Teresa Cristina Montero Ferreira, *Eu sou uma pergunta: Uma biografia de Clarice Lispector* (Rio de Janeiro: Rocco, 1999), 209–10.

17. See *A paixão segundo G.H.* (Rio de Janeiro: Editora do Autor, 1964).

18. In 'Anonimato' [Anonymity], 10 Feb. 1968, she states 'Escrevo agora porque estou precisando de dinheiro' [I am only writing now because I am in need of money] (DM 92). She praises anonymity, in spite of people's wish for personal fame. Later on, in 'Outra carta' [Another letter], 24 Feb. 1968, she states that not only do her newspaper *crônicas* reveal her intimacy, but also her novels: 'Estes não são autobiográficos nem de longe, mas fico depois sabendo por quem os lê que eu me delatei' [These novels are far from autobiographical, but afterwards I discover from the readers that I revealed myself in them] (DM 97).

19. For instance, 'Maria chorando ao telefone' [Maria crying on the phone], 23 March 1968 (DM 112–13). These female readers frequently offer her desserts, recipes, anonymous letters, plenty of flowers, once a perfumed ivy, or even a cooked octopus ('Ana Luísa, Luciana e um polvo' [Ana Luísa, Luciana and an octopus], 23 March 1968 (DM 110–12)). These female fans, interviewers and friends compliment her on her texts, discuss her stories and exchange advice and opinions with her; see, among others, 'Dies Irae', 14 Oct. 1967 (DM 33–5); 'Bolinhas' [Amphetamines], 9 Dec. 1967 (DM 59), and 'Um telefonema' [A telephone call], 4 Feb. 1968 (DM 88).

20. Divorce was only made legal in Brazil on 26 Dec. 1977, shortly after Clarice's death. It was later ratified by the 1988 Constitution.

21. 'A partida do trem', *Onde estivestes de noite* (Rio de Janeiro: Artenova, 1974), 24–48. The dog is mentioned on pp. 31, 43–7.

22. *Uma aprendizagem ou o livro dos prazeres* (Rio de Janeiro: Sabiá, 1969); *An Apprenticeship, or The Book of Delights*, trans. Richard A. Mazzara and Lorri A. Parris (Austin: University of Texas Press, 1986).

23. 'Brasília', *Para não esquecer*, 2nd edn (São Paulo: Ática, 1979), 34–52 at 45; repr. from *Visão do esplendor: Impressões leves* (Rio de Janeiro: Francisco Alves, 1975), 9–34. The latter volume consists of a selection of *crônicas* from *Jornal do Brasil* and stories from *Alguns contos* (1952). See also 'Brasília de ontem e de hoje' [Brasília, past and present], 7 Oct. 1972 (DM 678).

24. See Luiza Lobo, 'Clarice Lispector e Virginia Woolf', *Crítica sem juízo* (Rio de Janeiro: Francisco Alves, 1993), 226–36 at 28. On 16 Feb. 1944, in a letter to Álvaro Lins, Lispector denied that she had read Proust, Woolf or Joyce (see Ferreira, *Eu sou uma pergunta*, 75, 101; Lobo, 'Clarice Lispector e Virginia Woolf', 28). Later, however, on 22 May 1952, under the pen name of Teresa Quadros, she published in *O comício* a *crônica* that commented on the imaginary figure of Shakespeare's sister in Virginia Woolf's *A Room of One's Own* (see Ferreira, *Eu sou uma pergunta*, 173–7). This text was republished as 'Violência de um coração' [The Violence of a Heart] in an unidentified newspaper on 29–30 Oct. 1977 (see Peixoto, *Passionate Fictions*, 100–11).

25. In her *crônica* of 24 Feb. 1973, 'O primeiro livro de cada uma de minhas vidas' [The first book of each of my lives] (DM, 721–3 at 722–3), Lispector writes that at the age of 15 she read Katherine Mansfield by chance. Lispector was 15 in

1935, the year in which she and her family moved from Recife to Rio de Janeiro. In her *crônica* of 17 April 1971, 'Ao correr da máquina' [Following the course of the typewriter] (DM 529–32 at 529), she states that she read Woolf only after she had finished writing her first novel, *Perto do coração selvagem*.

26. These were *Água viva* (1973), *A via crucis do corpo* (1974), *A hora da estrela* (1977) and *Um sopro de vida (Pulsações)* (1978).

27. Gyorgy Lukacs, *Narrar ou descrever* (Rio de Janeiro: Civilização Brasileira, 1967).

28. See Henri Lefebvre, *The Construction of Space* (Oxford: Blackwell, 1988).

29. For instance, the short story 'Uma galinha' [A hen] was published at least four times in Lispector's selected works, firstly in the magazine *Senhor* [Rio de Janeiro] in 1959, and afterwards in *Laços de família* (1960). Later, the *crônica* (or short story) 'Atualidade do ovo e da galinha' [The facts about the egg and the chicken] was serialized in *Jornal do Brasil* on 5, 12 and 19 July 1969 (DM 313–17, 318–21, 322–4). The same paper had already featured other *crônicas* focusing on similar themes, such as 'O pintinho' [The little chick], 10 Feb. 1968 (DM 91–2), 'Uma história de tanto amor' [A story of so much love], 10 Aug. 1968 (DM 173), and 'Bichos — I' [Animals—I], 13 March 1971 (DM 517–20).

CHAPTER 7

'Fatos são pedras duras': Urban Poverty in Clarice Lispector

Marta Peixoto

> Estou me interessando terrivelmente por fatos: fatos são pedras
> duras. Não há como fugir. Fatos são palavras ditas pelo mundo.
> (*A hora da estrela*)[1]
>
> meu caminho não sou eu, é outro, é os outros. Quando eu
> puder sentir plenamente o outro estarei salva e pensarei: eis o
> meu porto de chegada. (*A descoberta do mundo*)
>
> Não dou pão a ninguém, só sei dar umas palavras. E dói ser tão
> pobre. (*A descoberta do mundo*)[2]

In one of the *crônica*s in *A legião estrangeira* (1964), Lispector deplores
her inability to write about the social injustice she sees all around her.
This self-criticism no doubt echoes and attempts to answer the criticism
levelled at her writing in the early 1960s for its lack of engagement with
the social problems in Brazil. In this *crônica* Lispector recalls her sobering
acquaintance as a child with severe poverty in the *mocambos* (riverside
shanty-towns) in Recife. Even later on, she writes in this *crônica*, despite
her continued awareness of social injustice and her sense of the urgent
nature of the problems it presents, she felt unable to approach it 'de um
modo "literário" (isto é, transformado na veemência da arte)' [in a
'literary' way, in other words, transformed into the vehemence of art].[3]
As is well known, in *A hora da estrela* (1977) poverty gains centre stage,
complex dimensions and a disquieting intensity. But Lispector did not
come upon this topic all of a sudden, or without having made many
other more or less successful incursions into it. This paper will discuss
some of those other, less-studied approaches to the topic of poverty in
Lispector's *crônica*s, in *A paixão segundo G.H.* and in the posthumous

story 'A bela e a fera, ou a ferida grande demais' [Beauty and the Beast, or the Wound Too Great].

In the weekly *crônicas* Lispector published in the *Jornal do Brasil*, a major Rio de Janeiro daily, between 1967 and 1973, urban poverty is a recurrent motif.[4] Most of the *crônicas* are set in Rio, and *cronistas* have traditionally engaged with events set in their own time and place. Poverty was then, as it still is now, an inescapable part of the urban landscape. In addition to the usual urban phenomena of beggars, the homeless and street-children, Rio de Janeiro, because of the hills that characterize its topography, has the particularity of placing the well-off and the very poor in close contiguity, in some of its most prestigious locations. Although there are many poor neighborhoods (*favelas* or shanty-towns) on the periphery of Rio, some are located on the hills right within the city. Since the end of the nineteenth century, poor people have established themselves precariously in areas with undesirable characteristics, at times on public lands. 'Ao longo do século XX,' writes Carlos Lessa, 'a pobreza do Rio distribuiu-se pelos neo-cortiços, pelos loteamentos improvisados nos eixos dos subúrbios e pelas favelas nas encostas dos morros e de zonas inundáveis. De um início discreto a favela impôs sua presença efetiva no espaço urbano e no imaginário do Rio de Janeiro a partir dos anos 20.' [Throughout the twentieth century, poor people in Rio lived in tenement houses, on improvised plots of land in the suburbs, and in *favelas* on the hillsides and on the borders of flood-prone lands. After its discreet beginnings, from the 1920s onwards the *favela* became imprinted definitively on the urban space and the imaginary of Rio de Janeiro.][5]

By the early 1960s, there were 147 known *favelas* in Rio, 33 of them on the hills contiguous to the middle-class or wealthy neighbourhoods in the southern part of the city,[6] where the rich and the poor can often see each other from their respective windows. Botafogo, Copacabana, Ipanema, Leme had their own *favelas* then and still do today. The *favelas* of the early 1960s, less numerous and densely-inhabited than the ones today, predated the aggravated conflict and violence brought about by the massive drug-trafficking of recent decades. But the dispossession of the *favelas* of the 1960s was perhaps even more stark, since they also predated improvements in material construction, in urban and social services and community organization, which, along with the movements that demand recognition for the citizenship rights (*cidadania*) of the inhabitants of poorer communities, have in some ways improved their material and symbolic circumstances.

Lispector, who had lived in Rio as a young girl between the ages of 12 and 24, returned to the city in 1959 after fifteen years of foreign residence in Europe and the United States. She spent the rest of her life in Leme, a small beach-front neighbourhood backed by a steep hill where there were two *favelas*. The idea of poverty as an unavoidable presence appears in the opening segment of the very first *crônica* Lispector wrote for the *Jornal do Brasil* (19 August 1967). This brief text of only one paragraph, 'As crianças chatas' [Annoying children], takes the form of a testimony that is both imaginary and involuntary. 'Não posso', it begins (DM 9); 'Não posso pensar na cena que visualizei e que é real. O filho está de noite com dor de fome e diz para a mãe: estou com fome, mamãe.' [I cannot. I cannot think of the scene I visualized and which is real. It is night time and a child, hurting from the pain of hunger, says to his mother: I am hungry, Mummy.] The reality of poverty—it is a real scene, Lispector notes, despite being imaginary—is an unwelcome invasion, words and images that force their way past the barrier of the writer's unwillingness ('não posso pensar'): 'I cannot think about it' but also 'I cannot bear to think about it'. Lispector imagines the child's insistent complaint and the mother's powerlessness and escalating exasperation, until finally, overcome by pain and fatigue, they both fall asleep, 'no ninho da resignação' [in their nest of resignation] (DM 9). While they lack food, Lispector herself will feed off the revolt that their predicament generates in her (DM 9): 'E eu não agüento a resignação. Ah, como devoro com fome e prazer a revolta.' [I cannot bear such resignation. Ah, how I devour revolt with hunger and pleasure.]

This *crônica* sets up a complicated dynamic between the writer and her characters, who, because they are part of the vast and grim reality of poverty, do not belong purely to the world of the imagination (if any character ever does). These are not creatures she has made up but characters who appear uninvited and derive their force from being all too real. In the division of attributes between characters and writer, it seems that the writer takes the better share: the characters' lot is hunger, pain and passive resignation while the writer takes pleasure in hungrily devouring a revolt elicited precisely by their predicament. She, unlike them, has both the hunger and the means to satisfy it, repeating symbolically the privilege she has in reality. Though the *crônica* can be seen to end on a false note, and is complicated by the fact that the topic of the hungry mother and child in itself skirts sentimentality (recalling Lispector's claim in the *crônica* from *A legião estrangeira* quoted above that she does not know how to speak of social injustice 'com a veemência da arte'), it is with this text that she begins her career as a *cronista* for the *Jornal do Brasil*. While obviously trying to make her writing more responsive to this dark social reality, she registers at the start both her effort and her resistance. This is a new imperative in Lispector's writing: no one goes hungry in any of the stories of *Laços de família*, for instance. The annoying son who pressures his mother with his hunger stands in a parallel position to the dispossessed characters who pressure the writer with their pain. It is also significant that it is a woman writer who 'hears' their painful dialogue, though the only maternal protection she offers is to register their cry and to imagine for them the shelter of resignation.

Another *crônica*, 'Eu tomo conta do mundo' [I take care of the world], returns to the topic of a troubled sense of maternal obligation, here writ large and approached from an ironic perspective, which registers both the intention and its hubris. The activity of taking care proves to be no more than a careful observation of the visual surfaces of the world and is thus completely self-enclosed, in no way affecting, for better or for worse, the objects of care, who include the dispossessed. The 10-year-old boy, emaciated and dressed in rags, merits the same detached observation as the thousand plants and trees of the Botanical Garden. 'Tomo conta dos milhares de favelados pelas encostas acima' [I take care of the thousands of slum-dwellers on the nearby slopes], the narrator states, as she extends to them the visual attentiveness also applied to the traces of water on the sands of the beach, to ants, bees and flowers. 'Nasci assim, incumbida' [I was born that way: encumbered], she says by way of explanation, but her witnessing remains purposeless (DM 421–2): 'Só não encontrei ainda a quem prestar contas' [Only I still have not found anyone I can report back to]. This caring does not in fact extend care (DM 421): 'Fico apenas sabendo como é o mundo' [I just end up knowing what the world is like]. Instead it multiplies the objects of care beyond all normal boundaries but also dissipates responsibility. Although her care is devoid of any effect on the real world, it does benefit the observer, and ultimately her reader. Lispector insists on this practice of sympathetic attention as a way of knowing, and this knowing of course has a direct bearing on her narrative art.

If in this *crônica* the narrator lets herself off the hook by ironically pretending that the poverty she observes is some way taken care of by her observation, another *crônica*, 'As caridades odiosas' [Odious charity] (DM 324–6), includes an acerbic statement of self-criticism. The *crônica* tells of two incidents in which the autobiographical narrator is moved to give to beggars: she buys a sweet for a street child who requests it and gives money towards the rent of a woman about to be evicted and whose baby attracts her in a bus: 'dá-dá-dá', the baby babbles, 'give-give-give.' The *crônica* hinges on the narrator's various and contradictory emotions that arise from being part of an unjust social order and in the position of the one who can give or withhold the gift: gratitude for being able to afford the boy a small pleasure, shame and guilt for not giving more, mixed with pride, revolt, self-hatred; unease, suspicion and anger at the woman, who, with the baby's innocent help, snared Lispector with what perhaps was a ploy, or more likely the plain truth. The understanding that this kind of charity does not reduce poverty in any systematic and effective way makes the giving hateful without blocking her other, disparate responses.

When the poor in question are not the anonymous poor in the streets or the *favelas* but a familiar presence in one's own home, the contradictory feelings on the part of Lispector's autobiographical narrator only increase. 'Ter empregadas, chamemo-las de uma vez de criadas, é uma ofensa à humanidade' [employing domestic servants, or let's just call them maids, is an offence to humanity] (DM 33), the narrator announces emphatically in one *crônica*, and in another specifies some of the tensions in this relationship (DM 54): 'Por falar em empregadas, em relação às quais sempre me senti culpada e exploradora, piorei muito depois que assisti a peça *As criadas* [de Jean Genet]. Fiquei toda alterada. Vi como as empregadas se sentem por dentro, vi como a devoção que às vezes recebemos delas é cheia de um ódio mortal.' [Speaking of housemaids, who have always made me feel guilty and exploitative, I felt much worse after seeing Genet's play *The Maids*. The play distressed me. I began to see how maids really feel inside, to realize that their occasional shows of devotion to us are full of mortal hatred.] Despite these many qualms, the domestic servant was a constant presence in Lispector's life, to judge by these autobiographical texts, and also appeared often in her fiction. Of the *crônica*s from *Jornal do Brasil* later published in *A descoberta do mundo*, seven deal with this topic while others refer to it in passing.

As part of the urban poor who can barely eke out a living from their employment in occupations nevertheless essential for the normal functioning of the city, the domestic servant moves between the worlds of poverty and middle- and upper-class comfort. Living her personal life on the hills or on the outskirts of the city of Rio, she has as her workspace the home of her well-off employers and participates with them in a contradictory relationship that still bears the traces of its historic predecessor, the relationship between masters and slaves. The modern relationship, marked by both intimacy and distance, on its simplest level entails a mere exchange of money for service, but, as Lispector is quick to note, it also enmeshes the employer in a position of complicity with an unjust social order, because the usual salary is less than sufficient to cover basic needs. Moreover, the relationship is vulnerable to the emotional pressures arising from its domestic setting, as well as from the hierarchical position and disparate social circumstances of the participants. In the *crônicas*, Lispector registers the less disquieting aspects of the relationship between employer and servant, and shows the writer concerned with understanding these women who are so close and at the same time so distant. Lispector reserves for her fiction—especially *A paixão segundo G.H.*—a view of that relationship that is more critical and fraught with negative emotions.

How can I write the other, Lispector seems to ask in these texts, if the other who observes me in my own kitchen bears the marks of a life of incalculable poverty—missing teeth, for instance, or a complete lack of formal education and social skills—and brings to mind other lives of equal deprivation? The origins of this relationship in slavery (which in Brazil was abolished in 1888) leave their traces even today. In the architecture of modern homes, for instance, the maid's room, often tiny and without windows, makes apparent her position of drastic inferiority. In G.H.'s luxury apartment, the maid's room has 'a dupla função de dormida e depósito de trapos, malas velhas, jornais antigos, papéis de embrulho e barbantes inúteis' [the dual function of sleeping quarters and storage space for old suitcases and clothes, out-of-date newspapers, leftover wrapping paper and useless bits of string].[7]

According to Sandra Lauderdale Graham, servants and masters in nineteenth-century Rio de Janeiro formed ambivalent relationships:

Despite their firmly fixed inequalities, a shared domesticity imposed its inevitable intimacies. Servants and masters had to live in one another's constant presence, repeating in daily routine the countless and complex exchanges that connected them. Masters could scarcely prevent servants from witnessing at close range the otherwise private habits and events of family life. Nor could servants long conceal from masters their idiosyncrasies and preoccupations. Familiarity and its necessary accommodations threatened to erode the carefully defined differences of their relationship.[8]

Despite the great changes in social habits that took place in the twentieth century, these tensions between masters and servants persist in Brazilian society beyond the time-frame of Lauderdale Graham's study into Lispector's time and later.

Lispector's narratives about domestic servants alternate between presenting them as alien figures and finding points of kinship and identification. The *crônica* 'O lanche' [The tea-party] includes both of these perspectives, as sympathy coexists with an amused, wistful estrangement. This *crônica* also offers a delicate portrayal of the give and take in the relation between mistress and servants, on the levels of both practical and symbolic exchanges. The narrator imagines a hypothetical, ghostly tea-party, where the guest list would be limited to all her former maids (DM 423):

Seria um chá — domingo, Rua do Lavradio — que eu ofereceria a todas as empregadas que já tive na vida. As que esqueci marcariam a ausência com uma cadeira vazia, assim como estão dentro de mim. As outras, sentadas, de mãos cruzadas no colo. Mudas — até o momento que cada uma abrisse a boca e, rediviva, morta viva, recitasse o que eu me lembro. Quase um chá de senhoras, só que nesse não se falaria de criadas.[9]

These ghostly maids, despite being Lispector's guests, are not her equals. That they speak their own words can be seen as a exercise of power, but they speak only on command, as it were, saying only the words their former employer is unable to forget. Like ghosts, they also revisit emotions and reopen wounds (DM 424):

— Pois te desejo muita felicidade — levanta-se uma — desejo que você obtenha tudo que ninguém pode te dar.
— Quando peço uma coisa — ergue-se outra — só sei falar rindo muito e pensam que não estou precisando [...].
— Trivial, não senhora. Só sei fazer comida de pobre. [...]
— Pois hoje de madrugada — me diz a italiana — quando eu vinha para cá, as folhas começaram a cair, e a primeira neve também. Um homem na rua me disse assim: 'É a chuva de ouro e de prata.' Fingi que não ouvi porque se não tomo cuidado os homens fazem de mim o que querem.
— Lá vem a lordeza — levanta-se a mais antiga de todas, aquela que só conseguia dar ternura amarga e nos ensinou tão cedo a perdoar crueldade de amor. — A lordeza dormiu bem? A lordeza é de luxo. É cheia de vontades, ela quer isso, ela não quer aquilo. A lordeza é branca.[10]

The domestic servants who provided the leisure and made possible the narrator's intellectual work are remembered for what had no practical use: their words, so moving, frank, humorous or precise that they became memorable, an effect close to that of poetry. Lispector recognizes in this way the maids' subjectivities and the elements of this relationship that go beyond an economic exchange. These gifts are not offered by the generous employer to the needy maid but vice versa. In the final paragraph, Lispector renders them a kind of homage by including their words as components of her text, using their phrases as modules to be recombined, added to or inverted, forming new statements and a new whole (DM 424):

— Comida é questão de sal. Comida é questão de sal. Comida é questão de sal. Lá vem a lordeza: te desejo que obtenhas tudo o que ninguém pode te dar, só isso quando eu morrer. Foi então que o homem disse que a chuva era de ouro, o que ninguém pode te dar. A menos que não tenhas medo de ficar toda de pé no escuro, banhada de ouro, mas só na escuridão. A lordeza é de luxo pobre: folhas ou a primeira neve. Ter o sal do que se come, não fazer mal ao que é bonito, não rir na hora de pedir e nunca fingir que não ouviu quando alguém disser: esta, mulher, esta é a chuva de ouro e de prata. Sim.[11]

Although what remains from this relationship has nothing to do with its main utilitarian purpose, the servants are still placed in a subservient position, but now on a symbolic level. Lispector's use of the servants' memorable words in this final paragraph can be seen as an homage but also as an appropriation, for she revises and changes them as she makes her own text.

In other *crônica*s Lispector also mentions servants' use of words, or their incapacity to use them. She seems to be attracted to the maids' verbal (or other) creativity and to any demonstration of intellectual curiosity on their part, which tend to attenuate differences and bring out unexpected similarities between the servants and their writer employer. In 'Uma mineira calada' [A quiet woman from Minas] (DM 53), the maid Aninha, 'uma mineira que mal falava e quando o fazia era com voz abafada de além túmulo' [a woman from Minas who hardly spoke, and when she did it was like a low voice from beyond the grave], nevertheless says she likes complicated books and wants to read one of Lispector's. Once again we find the metaphoric linkage of maids and ghosts ('voz de além túmulo' [a voice from beyond the grave]), underlining the simultaneous closeness and distance of the relationship, and the unease it provokes. In another *crônica*, a maid sings a beautiful melody without words, and answers, when Lispector

asks what she is singing: 'é bobagem minha mesmo' [it's just a silly
tune I made up] (DM 444). At this moment, Lispector perceives, with
sudden clarity, that the servant possesses a distinct and independent
subjectivity (DM 445):

Enquanto isso a empregada estende a roupa na corda e continua sua melopéia
sem palavras. Banho-me nela. A empregada é magra e morena e nela se aloja
um 'eu'. Um corpo separado dos outros, e a isso se chama de 'eu'? É estranho
ter um corpo onde se alojar, um corpo onde sangue molhado corre sem
parar, onde a boca sabe cantar e os olhos tantas vezes devem ter chorado. Ela
é um 'eu'.[12]

Rather than approaching the servant as a 'you' or a 'she', the external
object of practical commands, Lispector imagines for a moment her
interiority as an 'I' like other 'I's', sharing with her the position of the
first person.

If certain of the *crônica*s reveal a sense of kinship between employer
and servant, others situate the maids as if they were inhabitants of a
parallel universe. In 'Como uma corça' [Like a fawn], Lispector sketches
a delicate portrait of the maid Eremita, a predecessor of the lyrical
components of Macabéa in *A hora da estrela*. The abyss that separates
the experiences of the maid from those of her employer is figured as a
double life of the maid. The narrator imagines that the maid repeatedly
escapes into a forest, a mysterious and ancient world she shares with
animals and plants. Eremita's convenient disappearance into the natural
landscape affords her employer respite from the grim knowledge that
the dangerous other world the maid inhabits is a human and social
construction with which she, the employer, is in some way complicit.
'Ah, então decerto devia ser este o seu mistério: ela descobrira um
atalho para a floresta. Decerto nas suas ausências era para lá que ia.
Regressando com os olhos cheios de brandura e ignorância, olhos
completos. Ignorância que nela caberia e se perderia toda a sabedoria
do mundo.' [Ah, so *that* was her mystery: she had discovered a shortcut
into the forest. That was almost certainly where she vanished in her
moments of distraction. When she returned, her eyes were full of
mildness and ignorance, her eyes were complete. An ignorance that
fitted within her and where all the wisdom of this world could be
absorbed.] (DM 85)

The narrator's lack of knowledge of the problems, desires, and
fantasies that occupy the mind of the young woman with whom she
shares a close and daily contact becomes here the wise ignorance of

the maid: opaque to her employer she becomes opaque to herself. The discomfort that arises from the certainty that the girl also participates in another social and spiritual world, governed by unknown values and beliefs, is registered comfortingly as the certainty that the girl's apparent household duties disguise devotion to the natural elements. Her menial tasks—washing clothes, hanging them up to dry, mopping floors—might appear to be done as a service to her employers, but they actually engage Eremita with the elements she supposedly worships, the sun, the wind and the rain (DM 86): 'Ela se arranjava para servir muito mais remotamente, e a outros deuses' [She took care to serve much more remotely, and to serve other gods]. The girl's gestures that bear traces of a life of poverty, past or present, appear soothingly as the results of unknown but safely overcome dangers she faced in the forest (DM 86): 'A única marca do perigo que passara era o seu modo fugitivo de comer pão. No resto era serena. Mesmo quando tirava o dinheiro que a patroa esquecera sobre a mesa, mesmo quando levava para o noivo em embrulho discreto alguns gêneros da despensa. Roubar de leve ela também aprendera nas suas florestas.' [The only trace of the danger she had faced was her furtive way of eating bread. In everything else she was quite calm. Even when she stole money which her employer had left lying on the table or slipped the odd parcel of food to her boyfriend. For in her forests she had also learned how to steal with a light touch.]

This lyrical and gentle portrait, which tones down tensions, accepts differences of experience and values and pardons discreet thefts, also displays the predominant attitude in Lispector's *crônicas* about domestic servants. Guilt, tensions and estrangement are recognized but are also mitigated and effaced. In *A paixão segundo G.H.*, however, the kindly bourgeois mistress disappears, and the mistress–servant relation sketched out is more brutal and stark. The novel is structured as a monologue, with G.H. as the only character. The maid in question, Janair, has quit her employment the day before—no reasons are given for this—and G.H. at first cannot even recall her name. Their exchanges were marked by distance and anonymity (PGH 46): 'Não era de surpreender que eu a tivesse usado como se ela não tivesse presença: sob o pequeno avental, vestia-se sempre de marrom escuro ou de preto, o que a tornava toda escura e invisível — arrepiei-me ao descobrir que até agora eu não havia percebido que aquela mulher era uma invisível.' [It wasn't surprising that I had used her as though she had no presence: under her small apron she always wore dark brown

or black, which made her all dark and invisible—I shivered to discover
that until now I hadn't noticed that she was an invisible woman.] Here
G.H. makes harshly explicit the tactful invisibility that is the usual
condition of domestic employment, ascribing it, however, not to the
skilled performance of a service or to G.H.'s own convenient disregard
of the maid as a person but to the maid's very nature: because I don't
see her, she must therefore be invisible.

The apparent distance and indifference between employer and
servant soon reveal an underlying hatred. Even *in absentia* Janair
manages to offend her former employer by leaving the maid's room
neat and impeccably clean. On the wall, she sketched an unexpected
mural: a hasty and schematic drawing of a woman, a man and a dog.
G.H. sees in these graffiti-like drawings slurs directed against herself,
not only in the sketch of the woman but also, surprisingly, in the man
and the dog: the man because G.H. imagines that the life she leads,
without husband or children, could have been seen by the maid as a
man's life (PGH 45): 'E quanto ao cachorro — seria este o epíteto que
ela me dava? Havia anos que eu só tinha sido julgada pelos meus pares
e pelo meu próprio ambiente que eram, em suma, feitos de mim
mesma e para mim mesma. Janair era a primeira pessoa realmente
exterior de cujo olhar eu tomava consciência.' [And as for the dog ...
was that the name she used to call me? For years I had only been
judged by my peers and by my own circle, who were, when it came
down to it, made by me for me. Janair was the first outsider whose
gaze I really took notice of.]

But is this really an external perspective? Of all the meanings that
could be found in these enigmatic drawings, G.H. discovers in them
always and merely her own image. Once again, even at the moment
of attempting to read the maid's subjectivity by interpreting her
drawing, the maid remains to G.H. an invisible woman. G.H sees
herself alluded to or depicted everywhere, if not crushed and
murdered along with the cockroach, the main object of her struggle
with the abject. Janair is merely a shadowy and preliminary figure,
soon replaced by the cockroach. The drawings on the wall eventually
come to reveal the mutual hatred—but is it really mutual?—previously
imperceptible to G.H., between herself and Janair (PGH 49):
'tranqüila e compacta raiva daquela mulher que era a representante de
um silêncio como se representasse um país estrangeiro, a rainha
africana. E que ali dentro de minha casa se alojara, a estrangeira, a
inimiga indiferente. Perguntei-me se Janair teria me odiado — ou se

fora eu que, sem sequer a ter olhado, a odiara.' [Calm, compact fury on the part of the woman who represented silence as if she were representing a foreign country, the African queen. And she had lodged here in my home, that stranger, that indifferent enemy. I wondered if Janair had in fact hated me—or if it had been me who had hated her, without even looking at her.]

In Janair, G.H. sees an African queen, a brilliant metaphor that sums up her tensions and assuages her guilt. It conveys G.H.'s disquiet if not fear regarding the stability of current hierarchies and the fact that other, dissonant values might claim the maid's loyalty. The woman she disdains as an inferior may with a shift of perspective and nationality become her superior, though only in Africa, outside the realm of Eurocentric prestige. This hypothetical superiority disguises the sad constraints of Janair's actual social status and dissipates any guilt on the part of her employer. If Janair is a queen she cannot possibly suffer the negative consequences of a meagre salary or of racial discrimination. In Janair's absence, G.H. perceives that the maid's room 'era o retrato de um estômago vazio' [the portrait of an empty stomach] (PGH 48), but never links this insight to the possibility that the maid herself might in some way have shared that hunger. Like the three figures on the wall, who demonstrate no ties to each other, G.H and Janair lived side by side without truly interacting (PGH 44): 'Nenhuma das três figuras tinham ligação com a outra, as três não formavam um grupo: cada figura olhava para a frente, como se nunca tivesse olhado para o lado, como se nunca tivesse visto a outra e não soubesse que ao lado existia alguém.' [There was nothing linking the three figures together, and they didn't make up a group: each figure stared straight ahead, as though it had never looked sideways, as though it had never seen any of the others and did not realize that that anyone existed beyond itself.]

G.H., who was never able really to see Janair, will now belatedly use her vacated room as the setting for the traumatic meeting with the cockroach. If Janair is eventually identified with the cockroach and both of these with G.H. herself, as Solange de Oliveira argues,[13] that is because both Janair and the cockroach become *dramatis personae* in G.H.'s solipsistic inner drama. Although G.H.'s epiphanic experiences of contact with the abject (which also becomes the sublime) take as their point of departure a detailed survey of the residues and traces that the maid left behind, what ultimately matters is not the figure of the maid but its usefulness in delineating G.H.'s initial position as she begins her long trajectory toward contact with all that she had excluded from her superficial and well-ordered life. It is only later, in *A hora da estrela*, that Lispector's fiction gives centre stage to the problem of how—and to what end—literature might represent the interiority of those who live with basic deficits, '[os que] sofrem de leve fome permanente' [those who suffer a vague but permanent hunger] (HE 38).[14]

A similar use of the place of urban poverty as the springboard for visionary experiences occurs in one of the chapters of *A paixão segundo G.H.*, where the protagonist looks out at a *favela* on the hills facing her window, but immediately pries the image loose from its actual context by situating it in foreign lands (PGH 125): 'Além das gargantas rochosas, entre os cimentos dos edifícios, vi a favela sobre o morro e vi uma cabra lentamente subindo pelo morro. Mais além estendiam-se os planaltos da Asia Menor. Dali eu contemplava o império do presente. Aquele era o estreito de Dardanelos. Mais além as escabrosas cristas.' [Beyond the rocky cliffs, in the gaps between the concrete buildings, I saw the *favela* on the hillside, and I saw a goat walking slowly up the hill. The plains of Asia Minor stretched away beyond. From there I contemplated the empire of the present. Over there was the strait of the Dardanelles. Beyond that, the craggy peaks.]

In a *tour de force* of visionary equivalences, Lispector renders in shifting metaphors the non-prestigious, chaotic agglomerations and precarious constructions of the *favela* in terms of the prestigious ancient civilizations of Asia Minor, their rise and fall, their warring peoples and the later archeological work that uncovered their cities and treasures. (It might be pertinent to note here that, in the 1960s, one of the *favelas* in Lispector's neighbourhood, Leme, was called Morro da Babilônia [Babylon Hill].)[15] The shanties on the hill become the 'semi-ruínas das favelas' [the semi-ruins of the *favelas*] (PGH 129), their obvious poverty a potential for riches, in a complex set of overlapping pieces, where both the present city and ancient oxymoronic equivalents are alternately visible (PGH 128): 'Pois eu estava procurando o tesouro da minha cidade. / Uma cidade de ouro e pedra, o Rio de Janeiro, cujos habitantes ao sol eram seiscentos mil mendigos. O tesouro da cidade poderia estar numa das brechas do cascalho. Mas qual delas?' [For I was looking for my city's treasure. / A city of gold and stone, Rio de Janeiro, whose inhabitants in the sun were six hundred thousand beggars. The city's treasure might be in one of the openings in the rubble. But which one?] The surge and proliferation of metaphors, which transform sight into visionary seeing, although it aims for and may reach other truths, also becomes a way of canceling out the significance of the physical evidence before her, the *favela* in its actual and present poverty.

The landscape of the *favela* serves, then, as a canvas for the visionary seeing which also in its own way challenges and escapes the protagonist's understanding. Poverty, although not a prominent concern of the novel, can be seen as a kind of underlying surface, never dominant but intermittently visible through the layers superimposed upon it. Here and elsewhere in her texts, Lispector addresses a persistent dilemma regarding the representation of poverty. The options—to see (and understand and feel) or not to see—play themselves out in multiple variations, as the characters or the autobiographical narrator of the *crônicas* try out both seeing and refusing to see.

One of Lispector's most impressive achievements as a writer—in the short stories of *Laços de família* that established her reputation in Brazil, in *A paixão segundo G.H.,* as well as in other texts—is the capacity to represent inner crises, or, to put it more precisely, to represent a subjectivity in the grip of overwhelming and contradictory emotions, beyond the grasp of rational intelligence. In depicting, for instance, G.H.'s momentous contemplation of and brief physical encounter with a cockroach, Lispector's language proceeds by suggesting what neither character nor narrator can fully understand. Lispector's achievement is to take language to the point where language ceases to comprehend and master and must proceed by other means: a language that is telling because it cannot tell, does not know how to tell. 'Não sei contar,' says the narrator of 'Os desastres de Sofia' [The Disasters of Sofia] about what she intuits as a young girl when looking at her teacher in a moment of crisis (LE 21): 'Eu era uma menina muito curiosa e, para minha palidez, eu vi. Eriçada, prestes a vomitar, embora até hoje não saiba ao certo o que vi. Mas sei que vi. Vi tão fundo quanto numa boca, de chofre eu via o abismo do mundo.' [I was a very inquisitive child and, enough to make me go pale, I saw. Bristling, about to throw up, though to this day I cannot say for certain what I saw. But I know that I saw. I saw as deep as when looking into a mouth, all at once I saw the abyss of the world.] At these moments, Lispector's language bears witness to a crisis, or, to put it another way, her language suggests the momentousness of the crisis in its very incapacity to narrate it. In another metatextual passage, Lispector puts in precise and paradoxical terms the suggestive power of a language caught in the drama of the will to represent and the failure of representation (PGH 212–13):

A realidade é a matéria prima, a linguagem é o modo como vou buscá-la — e como não acho. Mas é de buscar e não achar que nasce o que eu não conhecia, e que instantâneamente reconheço [...] Por destino tenho que ir buscar e por destino volto com as mãos vazias. Mas — volto com o indizível. O indizível só me poderá ser dado através do fracasso de minha linguagem. Só quando falha a construção é que obtenho o que ela não conseguiu.[16]

When the 'reality' that Lispector's texts aim to capture is the social reality of poverty, she also comes to rely on the power of literature to represent by the circuitous route of charting its failure. The posthumous short story 'A bela e a fera, ou a ferida grande demais' represents urban poverty by highlighting the elite's usual indifference and the many modes of failure in its (occasional) efforts to see the poor. The primary centre of consciousness is a character far removed from the world of poverty, who confronts it against her will, and whose capacity for sympathy and understanding is limited, shot through with self-regard, prejudices and anger. The narrative posits that the wealthy and beautiful Carla undergoes a completely new experience when she is approached by a beggar with an open wound on his leg: 'E a ferida, ela nunca a vira tão de perto....' [And the wound, she'd never seen one so close up....].[17] If the novelty of this encounter lacks verisimilitude, it is nevertheless in keeping with the exaggerations and farcical situations of Lispector's late fiction. This story stages as farce a momentous encounter between poverty and wealth, seen mostly from the perspective of the wealthy, and followed by a rapid forgetting.

Carla belongs to the profoundly selfish elite, whose greatest self-protection is the refusal to see. When she comes upon the open wound on the beggar's leg, her response is a cry for help, but on her own behalf (BF 135): '"Socorro!!!" gritou-se para si mesma... "Socorre-me, Deus", disse baixinho.' ['Help!!!' she shrieked to herself... 'Help me, God', she whispered.] Momentarily losing grasp of all her usual rationalizations, she gives the beggar an unusually large sum of money, then flounders hysterically amid disorganized responses. These include absurd thoughts (Can this beggar speak English? Has he ever had caviar and champagne?) and the assimilation of the beggar to the figure of Christ (BF 142): 'Eu sou o Diabo, pensou lembrando-se do que aprendera na infância. E o mendigo é Jesus.' [I'm the Devil, she thought, remembering what she'd learned as a child. And the beggar is Jesus.] Her responses range from angry rejection—wanting to kick the beggar or kill all the beggars in the world—to a desperate sense of kinship, as she realizes that she too is a beggar of sorts, begging for her husband's affection (which she shares with his two mistresses) and for social acceptance. She eventually reaches points of extreme identification, presented both in a comic register (if she were to marry a third time, she would make the beggar her husband) and in more serious tones (BF 145): 'Parecia-lhe difícil despedir-se dele, ele era agora o "eu" alterego, ele fazia parte para sempre de sua vida [...] Por um motivo que ela não saberia explicar [...] ele era verdadeiramente ela mesma ' [It seemed to her difficult to say good-bye to him, he was now her *alter ego* 'I', he would be a part of her life forever. For a reason she didn't know how to explain, he was truly herself.]

All these responses, however, whether based on rejection or identification, end up referring to the woman herself rather than the beggar. While attempting to see him, she comes up with further modes of *not* seeing. She now recognizes the blindness to poverty that she had shared with other members of her class (BF 142):

Tomava plena consciência de que até agora fingira que não havia os que passavam fome, não falavam nenhuma língua e que havia multidões anônimas mendigando para sobreviver. Ela soubera sim, mas desviara a cabeça e tapara os olhos. Todos, mas todos — sabem e fingem que não sabem. E mesmo que não fingissem iam ter um mal-estar. Como não teriam? Não, nem isso teriam.[18]

But after her moment of uneasiness she returns to this same pretence. As she drives away with her chauffeur, already thinking that everything will soon return to normal, she realizes that she has forgotten to ask the beggar his name, again consigning him to the anonymous crowds of the poor whom 'everyone' pretends do not exist. Unlike the Beast in the fairy tale, the beggar and his situation remain obdurately untransformed. Meanwhile, Beauty rejoins her charmed circle, though more aware that its (and her own) glitter are not unconnected to the beggar's wound (BF 137): 'A cabeça dela era cheia de festas, festas, festas. Festejando o quê? Festejando a ferida alheia?' [Her head was full of parties, parties and more parties. Celebrating what? Other people's wounds?]

The central metaphor of the wound—poverty as a wound or an open wound—disguises its ideological thrust by its very ubiquity. 'A ferida da desigualdade social', 'a ferida exposta da cidade' [the wound of social inequality, the city's open wound][19] are commonplace metaphors that persist even in discourses that interrogate the basis of this symbolism. The sociologist Vera da Silva Telles discusses the difficulty that Brazilian social discourses have had until recently in linking the question of poverty to the crucial issue of affirming rights of citizenship for the poor. Remnants of this difficulty persist in '[uma] linha de sombra, em que se confundem direitos e ajuda, cidadania e filantropia, ao mesmo tempo em que se repõe esta espantosa indiferença diante do espetáculo da pobreza, que tanto caracteriza a sociedade brasileira' [a shadowy area, where a confusion between rights and aid, citizenship rights and philanthropy, perpetuates the amazing indifference toward the spectacle of poverty that so characterizes Brazilian society].[20] This traditional perspective naturalizes poverty by locating it literally in the natural world.

Visível por todos os lados, nas suas evidências a pobreza é percebida como efeito indesejado de uma história sem autores e responsabilidades. Nesse registro aparece como chaga aberta a lembrar o tempo todo o atraso que envergonha um país que se quer moderno, de tal modo que a sua eliminação é projetada para as promessas civilizatórias de um progresso que haverá algum dia, quem sabe, de absorver os que foram até agora dele excluídos.[21]

The very prevalence and visibility of poverty become motives for its invisibility. If poverty appears as a wound, this manifests a pathology that seems to be part of the natural world: 'desaparece como problema que diz respeito aos parâmetros que regem as relações sociais' [it disappears as a problem concerning the parameters that govern social relations].[22] In 'A bela e a fera' the beggar's poverty, perhaps caused by but certainly symbolized in his wound, is subsumed into the realm of natural pathology: it is a metaphor that sidesteps social forces and motivations to locate poverty conveniently in a natural world, without authors nor responsibilities.

In *A hora da estrela*, too, Lispector makes poverty visible by putting on display the social discourses that contribute to its dismissal. This novella, which the author published a month before her death, represents the culmination of the many incursions she had made into the theme of poverty throughout her other fiction. Using a metafictional register, the narrative discusses the act of narrating, especially the difficult act of creating a character who embodies severe deficits in material circumstances and whose suffering, while imaginary, is also real. From what perspective, with what investments does one narrate, or invent, an *other* whose circumstances are limited by destitution? The voice that presents Macabéa is not omniscient, nor does it achieve a transparent mimesis. It is a limited, partial voice that displays the multiple evasions, blind spots and short circuits in current social discourses on poverty.

The comfortably situated narrator, who writes while sipping white wine, begins his narrative moved by a surge of sympathy (HE 16): 'É que numa rua do Rio de Janeiro peguei no ar de relance o sentimento de perdição no rosto de uma moça nordestina' [Because on a street in Rio de Janeiro I caught a glimpse of the feeling of utter loss on the face of a girl from the North-East]. Quickly, however, the narrative comes to manifest extremes of identification—'Vejo [a nordestina] se olhando ao espelho e [...] no espelho aparece o meu rosto cansado e barbudo' [I see the girl from the North-East looking at herself in the mirror, and in the mirror my own face appears, weary and unshaven] (HE 28)—as well as the familiar negative attitudes—arrogance, indifference, repugnance, fear, hatred—through which poverty is seen and not seen in Brazil.

The kaleidoscopic modes of apprehension of the impoverished other, used most intensely by the narrator of *A hora da estrela* but also used in a more dispersed fashion by Lispector in other texts, display the well-known approaches to the other theorized by psychoanalysis: appropriation, projection, rejection, identification. If on the one hand they end up granting pride of place more to the perceiver than to the object perceived, they also show a narrator struggling with various forms of enmeshment, with positive and negative investments, and the criticism is directed back towards the one perceiving (and narrating) as well as towards an unjust social world. While showing the limits and the inadequacies of the discursive mechanisms that attempt to grasp the impoverished other, Lispector's texts also situate poverty not as a purely external problem but rather, in what is perhaps their greatest strength, as an issue that comes to involve and absorb the 'I' in the very processes of its constitution.

Notes to Chapter 7

1. Lispector, *A hora da estrela*, 5th edn. (Rio de Janeiro: José Olympio, 1979; hereafter abbreviated HE in the main text), 85: 'I'm getting terribly interested in facts: facts are hard stones. There's no escaping it. Facts are words spoken by the world.'

2. Lispector, *A descoberta do mundo* (Rio de Janeiro: Nova Fronteira, 1984; hereafter

DM), 166, 125: 'My path is not myself, it is someone else, it is other people. When I can fully feel the other, I will be safe and think to myself: I have arrived safely into harbour.' 'I do not give bread to anyone, I can only give words. And it hurts to be so poor.'

3. *A legião estrangeira* (Rio de Janeiro: Editora do Autor, 1964; hereafter LE), 149.

4. A selection of these *crónica*s was published posthumously as *A descoberta do mundo*.

5. Carlos Lessa, *O Rio de todos os Brasis: Uma reflexão em busca de auto-estima* [Rio of all the Brazils: A reflection in search of self-esteem] (Rio de Janeiro: Record, 2000), 296.

6. Ibid., 311.

7. *A paixão segundo G.H.*, 3rd edn. (Rio de Janeiro: Sabiá, 1972; hereafter PGH), 37. This description brings to mind Carolina Maria de Jesus, *Quarto de despejo* (Rio de Janeiro: Francisco Alves, 1960), where the title of this diary of a *favela* resident refers to a storage room for little used, if not useless, objects. As Carolina describes in detail her day-to-day effort to scrape together the bare means of survival, she conveys her sense of exclusion from the world of those who inhabit the 'living-rooms' of São Paulo. This diary, published by the same publishing house that brought out *Laços de família* that same year, was a best-seller during the time when Lispector must have been writing *A paixão segundo G.H.*

8. Sandra Lauderdale Graham, *House and Street: The Domestic World of Servants and Masters in Nineteenth-Century Rio de Janeiro* (Austin: University of Texas Press, 1992; first edn. 1988), 4.

9. 'It would be a tea-party this time—on a Sunday afternoon in the Rua do Lavradio—to which I would invite all the housemaids I had ever employed. Those I had forgotten would indicate their absence with an empty chair, just as they do inside me. The others would be seated, their hands folded on their laps. Silent—until the moment when each of them would open her mouth and, brought back to life, dead and alive at the same time, would recite the things I remember them saying. It would almost be a society ladies' tea-party, except that on this occasion there would be no talk about housemaids.'

10. '—I wish you every happiness—one of them gets to her feet.—I hope you get everything no one can give you. / —Whenever I ask for something—another rises from her chair—I can't help laughing when I talk, so people don't take me seriously. / —Not trivial, no ma'am. I only know how to cook poor man's food. / —Early this morning—the Italian maid tells me—on my way to work, the leaves started falling along with the first snow. A man on the street said to me: "It's raining gold and silver." I pretended I hadn't heard him because, if I'm not careful, men are always taking advantage of me. / —Here comes Her Ladyship— the oldest of all my former housemaids gets up, the one who could only manage to show soured affection and who taught us so early in life how to forgive love's cruelty.—Did Your Ladyship sleep well? Her Ladyship is deluxe. She is full of whims: she wants this, she doesn't want that. Her Ladyship is white.'

11. '—Good food is all to do with salt. Good food is all to do with salt. Good food is all to do with salt. Here comes Her Ladyship: I hope you get everything no one can give you, that's all I ask when I die. That's when the man said that the rain was gold, and no one can give you that. Unless you're not afraid to stand in the dark, bathed in gold, but alone in the dark. Her Ladyship is the poor's idea of deluxe: leaves or the first snow. Tasting the salt in what you eat, not hurting

what is beautiful, avoiding laughing when you are asking for something, never pretending that you didn't hear when someone says: This, woman, this is gold and silver rain. Yes.'

12. 'Meanwhile the maid is hanging out the washing on the clothes-line, still humming that tune without words. I let it wash over me. The maid is dark and skinny, and living within her is an "I". A body that is separate from other bodies, and that's what's called an "I"? It is strange to have a body in which to live, a body where wet blood flows incessantly, where the mouth can sing, and the eyes must have wept so many times. She is an "I".'

13. Solange Ribeiro de Oliveira, *A barata e a crisálida: O romance de Clarice Lispector* (Rio de Janeiro: José Olympio, 1985), 46–54.

14. For an analysis of this novel, see Marta Peixoto, *Passionate Fictions: Gender, Narrative, and Violence in Clarice Lispector* (Minneapolis: University of Minnesota Press, 1994), 89–99.

15. Elizabeth Bishop wrote a poem about the police killing of an accused man, 'The Burglar of Babylon', set in this same *favela*: *The Complete Poems, 1927–1970* (New York: Farrar, Strauss, Giroux, 1979), 112–18.

16. 'Reality is raw material, language is the way I go about seeking it—and how I can't find it. But it is from seeking and not finding that what I did not know and instantly recognize is born. It is my fate to seek and it is my fate to return empty-handed. But—I return with the unsayable. The unsayable can only be given to me by means of the failure of my language. Only when the construction fails do I achieve what it could not.'

17. 'A bela e a fera, ou A ferida grande demais' (hereafter BF), *A bela e a fera* (Rio de Janeiro: Nova Fronteira, 1979), 145.

18. 'She was fully aware that up to now she had pretended that there weren't people who went hungry, who spoke no languages, anonymous crowds begging just to survive. She *had* known this, but she had turned her head away and covered her eyes. Everyone, yes, everyone knows and pretends they don't know. And even if they didn't pretend, they were going to feel uncomfortable. How could they possibly not? No, they wouldn't, not even this.'

19. Adair Rocha, *Cidade cerzida: A costura da cidadania no morro Santa Marta* [Mended city: the stitching together of citizenship rights in the Santa Marta *favela*] (Rio de Janeiro: Relume Dumará, 2000), 93–4.

20. Vera da Silva Telles, *Pobreza e cidadania* [Poverty and citizenship rights] (São Paulo: Editora 34, 2001), 31.

21. Ibid.: 'Visible from all sides, poverty is perceived from its outward signs as the undesirable effect of a story lacking protagonists and responsibilities. In this sense it appears as an open wound that is a constant reminder of the backwardness that embarrasses a country eager to be modern, to such an extent that the elimination of it is projected onto the forces of progress promising civilization, which, some day, will gather to it all those hitherto excluded from its embrace.'

22. Ibid., 32.

CHAPTER 8

The Black Maid as Ghost: Haunting in *A paixão segundo G.H.*

Lúcia Villares

In this article, I aim to offer a close textual analysis of the first four chapters of Lispector's *A paixão segundo G.H.* [*The Passion according to G.H.*] (1964), with specific reference to the experience of 'haunting' and its sociological significance. I will try to demonstrate that, at the core of *A paixão segundo G.H.*, there is an experience of haunting. This experience is closely linked with the acknowledgement of the presence of a black maid as an individual in her own right. This, in turn, forces the protagonist to confront the ideology of whiteness in the opening chapters of the novel, causing her personal and national identity to collapse. From this point onwards, the novel becomes a detailed description of a journey into abjection. My contention is that race and class—as well as gender—are crucial to the understanding of the political implications of this work.

In examining the sociological implications of haunting in connection with this novel, I shall draw on the insights offered by the North-American sociologist Avery Gordon in her work entitled *Ghostly Matters: Haunting and the Sociological Imagination*. The expression 'ghostly matters' in her title is particularly revealing because it encapsulates two meanings. It can mean hallucinatory, disembodied material, but it also permits a reading such as 'despite it being *ghostly*, it *matters*'; or, to put it differently, ghostly substances can be relevant. Especially, one might add, if we think in terms of cultural memory. As Gordon explains: 'Ghostly matters are part of social life. If we want to study social life well, and if in addition we want to contribute, in however small a measure, to changing it, we must learn how to identify haunting and reckon with ghosts.' Her thesis is that haunting 'recovers the evidence of things not seen' and that through haunting one becomes aware of 'lost subjects of history—the missing and lost ones and the blind fields they inhabit'.[1]

The concept of 'haunting' as developed by Gordon illuminates the political and ethnic significance of Lispector's book. Indeed, through the experience of haunting, the main female character G.H. comes to recognize the 'subjective existence' of someone who is made invisible in Brazilian society: her former black maid Janair. The recognition of Janair as an individual provokes a collapse of G.H.'s identity-structure. Part of this identity-structure had been based on an idea of the nation that had excluded the visibility of the maid. In other words, the black maid could only be included in the country that the female protagonist thought she belonged to as long as she remained invisible as a subject. When she becomes visible, the whole identity-structure that G.H. had nurtured falls apart.

The novel, narrated in the first person by G.H., thus attempts to describe a violent crisis of identity. G.H.'s identity-crisis is triggered when she enters the maid's room to re-arrange it after the latter's impromptu departure. She sees an inscription that Janair had left on the wall. The book therefore enacts a confrontation between two women in asymmetrical social positions: a woman who sees herself as modern (G.H.) and another woman (Janair) who—while sharing the same female condition—is deprived of any hopes of liberating herself on account of the limitations of her social and economic circumstances. It is precisely this confrontation that forces the main character to undergo a deep re-evaluation of her self-identity. As she announces right at the beginning: 'Ontem [...] perdi durante horas e horas a minha montagem humana' [Yesterday I lost my human constitution for hours and hours].[2]

The cause of the collapse of her sense of identity is the fact that, through her ghostly presence, Janair becomes visible as a black person who has her own consciousness, her own gaze and her own feelings. Upon becoming aware of this critical consciousness, G.H. is forced to confront her own whiteness, suddenly made visible. Such visibility is unbearable, leading to the breakdown of her sense of identity. She does not know who she is anymore. This may contribute to explain why the maid is endowed with a full first name, while the main character/narrator, throughout the entire novel, is simply named by her initials G.H. Something is missing in the main character's name that can only be completed by the ghostly presence of Janair, the black maid.

During the opening four chapters, Clarice Lispector repeatedly builds a tension between two worlds. One is the world of things known, where G.H. has been living: her flat, her lifestyle, her gender-identifications. This includes a notion of personal national identity, although the words 'Brazil' or 'Brazilian' are never mentioned. The second world is the world of productive forces and manual labour: the world to which the black maid belongs, which is also the world of the unknown, the foreign. For despite being an everyday feature of Brazilian life, only during the 1980s did the profession of domestic servants start to be legally recognized and protected by labour regulations. Indeed, one needs to keep in mind that in Brazil at the time when Lispector was writing, there was a very clear demarcation separating members of the middle classes and their servants. The architecture of the apartment buildings where the middle classes live to this day often reflects this social apartheid. The so-called 'social' and 'service' areas are clearly divided, with separate entrances and lifts. Servants are only allowed to circulate in the social area when on duty.

Throughout the first four chapters, one can notice that each of these worlds is associated with a range of imagery that reinforces the contrast and difference between them:

G.H.'s world	Janair's world
known	foreign
dark	light
dilettantish	productive
moist	dry
fed	hungry

The first chapter functions as an introduction, in which the narrator gathers courage, internal resources and the reader's compliance to embark in this journey of retelling the terrifying experience that happened to her. There is no external action at all. Everything in this chapter happens in the mind of G.H.

In Chapter 2, we make more contact with the narrator's 'external life'. We are given external character-indications such as name (albeit only initials), class and gender. Here, for the first time, there is a mention of physical movement from G.H. (22): 'Ontem de manhã — quando saí da sala para o quarto da empregada — nada me fazia supor que eu estava a um passo da descoberta de um império' [Yesterday morning—when I went out of the dining room to go to the maid's room—I had no way of knowing that I was one step away from discovering an empire]. But this movement is mentioned as something that has happened and is stored in the character's personal memory. So we are still inside the character's mental world. Throughout the whole chapter, G.H. remains seated at the breakfast table, rolling little balls of bread in her fingers.

The above statement also constitutes the first time that the maid is alluded to. Despite the fact that she is not there, she has a fundamental role to play. She is a 'virtual reality' whose force springs precisely from her absence. Her image unsettles G.H.'s previously secure sense of identity and leads her to acknowledge its superficiality (24): 'o resto era o modo como pouco a pouco eu me havia transformado na pessoa que tem o meu nome. E acabei sendo o meu nome. É suficiente ver no couro de minhas valises as iniciais G.H. e eis-me. Também dos outros eu não exigia mais do que a primeira cobertura das iniciais dos nomes.' [The rest was how little by little I had transformed myself into the person who bears my name. And I ended up being my name. All you need to do is see the initials G.H. in the leather of my suitcases and there you have me. And from others too I had demanded nothing more than knowing the bare cover-up of the initials of their names.] Initials thus become a kind of superficial, 'masking' identity. They reflect a socially-accepted identity that covers the real self, who is neither seen nor understood. There is consequently a need to strip off this false identity so as to be able to get in contact with what the self really is (26–7): 'acho que estou precisando de olhar sem que a cor de meus olhos importe, preciso ficar isenta de mim para ver.' [I think I just need to be able to look without the colour of my eyes mattering. I need to be able to get outside myself to be able to see.]

G.H.'s description of her apartment, yet another external indication of status, is equally revealing (29): 'o apartamento me reflete. É no último andar, o que é considerado uma elegância. Pessoas de meu ambiente procuram morar na chamada "cobertura". É bem mais que uma elegância. É um verdadeiro prazer: de lá domina-se a cidade.' [My apartment reflects me. It's on the top floor, which is considered very elegant. People in my circle try to live in what's called the penthouse. It's far more than elegance. It's a real pleasure: you can dominate the city from up there.] Such a description gives us a clear sense of G.H. being part of an elite and enjoying the power that comes from it. Lispector plays with irony here, with the double meaning of the Portuguese word 'cobertura' (penthouse/cover-up).

She is linking 'cobertura das iniciais' (cover-up of her initials)—a social mask that hides her more real sense of self—and the fact that she enjoys the 'elegance of living in a penthouse' (also 'cobertura').

In Chapter 3, the character finally moves. If the second chapter was set in the dining room, this chapter is now set in the service area, as G.H. sets out to walk from the dining room to the maid's room. She is determined to go and clear up the recently-vacated room, which she expects is probably filthy. Although G.H. is a dilettantish sculptor, she enjoys tidying her house, to such an extent that she wryly comments that, were it not for the fact that she was 'pretty well-off', she would probably get a job as a maid 'numa grande casa de ricos, onde há muito o que arrumar' [in a great big house belonging to someone rich, where there is a lot to tidy] (33). The sarcasm springs out from the fact that G.H.'s comment blatantly ignores the depth of the class (and race) gulf separating her from a maid. G.H. is able to imagine this work as an enjoyable activity only because she is not pressed to do it to earn her living.

On the way to the maid's room, G.H. stops to smoke a cigarette in the open area separating the kitchen from the servants' quarters. As she leans against the waist-high wall, she stares at the huge internal empty space onto which all the kitchens and service-areas of the building open. This space is described as the building's 'belly' or 'bulge', further as looking like a factory (35): 'a área interna era um amontoado oblíquo de esquadrias, janelas, cordames e enegrecimentos de chuvas, janela arreganhada contra janela, bocas olhando bocas. O bôjo de meu edifício era como uma usina. A miniatura da grandeza de um panorama de gargantas e canyons.' [The inner yard was an oblique montage of over-lapping right angles, windows, clothes-lines and dark patches of rain damage, window grinning at window, mouths looking into mouths. My building bulged out like a factory. The miniature version of a vast panorama of gorges and canyons.]

G.H. experiences this sight as something threatening. She imagines the work of the numerous unqualified labourers who built the architectural 'monument' she is looking at (36): 'algo da natureza fatal saíra fatalmente das mãos de centenas de operários práticos que havia trabalhado canos de água e de esgôto, sem nenhum saber que estava erguendo aquela ruína egípcia para a qual eu olhava' [something fatal by nature had fatally grown forth from the hands of the hundred practical workmen who had installed water pipes and drains, quite unaware that they were erecting the Egyptian ruin at which I was staring]. There is something of the 'foreign' (Egyptian ruin) in this 'internal' service area of her block of flats. It seems that the subjectivity of manual workers, their participation in the building of this block of flats, is felt to be foreign in relation to the character's internalized image of the nation. Their humanity is transferred to the elements of the architecture: windows are seen as mouths, gorges as throats.

The fact that this space is described as an 'Egyptian ruin' is extremely meaningful. The word 'ruin' suggests the presence of ghosts. Despite having suffered partial destruction, ruins still keep traces of the time when they were inhabited. But why 'Egyptian'? On one level, it signifies something 'foreign', not Brazilian. But the word also conjures up the idea of a pyramid and the mystery that surrounds it. Those who dare penetrate the pyramid, by definition a sacred building that should remain forever closed, risk unleashing the fury of the gods. This gives us a sense of what is at stake for G.H. when she looks at that which is not supposed to be seen. The word 'Egyptian' furthermore conveys a sense of ancient times; we are dealing with elements that are millennia old, that do not belong to the present as we usually see it. G.H. is getting in touch with a cultural memory that has been repressed and suppressed for many centuries.

In Chapter 4, the ghost finally appears. As soon as G.H. enters the maid's room, she is dazzled by what she sees (37): 'É que em vez da penumbra confusa que esperara, eu esbarrava na visão de um quarto que era um quadrilátero de branca luz; meus olhos se protegeram franzindo-se' [Because instead of the bewildering shadows that I was expecting, I was struck with the vision of a room that was a quadrangle of white light: my eyes squinted in self-protection]. The white light that fills the room has a dazzling, threatening effect on the protagonist's eyes. This might represent G.H.'s first confrontation with the ideology of whiteness, which, as we shall see further on, will trigger the character's personal disintegration. The room is then specifically compared to a minaret (38): 'Como um minarete. Começara então a minha primeira impressão de minarete, solto acima de uma extensão ilimitada. Dessa impressão eu só percebia por enquanto meu desagrado físico.' [Like a minaret. That was the beginning of my first impression of a minaret: free-floating above a limitless expanse. At the time, I perceived only the physical discomfort that impression provoked in me.] The word 'minaret' reinforces the sense of the non-national, the foreign, the strange. In a mosque, the minaret is the small compartment on top of the tower, where the

Muslim priest calls the faithful to say their daily prayers. A minaret, in a Catholic country like Brazil, is seen as something unusual, strange. It also places the room in a space 'above reality', as if we were entering a different world, where the usual rules governing what is considered 'normal' have been provisionally suspended.

Then G.H. sees the mural that the maid has drawn on the wall—something that 'não era um ornamento: era uma escrita' [was not there for decoration; it was writing] (40). The word 'escrita' is significant. In this social set-up, Janair—who was probably illiterate—was not supposed to have her right to speak, her voice, let alone her own writing. In describing the mural as a 'writing' instead of simply decoration, the narrator is emphasizing Janair's intention to communicate, to assert her voice; picturing her now as a subject, not as a mere object. The mural features a woman, a man and a dog, drawn with charcoal straight onto the wall (39): 'quase em tamanho natural o contorno de um homem nu, de uma mulher nua e de um cão que era mais nu do que um cão' [outlines, almost life size, of a naked man, a naked woman, and a dog that was more naked than a dog]. They are more than just drawings, they are full of a mysterious, un-'natural' energy (39): 'Mesmo o cachorro tinha a loucura mansa daquilo que não é movido por força própria' [Even the dog had the tame madness of something that is not driven by a force of its own].

The drawings merely outline contours, empty shapes. Just like ghosts, therefore, the three figures are bodies without matter. Moreover, these almost prehistoric images have the appearance of mummies, floating in the air (39): 'À medida que mais e mais me incomodava a dura imobilidade das figuras, mais forte se fazia em mim a idéia de múmias' [As the figures' harsh motionlessness bothered me more and more, the idea of mummies grew stronger in me]. Mummies, like ghosts, are 'undead'. They retain the bodily material of the dead person, preserving a possibility of their coming alive again. Although the black maid has departed, her presence is still very strongly felt in the inscription that she left on the wall (41–2): 'Coagida com a presença que Janair deixara de si mesma num quarto de minha casa, eu percebia que as três figuras angulares de zumbis haviam de fato retardado minha entrada como se o quarto ainda estivesse ocupado' [Constrained by the presence of herself that Janair had left behind in a room in my home, I noticed that the three angular zombie figures had actually kept me from going in, as though the room were still occupied]. 'Zombie' is another word for the 'undead'.

Inhabitants of ruins, mummies, zombies: far from being simple etchings on the wall, these figures become endowed with a life of their own.

According to Gordon, ghosts 'recover the evidence of things not seen'. As she puts it, haunting allows us to become aware of 'lost subjects of history—the missing and lost ones and the blind fields they inhabit'.[3] In French, ghosts are also called 'revenants': those who return. Ghosts, when they appear, are in fact returning. This 'coming back', this sense of repetition—mirrored at a structural level in the novel through the repetition of the last line of each chapter as the first line of the next—suggests that we are dealing with repressed material. Something that has always been there, but which has remained unseen and unrecognized. Such a 'return' becomes more explicit later on, in Chapter 8, when G.H. tries to explain why she was losing contact with her 'normal self' (70): 'A vida se vingava de mim, e a vingança consistia apenas em voltar, nada mais. Todo caso de loucura é que alguma coisa voltou. Os possessos, eles não são possuídos pelo que vem, mas pelo que volta. Às vezes a vida volta.' [Life was taking its revenge on me, and that revenge consisted merely in coming back, nothing more. Every case of madness happens because something has come back. People who are possessed are not possessed by something that comes but rather by that which comes back. Sometimes life comes back.] Madness and possession are therefore understood not as diseases to be suppressed but as healing processes where repressed elements 'come back', asking to be acknowledged and eventually incorporated into the conscious self.

Janair's face also returns to haunt G.H. In Chapter 4, after the sculptor sees the inscription on the wall, she finally remembers the maid's black face (41): 'Revi o rosto preto e quieto, revi a pele inteiramente opaca que mais parecia um de seus modos de se calar, as sobrancelhas extremamente bem desenhadas, revi os traços finos e delicados que mal eram divisados no negror apagado da pele.' [I pictured again her quiet, black face, pictured her completely opaque skin that seemed more like one of her ways of keeping quiet, extremely well defined eyebrows, I pictured again the fine, delicate features that were barely discernible against the faded blackness of her skin.]

At this point G.H. also becomes conscious of the feelings that her maid nurtured towards her: feelings of hatred, no doubt as a result of her situation of oppression (40–1): 'De súbito, dessa vez com mal-estar real, deixei finalmente vir a mim uma sensação que durante seis meses, por negligência e desinteresse, eu não me deixara ter; a do silencioso ódio daquela mulher' [Suddenly, with real discomfort now, I finally allowed there to come over me a sensation that, through negligence and lack of interest, I had, for six months, not allowed myself to feel: the sensation of that woman's silent hatred]. For six months these two women lived in close contact with each other, with G.H. programmed to ignore the physical and emotional presence of Janair. The tension and all the emotional conflicts that could have emerged from a situation of oppression were thus systematically made invisible and ignored. Neglect and lack of attention maintained the repression. This is how the narrator describes the invisibility of the black maid (41): 'Não era de surpreender que eu a tivesse usado como se ela não tivesse presença: sob o pequeno avental, vestia-se sempre de marrom escuro ou preto, o que a tornava toda escura e invisível — arrepiei-me ao descobrir que até agora eu não havia percebido que aquela mulher era uma invisível' [It wasn't surprising that I had used her as though she had no presence: under her small apron she always wore dark brown or black, which made her all dark and invisible—I shivered when I realized that that woman was an invisible woman].

The room disturbs G.H. because of its 'non-national' characteristics, which embody the hatred that Janair felt for her (43; my emphasis):

o quarto me incomodava fisicamente [...] O som inaudível do quarto [...] um chiado neutro de coisa, era o que fazia a matéria de seu silêncio. Carvão e unha se juntando, carvão e unha, calma, tranqüila e compacta raiva *daquela mulher que era a representante de um silêncio como se representasse um país estrangeiro, a rainha africana. E que ali dentro de minha casa se alojara, a estrangeira, a inimiga indiferente.*[4]

Janair, as an African queen, symbolizes a repressed black culture that had had no space to be expressed and acknowledged inside the idea of nation that G.H. had internalized. Janair is the foreigner, the one that cannot be assimilated, but needs to be left as an 'other', an 'outsider'.

The room unsettles the narrator so much that she feels a powerful urge to wash it, to flood it with water to take away all traces of this 'foreign' woman and 'foreign' world. This little square of light and dryness needs to be transformed back into something familiar. The marks of its 'difference' must be effaced (44): 'jogaria no quarto vazio baldes e baldes de água que o ar duro sorveria, e finalmente enlamearia a poeira até que nascesse umidade naquele deserto, destruindo o minarete que sobranceava altaneiro um horizonte de telhados. [...] Uma cólera inexplicável, mas que me vinha toda natural, me tomara: eu queria matar alguma coisa ali' [I would throw bucket after bucket of water into the empty room that the harsh air would drink up, and finally I would soak the dust until moisture was born into that desert, destroying the minaret that so haughtily surveyed a horizon of rooftops. An unexplainable anger, but one that came over me quite naturally, had invaded me: I wanted to kill something there.]

In the narrating character's imagination and her rage, this cleansing would reconcile these two worlds by killing off the foreign, the 'other' ('eu queria matar alguma coisa ali'), and salve the pain of her identity crisis.

Why is it that the inscriptions on the wall distress G.H. so much? The most obvious explanation lies in the fact that these ghostly inscriptions, marking the apparition of Janair's consciousness as a black person, simultaneously make G.H.'s whiteness visible. The visibility of a previously invisible whiteness is unbearable. In G.H.'s own words (40), 'Havia anos que eu só tinha sido julgada pelos meus pares e pelo meu próprio ambiente que eram, em suma, feitos de mim mesma e para mim mesma. Janair era a primeira pessoa realmente exterior de cujo olhar eu tomava consciência.' [For years I had only been judged by my peers and by my own circle, who were, when it came down to it, made by me for me. Janair was the first outsider whose gaze I really took notice of.] The fact that Janair has her own consciousness, her own gaze, breaks an accepted 'social pact' that ensured that whiteness remained ethnically invisible. Janair's own consciousness as a black person is thus unbearable. Her assumption of the gaze unmasks a farce, challenging her invisible existence as a servant, never allowed a gaze of her own.

While whiteness is often seen as normal, blackness is seen as different, abnormal. Blacks may be invisible to society as individuals, and often as citizens too, but paradoxically blackness as a racial marker is ostensibly visible. Indeed, as Richard Dyer explains, one of the characteristics of whiteness is that of being ethnically unmarked; as a synonym of normality, it does not need to be mentioned:

As long as race is something only applied to non-white peoples, as long as white people are not racially seen and named, they/we function as a human norm. Other people are raced, we are just people. [...] There is no more powerful position than that of being 'just' human. The claim to power is the claim to speak for the commonality of humanity. Raced people can't do that—they can only speak for their race. But non-race people can, for they do not represent the interest of a race. The point of seeing the racing of whites is to dislodge them/us from the position of power, with all the inequities, oppression, privileges and sufferings in its train, dislodging them/us by undercutting the authority with which they/we speak and act in the world.[5]

Janair's ghost, introducing a different point of view, that of a black consciousness, makes G.H.'s position as white explicit. The main feature associated with whiteness is the violence that sustains whites in their position of power. In becoming visible, such an asymmetrical situation demands to be redressed.

Thus far, this analysis has concentrated on the first four chapters of *A paixão segundo G.H.*, since they stage Janair, whose ghostly apparition triggers an identity crisis in G.H. The next nineteen chapters will develop a slow, complex process during which G.H. increasingly loses her sense of personal identity. This process of 'despersonalização', entailing identification with the body of a dying cockroach, runs parallel to an investigation into her gender-identity. This process is marked by G.H. immersing herself in what is considered dirty, revolting, abject. Contact with defilement, vomit, nausea dominates most of the narrative for the next nineteen chapters. It seems that examining whiteness leads the character to plunge into abjection.

This is how Julia Kristeva describes the experience of abjection: 'there looms, within abjection, one of those violent, dark, revolts of being, directed against a threat that seems to emanate from an exorbitant outside or inside, ejected beyond the scope of the possible, the tolerable, the thinkable. It lies there, quite close, but it cannot be assimilated.'[6] Following the work of Mary Douglas on the anthropological significance of defilement,[7] Kristeva goes on to say: 'It is not lack of cleanliness or health that causes abjection, but what disturbs identity, system, order. What does not respect borders, positions, rules.'[8] In Lispector's novel, G.H. was used to following invisible borders of whiteness, class and gender. Seeing those borders has a devastating effect on the protagonist's sense of self-identity and upon her sense of normality. The mere recognition of those borders is experienced as breaking them. This throws the subject into a space that is a non-space, the space of abjection, of dirtiness, the space of the unclean and the improper. As Kristeva says, 'the abject [...] is radically excluded and draws me toward a place where meaning collapses'.[9] The abject is the realm of the unspeakable and the unthinkable. This passage at the end of Chapter 4 reflects such a feeling of collapse (45): 'e o peso do primeiro desabamento abaixava os cantos de minha boca, me deixava de braços caídos. O que me acontecia? Nunca saberei entender mas há de haver quem entenda. E é em mim que tenho de criar esse alguém que entenderá.' [And the force of the first collapse turned down the corners of my mouth, left me with my arms hanging limply. What was happening to me? I shall never be able to understand it, but there must be someone who can. And I shall create inside myself that someone who can understand.]

This lack of 'understanding' and the need to create inside herself the one who will understand is the novel's main drive. How to incorporate the examination of whiteness, the collapse of her ideas about the world and about herself? There is a need to create a special space where an 'understanding' could take place.

This room that dazzles because of its whiteness, this Muslim 'minaret' floating above the Catholic Rio de Janeiro, represents that special space. It is the architectural compartment—created by Lispector—to place G.H.'s exploration into abjection. However, the immense power of abjection is never contained. Repulsion is a feeling that will inhabit G.H. throughout the novel (45): 'É que apesar de já ter entrado no quarto, eu parecia ter entrado em nada. Mesmo dentro dele, eu continuava de algum modo do lado de fora. Como se ele não tivesse bastante profundidade para me caber e deixasse pedaços meus no corredor, na maior repulsão de que eu já fora vítima: eu não cabia.' [Because in spite of already having come into the room, I seemed to have come into nothingness. Even though inside it I somehow stayed on the outside. As though it were not deep enough to hold me and left parts of me out in the hallway, in the greatest repulsion I had ever experienced: I didn't fit.]

This room, detached and separated from the level of 'normality', is a space where whiteness can be examined and the abject can be explored. Interestingly, however, gender seems to play a key role in this process of plunging into abjection. In Chapter 4, when she first confronts Janair's inscription on the wall, G.H. imagines Janair seeing her as a man (40): 'Olhei o mural onde eu devia estar sendo retratada... eu, o Homem' [I looked at the drawing on the wall which must have been portraying me... me, the Man].

Examining whiteness forces us to reassess our concepts of 'self', personal identity and a whole ontology based on white identity being opposed to a black 'other'. 'Being white' becomes the unexamined attribute of a subject defined by contrast to a marked 'other', in this case a black female other. To reject this ontology, to examine race, is to face the need to rebuild new concepts of identity. The last quotation ('eu, o Homem'), however, reveals that gender is also a relevant social mark here. To exclude Janair was also to exclude femaleness. Janair's gaze brings a 'double' accusation. In G.H.'s imagination, Janair sees her as different not simply in terms of race and class, but also in terms of gender.

As Ross Chambers argues in her article 'The Unexamined': 'There are plenty of unmarked categories (maleness, heterosexuality, and middle classness being obvious ones), but whiteness is perhaps the primary unmarked and so unexamined—let's say "blank"—category.'[10] Adhering to unexamined whiteness, G.H. had also adhered to an unexamined 'maleness', denying her own femaleness, possibly the only social mark she had in common with Janair.

The cockroach—the novel's third protagonist, which G.H. confronts from the end of Chapter 5 to the end of the novel—may represent a lost gender-link between Janair and G.H. It is as if Janair needed to return to haunt G.H. again, this time transformed. She returns not as an 'African queen', as pure blackness, but as a miscegenated, mixed-raced 'mulata'. After unsuccessfully trying to kill the cockroach, G.H. describes how she sees the insect (56): 'a barata não tem nariz. Olhei-a, com aquela sua boca e seus olhos: parecia uma mulata à morte.' [The cockroach doesn't have a nose. I looked at it, with that mouth it had, and its eyes; it looked like a dying mulatto woman.]

It is the cockroach that 'forces' individuals to assume their gender identities, as they are lured inside the room (59–60): 'A entrada para este quarto só tinha uma passagem, e estreita: pela barata. [...] E quem entrasse se transformaria num "ela" ou num "ele". Eu era aquela a quem o quarto chamava de "ela". Ali entrara um eu a que o quarto dera uma dimensão de "ela".' [There was only one way into this room, and it was a narrow one: through the cockroach. And whoever came in would be transformed into a 'she' or into a 'he'. I was the one the room called 'she'. An I had come in, but the room had then given it the dimension of a 'she'.]

The cockroach functions as a 'passage', a 'filter' determining the way reality penetrates our consciousness. This filter forces one to recognize gender. Sexuality, fertility, procreation are elements that cannot be ignored here. G.H. sees herself as another link in a historical chain of female individuals (65): 'E terminara, também eu toda imunda, por desembocar através dela [a barata] para o meu passado que era o meu contínuo presente e o meu futuro contínuo — e que hoje e sempre está na parede, e minhas quinze milhões de filhas, desde então até eu, também lá estavam' [And, all impure myself, I had ended up embarking, through the cockroach, upon my past, which was my present continuum and my continuous future—and which is on the wall today and for ever, and my fifteen million daughters, born between then and now, were also there]. This is how G.H. refers to the cockroach's eyes in Chapter 11 (77): 'Os dois olhos eram vivos como dois ovários. Ela me olhava com a fertilidade cega do seu olhar. Ela fertilizava a minha fertilidade morta.' [The two eyes were alive like two ovaries. It looked at me with the blind fertility of its look. It was fertilizing my dead fertility.] If, in adhering to unexamined whiteness, G.H. had repressed her female characteristics, now, in this room, she cannot escape them. As a consequence, they are experienced as enlarged, almost overwhelming.

According to Kristeva, the female body and its procreative power also belongs to the realm of abjection:

In societies where it occurs, ritualization of defilement is accompanied by a strong concern for separating the sexes, and this means giving men rights over women. The latter, apparently put in the position of passive objects, are none the less felt to be wily powers, 'baleful schemers' from whom rightful beneficiaries must protect themselves. [...] That other sex, the feminine, becomes synonymous with a radical evil that is to be suppressed.[11]

We could say that the cockroach concentrates two aspects that need to be excluded into the realm of abjection: not being white ('mulata') and being female (with the frightening power of procreation this entails). In this context, it is not surprising that G.H. sees the cockroach as female (93; my emphasis): 'No entanto ei-la, a barata neutra, sem nome de dor ou de amor. Sua única diferenciação de vida é que ela devia ser macho ou fêmea. Eu só a pensara como fêmea, *pois o que é esmagado pela cintura é fêmea.*' [There it was, nonetheless, the neutral cockroach without love or pain to its name. Its only differentiation in life was that it had to be either male or female. I had only ever thought of it as female *since whatever is crushed at the waist must be female.*]

The cockroach's body, 'crushed at the waist', mimics what corsets used to do to the female body (and what prevailing images of female beauty still impose): the tightening of the waist to emphasize the female form but to conceal suggestions of fertility, pregnancy and an autonomous sexuality. The insect's crushed body, therefore, pictures the engendering of female bodies, its 'shaping' to conform to images of femininity.

In conclusion, the novel describes a process where a middle-class woman confronts the limits of her own identity as a 'modern woman'. Lispector achieves this by opening up a space where abjection can be explored. In that space, the comfortable parameters determining G.H.'s gender, national and personal identity—parameters within which Janair's blackness was the abnormal, her subjectivity non-existent and G.H.'s own whiteness invisible—collapsed when Janair's black consciousness was made explicit. It was Janair, as a ghost, who caused G.H's identity crisis. It was not as a maid that Janair's triggered this process, but as a 'black African'. If Janair had not disappeared to leave her inscription on the wall she would have continued to exist merely as another invisible black maid. The ghost (the inscription and then the cockroach) is therefore necessary, in order that Janair's black consciousness become visible. The presence of the 'African queen', as an autonomous subject with an autonomous culture, is crucial in this novel. As G.H. puts it earlier on (114): 'eu era o petróleo que só hoje jorrou, quando uma negra africana me desenhou na minha casa, fazendo-me brotar de uma parede' [I was the oil that gushed forth only today, when a black African woman drew a picture of me in my own home, making me burst forth from a wall]. The words 'petróleo' and 'jorrou' seem to put G.H.'s experience of disintegration as something positive, valuable and useful. They also represent G.H.'s non-white, non-male, primitive aspects that had been excluded from her personal and national identity.

Despite the sensation of ecstasy at the end of *A paixão segundo G.H.*, when G.H. finally reaches a fusion with 'pure living matter', with the 'neutral', as a whole the novel is very pessimistic. The last signs of the text—dashes—are signs of silence. Together with any sense of personal identity, the narrator also relinquishes any effort at expression, giving up the use of language. This work, I would contend, is more than a philosophical enquiry into the substance of the self. Lispector did not imagine a new personal identity emerging from such an experience of internal disintegration. Rather, one could argue that the narrative shows how, in the 1960s, at the time when Lispector was writing, consciousness of one's own whiteness, together with the apprehension of one's female condition, was experienced as something that the self could not survive.

Notes to Chapter 8

1. Avery F. Gordon, *Ghostly Matters: Haunting and the Sociological Imagination* (Minneapolis: University of Minnesota Press, 1997), 195.
2. Clarice Lispector, *A paixão segundo G.H.* (Rio de Janeiro: Editora do Autor, 1964), 10.
3. Gordon, *Ghostly Matters*, 195.
4. 'The room bothered me physically. The room's inaudible sound, a neutral thing-screeching, was what made up the matter of its silence. Charcoal and fingernails joined together, charcoal and fingernails, the calm, compact fury *on the part of the woman who represented silence as if she were representing a foreign country, the African queen. And she had lodged here in my home, that stranger, that indifferent enemy.*'
5. Richard Dyer, *White* (New York: Routledge, 1997), 1, 2.
6. Julia Kristeva, *Powers of Horror: An Essay on Abjection*, trans. Leon S. Roudiez (New York: Columbia University Press, 1982), 1.
7. Mary Douglas, *Purity and Danger* (London: Ark Paperbacks, 1984).
8. Kristeva, *Powers of Horror*, 4.
9. Ibid., 2.
10. Ross Chambers, 'The Unexamined', in *Whiteness: A Critical Reader,* ed. Mike Hill (New York: New York University Press, 1997), 189.
11. Kristeva, *Powers of Horror*, 70.

CHAPTER 9

Clarice Lispector and the Question of the Nation

Paulo de Medeiros

Enquanto eu tiver perguntas e não houver resposta continuarei
a escrever. (*A hora da estrela*)[1]

Clarice Lispector may always have been foremost a question, as Teresa
Cristina Montero Ferreira highlights in her recent biography,[2] and a
question without an answer, or for which there must be a continuously
renewed myriad of answers, as the uninterrupted stream of studies of
her work well attests. However, one question that seems to impose
itself, considering the high esteem and visibility accorded to her texts
both in Brazil and outside, has never been more than roughly sketched.
Given that the name of Clarice Lispector has come to stand not only
for a group of extremely complex works but also for a watershed in
twentieth-century Brazilian literature, and that perhaps, for many with
little or nothing more than a passing acquaintance with that literature,
Clarice Lispector has come to embody it, it would seem only logical
to question the involvement of Lispector's textuality in the issue of
national representation. Perhaps the reason such a question has not been
really addressed has much to do with the way in which Lispector's texts
have been received, which has privileged a sense of hermetic complexity
allied with an abstract, individualistic prose. Questions around the
problematics of identity were postulated from the beginning but
without venturing into aspects bearing upon collective rather than
individual identity. Without for a moment thinking that all writing
always has to be concerned with a representation of the nation, none
the less I am intrigued at how a writer's texts can achieve such an iconic
status and not be seen as key representations of the nation.

One point that has received constant attention and is closely linked with the question of the nation is Lispector's 'foreignness' and her own status as a Brazilian. It has become a cliché to refer to Lispector's birth in the Ukraine, on transit from Russia to Brazil, where she arrived as an infant. Likewise, the view of Lispector as different, as foreign, used to explain the impact and strangeness of her texts, has become common. Thus, Nádia Gotlib at the very beginning of her biography of Clarice Lispector quotes Antônio Callado as saying that 'Clarice era uma estrangeira. Não porque nasceu na Ucrânia, criada desde menininha no Brasil, era tão brasileira quanto não importa quem. Clarice era estrangeira na terra.'³ [Clarice was a foreigner. Not because she was born in the Ukraine, for, brought up in Brazil since she was a little girl, she was as Brazilian as could be. She was a foreigner on this earth.] Lispector herself was very aware of this, and regardless of how she might have felt about her image as a writer, or how much she might have constructed it, she was adamant about her Brazilian status: 'Sou brasileira naturalizada, quando, por uma questão de meses, poderia ser brasileira nata. Fiz da língua portuguesa a minha vida interior, o meu pensamento mais íntimo, usei-a para palavras de amor.'⁴ [I am a naturalized Brazilian when, but for a couple of months, I could have been Brazilian from birth. I created my inner life in the Portuguese language, I used it to structure my most intimate thoughts and to speak words of love.]

Another strand that has been receiving ever more attention lately and which is still related to the question of the nation, at least inasmuch as literary representations of the nation are inextricably linked to questions of ethnicity and to questions of cultural heritage, is Lispector's Jewish identity, or, to be more precise, the links seen by some critics between Lispector's textuality and a Jewish cultural background, be it at the level of the language itself and a possible influence from Yiddish, the use of biblical references, and the pursuit of certain lines of enquiry into existence and nothingness. In this vein, the collective volume *A narração do indizível*, edited by Regina Zilberman, is exemplary. Zilberman's introduction reflects well the different levels in which the study of Lispector has been progressing: 'Judia, mas não sionista, do sexo feminino, mas não feminista militante, escritora recatada, mas mulher vaidosa, Clarice Lispector constitui hoje um dos portos seguros da crítica e da história da literatura brasileira. Vertentes ligadas às questões de género e etnia encontram em seus livros sugestões enriquecedoras de suas próprias práticas teóricas.'⁵ [Jewish but not Zionist, of the female sex but not a militant feminist, a reclusive writer but a vain woman, today Clarice Lispector is one of the pillars of Brazilian history and criticism. Critical approaches associated with questions of gender and ethnicity use her books as sources for examples that illustrate their own theoretical practices.]

However, none of these critical approaches really touches on the question of the nation, or even on how Lispector's texts might function as representations of it. To my knowledge only in two instances can one speak of a sketching out of such a question. One of them comes as the introduction to a detailed study of Lispector's works, Carlos Mendes de Sousa's *Clarice Lispector: Figuras da escrita* (2000). In it, the author does suggest a correlation between Lispector and the idea of the nation, inasmuch as he ponders on the relationship between Lispector, personally and as writer, and the situation of Brazil as a self-fashioning society, conscious of the immensity of its national territory and keenly desirous of an equivalent hegemonic role. But this is primarily invoked so as to allow De Sousa to relate the practice of Lispector's writing to models of deterritorialization as conceptualized by Gilles Deleuze.[6] This is indeed a fruitful and thought-provoking approach but one that leaves the question of the nation behind.

The other instance is a short article by Débora Ferreira, with the suggestive title of 'O imaginário nacionalístico na obra de Clarice Lispector'.[7] None the less, this critic hardly manages to go beyond raising the issue, since for her, in the works actually referred to, *A paixão segundo G. H.* and especially *A hora da estrela*, what is sought primarily is a representation of women in Brazilian society, primordially as non-subjects, either objectified or marginalized.[8] This is not to say that Débora Ferreira totally misses the point of the question. Indeed, when she quotes Maria José Barbosa, saying that 'women also partake in linguistic, social and cultural modes of domination, as they incorporate patriarchal models into their lifestyle and then disseminate them', Ferreira is approaching a relevant issue in terms of how Lispector's texts enact representations of the nation.[9] For of course women, even more than men, are reproducers of the cultural order upon which any idea of the nation rests. Whether Lispector's texts reproduce, or rather subvert, such a cultural order, however, is precisely one of the points I wish to examine. In any case, no matter how closely linked the reproduction, reflection and criticism of social issues might be to the question of the nation, social criticism should not be confused with a reflection on national representations.

For a long time, especially owing to the horror of the Holocaust, which can be seen, in part, as the culmination of xenophobic ultra-nationalism, discussions of nationalism and of representations of the nation were all but shunned by academic thinkers. However, in part owing to the seminal work of Benedict Anderson in *Imagined Communities* and others,[10] in part to the rebirth of violent, ethnic-based forms of nationalism all over the world and especially after the collapse of the Soviet Union, the study both of nationalism as ideology as well as of representations of the nation has been a burgeoning field in the last two decades. The role of women in the construction of images of the nation, or in their representation, however, has not really been a matter of great concern. Few theoretical studies of the relation between women and the question of the nation have been published and case-studies of particular examples are also scarce.[11] Débora Ferreira has rightly noted the discrepancy between the study of elite (male) intellectual representations of the nation and the exploration of a possibly different, female approach to the same question.[12] If limited in comparison to more traditional approaches to nationalism and the forms of representing the nation, these studies nonetheless provide a variety of key theoretical issues that can be usefully applied to other specific circumstances and authors. Referring specifically to Brazil, Regina Zilberman's *A terra em que nasceste: Imagens do Brasil na literatura* is especially useful insofar as it provides a synthesis of issues and offers an analysis of how the figure of 'woman' has been variously used to represent Brazil as a nation: 'Originários de um programa cujas intenções ultrapassam o âmbito estético, *Iracema* e *Inocência* dramatizam uma questão que afeta, ainda hoje, o Brasil e o contingente de mulheres da sociedade nacional.'[13] [Originating from a project with intentions beyond the dimension of the aesthetic, *Iracema* and *Inocência* dramatize a question that affects Brazil and its female population even today.]

The correlation between the figure of woman and the territory is a commonplace of nationalistic, patriarchal imagination. Even so, in the case of Brazil this process is truly inescapable. Not only did José de Alencar with *Iracema* produce a myth of national origin that made sense for the society of his time and cannot be avoided even nowadays, he also positioned the Brazilian nation as a woman. That is the view Zilberman expresses when she writes that Alencar, though drawing on established precepts and images inherited from colonial times, 'chegou a um resultado que não se resume a uma colagem: de um lado, por consolidar padrões conhecidos e acatados pelos segmentos dominantes, os de seus leitores; de outro, por produzir novos padrões, o mais importante sendo o que via o Brasil como mulher'[14] [reached a result that was not a mere collage: on one hand by consolidating models known and respected by the dominant sectors, those represented by their readers; on the other, by producing new models, the most important of these representing Brazil as a woman]. Zilberman adduces a number of other examples that show a view of Brazil as woman. One that she could also easily have brought forth is the Brazilian national anthem. In lines such as 'Ó Pátria amada! / Dos filhos deste solo és mãe gentil, / Pátria amada, / Brasil!' [O Beloved Homeland! You are the kindly mother of the children of this soil. Beloved Homeland, Brazil!] the identification of the territory, the nation and the figure of a mother is explicit as it had already been in Brazil's first anthem, which, even though it celebrated foremost the resistance to colonial domination and independence, nevertheless starts by affirming the nation as mother: 'Já podeis da Pátria filhos, / Ver contente a mãe gentil; / Já raiou a liberdade / No horizonte do Brasil'[15] [Children of the Homeland, now you see that the kindly mother is content; Liberty has dawned on Brazil's horizon].

Floya Anthias and Nira Yuval-Davis have outlined five major ways in which, according to them, women tend, even if not exclusively, to relate to the nation. These are: (a) as biological reproducers of members of ethnic collectivities; (b) as reproducers of the boundaries of ethnic/ national groups; (c) as participating centrally in the ideological reproduction of the collectivity and as transmitters of its culture; (d) as signifiers of ethnic/national differences—as a focus and symbol in ideological discourses used in the construction, reproduction and transformation of ethnic/national categories; (e) as participants in national, economic, political and military struggles.[16] As a woman, Lispector can be said to have fulfilled several of the functions expected of her as citizen both in terms of biological reproduction as well as of representing the cultural order. Indeed, she seems to have been uncannily aware of these when she petitioned the President of Brazil in 1942 to expedite her petition for naturalization, just before her marriage to a diplomat, at whose side she would travel to other countries—Italy, Switzerland and the United States—as a literal representative of her country, whose children she expressly mentions wanting to bear.[17]

If at 21 Lispector could still envision her contribution to the nation in those traditional terms, she already looked forward towards writing as her future. It is through her writing that Lispector more strongly attempted a transformation of the idea of the nation. The two novels to have received most critical attention are *A paixão segundo G.H.* (1964) and *A hora da estrela* (1977). Both texts constitute high marks of different stages of her writing, both can be viewed as synthesizing, albeit in different ways, her writing project, and both are significantly reflective of their historical moments.[18] Written in a moment of crisis in Brazilian society, and published in the year of the coup that deposed Goulart, initiated the military regime and eliminated political parties, *A paixão segundo G.H.* could not help but be cryptic, and its lack of any direct reference to the nation must be viewed as symptomatic.

Thus, the absence of the black maid whose room G.H. enters, can be said to be significant precisely because it is an absence—both permitting and forcing G.H. to go through the process of self-discovery she undergoes in the novel. In a sense the confrontation with the other of herself, herself as other, is only possible because she does not have to confront her real social other. And does this not constitute an acute representation of Brazil as a nation deeply committed to erasing the importance of its African heritage, even though without it Brazilian identity, collectively and often individually as well, would dissolve into meaninglessness?

A paixão segundo G.H. and *A hora da estrela* share many similarities, even though they are highly different texts. In both, I would argue, Lispector uses the figure of a woman to represent the Brazilian nation, its search for meaning, love, redemption and itself. But above all what the two novels share is the fact that each is a rather limited representation of the nation. Indeed, the power of each representation is directly proportional to its limitation. One could go so far as to see both G.H. (the artist who narrates her own descent into introspection and passage through the inhuman) and Macabéa (the 'heroine' of *A hora da estrela*, poor, exploited, and without much of a chance for survival) as different portraits of the author, that is, of different aspects within Clarice Lispector. Obviously, I do not mean to say that the fictional characters are simply autobiographical snapshots of the author. None the less, the two novels, perhaps especially *A hora da estrela*, draw the reader into a complex but never gratuitous game of identity-formation.

Whereas *A paixão segundo G.H.* was published in a climate of open repression, by 1977 much had changed in Brazilian politics even though much might have remained the same in terms of social conflicts. With *A hora da estrela*, Lispector writes not only what would be her last novel but also one that, for all its apparent ease of reading and comprehension when compared to her previous works, must also be seen as one of the most complex. In this short novel, Lispector sets forth a revision of the idea of Brazil as a nation, which, though it uses traditional elements, manages to subvert them at the same time that it reproduces and preserves them. Such an effect might appear paradoxical but it is above all consistent with her other texts.

It is consistent inasmuch as they too must be understood as deeply paradoxical, both revolutionary in their own terms as regards the established canon of Brazilian literature and reproducing in turn the process of renewal and change by rupture that characterizes works later considered canonical throughout Brazilian literary history. And it is consistent as regards other literary representations of the nation, which had imposed themselves previously, starting with probably the most influential example: José de Alencar's *Iracema* (1865). Lastly, *A hora da estrela* could also be aligned with other national representations in Latin America (and elsewhere), which rely in a strict correlation between family romance and a national project, as Doris Sommer has thoroughly demonstrated. In her seminal *Foundational Fictions: The National Romances of Latin America*, Sommer analyses the direct involvement between familiar romance and national projects in a variety of texts from the different Latin American countries:

Unlike the competitive comparison between nationalism and religion, the interchangeability between nation and sex here is mutually reinforcing. [...] At least this mutual incitement of love and country is felt in the Latin American novels that helped to train generations of patriots in the appropriately productive passions of liberal intercourse.

By assuming a certain kind of translatability between romantic and republican desires, writers and readers of Latin America's canon of national novels have in fact been assuming what amounts to an allegorical relationship between personal and political narratives [...].[19]

Consequently, I would argue, Lispector writes *A hora da estrela* as an allegory of the nation and makes Macabéa into a figure of Brazil as a woman. Perhaps her choice of a male narrator, who invents Macabéa but who in turn, of course, is also invented by Lispector herself— besides serving other textual functions allied to the complexity of textual introspection and a form of postmodern metanarrativity, which informs all of Lispector's works but is especially visible in the later works[20]—is foremost a way for Lispector to show how, in the writing of *A hora da estrela*, she incorporates those male-scripted models from the past and reinvents them in the process. For as a revisionist allegory of the nation, Lispector's text explodes her models, just as throughout the text the reader is alerted to many moments of explosion (28): 'Agora (explosão) em rapidíssimos traços desenharei a vida pregressa da moça até o momento do espelho do banheiro' [Now (bang) with a few rapid strokes I shall sketch out the girl's previous history up to the moment in front of the mirror in the bathroom].

A hora da estrela, inasmuch as it is an allegory of the nation, confronts previous imaginings. The original model to which *A hora da estrela* must refer, that it must incorporate and subvert, is necessarily Alencar's *Iracema*. As a national allegory and a 'foundational fiction',[21] *Iracema* is a love story in which the desire of Iracema for Martim, the Portuguese soldier, is the key for the establishment of Brazil as a nation. Iracema is the indigenous Brazilian 'virgin of honey lips', and she is closely associated with nature. Disobeying her father and desecrating her vow of virginity, Iracema marries Martim and has a son by him, before necessarily dying. I say necessarily because, even though Iracema is chosen by Alencar to embody Brazil, her function is necessarily a biological one, and once she has given birth to a son who, a literal embodiment of the miscegenation seen as key to the new nation, will constitute the new Brazilian, she ceases to have a function, except as a motive for longing and remembrance of the irretrievable past. Furthermore, having not only gone against the rule of the father but also having literally disobeyed her father's law, she had to die as her father himself had predicted. In a sense, that is Iracema's destiny.

Lispector's novel both refers to Alencar's model and subverts it. First of all, *A hora da estrela* is also a love-story. If there is any development at all to the character of Macabéa, it is due to her encounter with Olímpico, their incipient romance and his quick rejection of her for her colleague Glória. One of Macabéa's distinguishing features is also her virginity, and of course she also dies at the end of the novel. But it is not through its similarities to the plot of *Iracema* that Lispector's novel can be read as an allegory of the nation. Indeed, they would clearly be insufficient. Rather, it is by paying attention to the way in which Lispector subverts many of the precepts of *Iracema* that one may venture to relate the two texts. It might seem excessive to say that *A hora da estrela* is a love-story, given the short encounters between Macabéa and Olímpico and given that their conversation is more often a form of miscommunication than an exchange between two beings approaching each other. The novel is more precisely a failed love-story, and that failure is as important for Lispector's project as the successful seduction of Martim by Iracema can be said to have been for Alencar's.

Whereas the success of the relationship between Iracema and Martim is crucial to the success of the nation, the failure of a relationship between Macabéa and Olímpico is just as necessary to present a new model of the national allegory, which even rejects the original model as the fantasy it was. When Olímpico abandons Macabéa for Glória, he is simply selecting a mate who might better serve his designs of social climbing and of reproducing himself, which is first and foremost a form of satiating himself. Glória is doubly attractive to Olímpico, both as an object of sexual desire—fake blonde and plump—and as a source of attachment to a privileged place, having been born in Rio, free from any stigma of being a northern migrant. Glória is the embodiment of a stereotyped cliché about the sensuality of Brazilian women but several notches lower (64): 'Glória era toda contente consigo mesma: dava-se grande valor. Sabia que tinha o sestro molengole de mulata, uma pintinha marcada junto da boca, só para dar uma gostura, e um buço forte que ela oxigenava.' [Glória was very full of herself: she thought she was really something. She knew that she had a mulatta's sex appeal, a beauty spot drawn above her mouth, just to add a touch of glamour, and stubborn facial hair on her top lip that she bleached.] Besides, with a butcher for a father, Glória symbolizes plenty of food as well as a link to the world of violence and killing Olímpico so admires (59–60): 'ele soube que Glória tinha mãe, pai e comida quente em hora certa. Isso tornava-a material de primeira qualidade. Olímpico caiu em êxtase quando soube que o pai dela trabalhava num açougue. Pelos quadris adivinhava-se que seria boa parideira.' [Olímpico soon learned Glória had a mother, a father and a hot meal on the table at the same time every day. This turned her into top quality material. Olímpico swooned when he found out that Glória's father worked in a butcher's shop. He could tell from her hips that she would be a good breeder.]

By rights, the new couple symbolizing the nation should be that formed by the two migrants from the northeast: the virginal typist Macabéa and the strong metal-worker with political ambitions, who had not hesitated to kill a man before and even derived from that act and his secret knowledge of it a form of identity and personal power. And, had Lispector chosen to give us such a pair to found a new myth of the nation, she would have been following Alencar's model and adapting it to a late-twentieth-century context, where Brazil has been independent for a long time but the social inequalities remain and the exodus of the dispossessed from the Northeast continues. What is more, she would also have then reflected the heritage of engaged and regionalist writing that had been so influential in Brazilian literature.

Macabéa is as virginal as Iracema, and as desirous of a warrior lover as her (35): 'Devo dizer que ela era doida por soldado? Pois era.' [Should I tell you that she was crazy about soldiers? Well she was.] But it is Glória, a mixture of a good Portuguese 'wine' and hidden African blood (59), who can provide Olímpico with honey (65): 'Glória [...] lhe daria mel de abelhas e carnes fartas' [Glória would give him bees' honey and ample flesh]. There is no possibility for redemptive miscegenation (the Indian is absent, the African disguised) just as there is no chance at ennobling solidarity between the oppressed.[22] It might seem ironic that Alencar, a man, chose Iracema, a strong woman full of vitality, to represent Brazil, whereas Lispector, a woman, chose the sickly and weak Macabéa to represent the same nation, a nation moreover that in spite of all its problems can not only be said to represent enormous power and potential in the continent but at the time of publication was beginning to show strong public signs of the social unrest that would lead to a return to democracy.

Marta Peixoto, in a sustained analysis of *A hora da estrela* from the perspective of narrative violence, does not hesitate to classify Macabéa insistently as a victim: 'This young woman, a bona fide social victim, is a native of the Northeast [...] The protagonist, recently arrived in Rio, hungry, marginalized, displaced, represents others in her situation, a fragment of a vast social reality.'[23] Peixoto's study is both extensive and thoughtful, and she is also aware of how exaggerated Macabéa's marginalization is and that this contrasts as well with other affirmations by the narrator, which show not only a form of identification with her but also a sort of attraction to her. In any case, there can be no doubt that Macabéa certainly is a negative image of Iracema in most respects, especially when it comes to her physical appearance and vitality.

But there is no irony in Lispector's subversion of Iracema. Or rather, the irony is there, but it is of an altogether different nature: rather than presenting an idolized, exotic Indian princess who in spite of all her strength is only too ready to submit herself to the wishes of the European warrior, Lispector chooses an almost faceless woman— symbolically but also literally, at least in the eyes of Glória who asks her point blank (65), 'Oh mulher, não tens cara?' [Hey girl, don't you have a face?] And it is not only Glória who cannot see Macabéa. For others too, Macabéa is practically invisible until she lies dying in the street after having been hit by the yellow Mercedes driven by a foreigner who did not stop to look at her: 'Ninguém olhava para ela na rua, ela era café frio' [No one looked at her in the street, for she was like cold coffee] (27); 'Algumas pessoas brotaram no beco não se sabe de onde e haviam se agrupado em torno de Macabéa sem nada fazer assim como antes pessoas nada haviam feito por ela, só que agora pelo menos a espiavam, o que lhe dava uma existência' [Some people had sprung up from nowhere in the dead-end street and gathered round Macabéa without doing anything, just as nobody had ever done anything for her, except that at least people were peering at her now and this gave her an existence] (81).

Right at the beginning of the novel, immediately following the announcement of her dismissal by her boss Raimundo Silveira, who nevertheless after 'seeing something in her face' decides to postpone it indefinitely, Macabéa goes to the bathroom in order to be alone and cannot see her reflection in the mirror (25): 'Olhou-se maquinalmente ao espelho que encimava a pia imunda e rachada, cheia de cabelos, o que tanto combinava com a sua vida. Pareceu-lhe que o espelho baço e escurecido não refletia imagem alguma. Sumira por acaso a sua existência física?' [She examined herself mechanically in the mirror above the filthy hand basin, badly cracked and full of hairs: it matched her life so well. It seemed to her that the dark, tarnished mirror did not reflect any image. Could her physical existence have vanished, by any chance?] This moment of the confrontation before the mirror is crucial in several senses: one might be tempted to recall Lacan's mirror stage, the moment at which a child for the first time upon seeing its own reflection on a mirror recognizes it as belonging to him- or herself and thus assumes consciousness of the Self.[24] But Macabéa is often described as not having any such conception of her self.

For instance, as Olímpico and Macabéa converse seating on a park bench, he suggests that they talk about her, to Macabéa's surprise:

Ela: — Falar então de quê? / Ele: — Por exemplo, de você. / Ela: — Eu?! / Ele: — Por que esse espanto? Você não é gente? Gente fala de gente. / Ela: — Desculpe mas não acho que sou muito gente. (48)[25]

A datilógrafa vivia numa espécie de atordoado limbo, entre céu e inferno. Nunca pensara em 'eu sou eu'. Acho que julgava não ter direito, ela era um acaso. Um feto jogado na lata de lixo embrulhado em jornal. Há milhares como ela? Sim, e que são apenas um acaso. (36)[26]

Given Macabéa's almost complete lack of consciousness of herself as an individual and given the narrator's cruel but sharp characterization of her existence as a form of suspended life ('atordoado limbo' [dizzy limbo]) or aborted altogether ('feto jogado na lata de lixo' [a foetus thrown in the dustbin]), an existence she shares with the masses, there can hardly be any talk of a recognition of the Self, and so Lacan's mirror stage is not only reversed but actually denied as altogether inapplicable.

Accordingly, instead of representing the nation in the image of an exceptional woman, Lispector does so through an absolutely undistinguished woman, a woman like thousands of others, a woman who is always already representing even being herself (36): 'Quando acordava não sabia mais quem era. Só depois é que pensava com satisfação: sou datilógrafa e virgem, e gosto de coca-cola. Só então vestia-se de si mesma, passava o resto do dia representando com obediência o papel de ser.' [When she woke up, she no longer knew who she was. Only later would she think with satisfaction: I am a typist and a virgin, and I like Coca-Cola. Only then would she put her self on, and spend the rest of the day obediently playing the role of being.] But Macabéa is not as weak or pitiful as one might be tempted to think. The discourse of the narrator, as Peixoto remarks, is highly ambivalent about Macabéa. Fertility, a key element as it is precisely through biological reproduction that women are most often adduced to literally embody the nation, is a prime example. Macabéa is repeatedly described as infertile, and her ovaries as dried up (58–60). This is perhaps one of the greatest contrasts between *A hora da estrela* and *Iracema*, since giving birth to Moacir, the child who would be the 'first Brazilian', is Iracema's key function, after which she must die according to the logic order of the foundational, patriarchal discourse deployed by Alencar.

By displacing fertility and the promise of reproduction to the figure of Olímpico—'Olímpico era um diabo premiado e vital e dele nasceriam filhos, ele tinha o precioso sêmen' [Olímpico was an accomplished and vibrant devil who would father children, he had the precious semen] (58)—and Glória, however, Lispector is not simply

displacing the original couple, nor does she deny biological reproduction its privileged position in imagining the nation. Proof to the
contrary could be identified at the very beginning of the narrative (or
one of its multiple beginnings), which is precisely a celebration of
reproduction in its most elemental form (11): 'Tudo no mundo
começou com um sim. Uma molécula disse sim a outra molécula e
nasceu a vida.' [Everything in the world began with a yes. One
molecule said yes to another molecule and life was born.] Besides,
Macabéa herself, at one point, rather than lacking fertility can be said
to possess it excessively, so that she would not even need Olímpico or
anyone else to reproduce. This startling comment comes as almost an
afterthought of the narrator (60): 'Esqueci de dizer que era realmente
de espantar que para o corpo quase murcho de Macabéa tão vasto
fosse o seu sopro de vida quase ilimitado e tão rico como o de uma
donzela grávida, engravidada por si mesma, por partenogênese.' [I
forgot to say that it was really amazing to observe how Macabéa's
almost parched body could contain such a vast and almost unlimited
breath of life, as rich as that of a pregnant maiden, impregnated by
herself, by parthenogenesis.]

One can readily see that it is no afterthought when one compares
that passage with the beginning of the narrative. Macabéa, the virgin
who can make herself pregnant, also has strange dreams 'nos quais
apareciam gigantescos animais antediluvianos como se ela tivesse
vivido em épocas as mais remotas desta terra sangrenta' [in which
giant antediluvian animals appeared as if she had lived in the most
distant ages of this bloodthirsty land] (60), and the narrator also refers
to such prehistoric monsters as he questions the possibility of ever
starting his story (11): 'Como começar pelo início, se as coisas aconte-
ceram antes de acontecer? Se antes da pré-pré-história já havia os
monstros apocalípticos?' [How can one start at the beginning, if things
have happened before they actually happen? If apocalyptic monsters
already existed before pre-prehistoric times?] If one chooses to adopt
this view, then it is clear that Macabéa has always already existed, that
she is as ancient as the earth. And that, in the national imagination, is
always of the essence, for even though most nations are exceedingly
modern (being indeed a product of modernity), they always invent
themselves as ancient. Benedict Anderson singles out the American
nations—he makes an exception of Brazil, but that is only because
Brazil did not proclaim itself a republic upon independence but rather
an Empire—for initiating precisely such a modern process and thus

constituting themselves as a sort of 'real models of what such states should "look like"'.[27]

In a sense what makes Brazil different from other 'modern' nation-states in the American continent is precisely that in hanging on to an archaic system, the monarchy, it made much more visible than any other country the desire and need for any nation to hold on to the ghosts of the past even as it proclaimed a radical rupture with such a past. As Eric Hobsbawm makes exceedingly clear, 'modern nations and all their impedimenta generally claim to be the opposite of novel, namely rooted in the remotest antiquity, and the opposite of constructed, namely human communities so "natural" as to require no definition other than self-assertion'.[28] Macabéa also assumes such a 'natural' existence (33): 'Vagamente pensava de muito longe e sem palavras o seguinte: já que sou, o jeito é ser' [She wondered vaguely, from very far away, and without words the following thought came to her: since I am, the knack is to be]. In the historical realm Brazil enacted this paradoxical claim to antiquity in novelty, since, as Sommer points out, 'Brazilians, by contrast [to other Latin-American nations], managed to have their king and rule him too. Pedro II, a doubly legitimate monarch because of Iberian descent and Brazilian birth, was an emperor on their own constitutional terms.'[29] And at the fictional level Alencar certainly provided Moacir, the future of the nation, with an equal pedigree: son of a Portuguese captain and an Indian princess.

Macabéa's origins seem to be the opposite, a misplaced 'nordestina', orphaned so long ago that she no longer remembers ever having parents, and of whom it is known that her roots were bad (27): 'Ela nascera com maus antecedentes' [She was the descendant of bad ancestors]. Moreover, Macabéa feels passion for the very first time when the fortune-teller predicts that she will marry a rich, blond foreigner named Hans (78). Iracema also fell in love with a foreigner, but Martim, being Portuguese, was obviously the inevitable choice for her within the logic of nationalism. Not so with this imagined Hans, a German or a 'gringo'—it does not really matter, just as the colour of his eyes can also be blue, green or brown, for only his being a foreigner and rich is at stake—who materializes ironically as the driver of the Mercedes who kills Macabéa without stopping to look at her. However, this apparent lack of antecedents is a necessary prerequisite so as to inscribe Macabéa in a much more remote past, a past that would thus give her even more legitimacy as a figure of the nation.

For Macabéa is both 'new'—to the narrator, to the readers and, I would argue, as an image of the nation—and antediluvian, a biblical figure (30–1): 'mas tudo o que é novo assusta. Embora a moça anônima da história seja tão antiga que podia ser uma figura biblíca.' [But then everything new is a shock. Although the anonymous girl in this story is so ancient that she could be a biblical figure.] And Macabéa's apparent treason—her desire for the foreigner—ends up, not unlike Iracema's case, reinforcing her capacity to symbolize the nation. Not so much because, by killing her, the foreigner would be revealed as a threat to the nation, but rather because Macabéa is more herself in death. Macabéa who leaves the fortune-teller's house a changed woman, 'grávida de futuro' [pregnant with future] (79), finds her true self only as she lies dying as if reborn (80): 'Hoje, pensou ela, hoje é o primeiro dia de minha vida: nasci' [Today, she thought, today is the first day of my life: I am born].

Is this novel then a tragic, ironic, bitter-to-the-core reversal of the foundational myth Alencar left as heritage to the nation? Is Macabéa not only a figure of the nation but above all a violent cry of accusation? 'Porque há o direito ao grito. Então eu grito' [For everyone has a right to shout. So I shout], the narrator tells us (13). Is Macabéa a living wound representing the millions of the oppressed whose life is disposable and who cannot but dream of a future that will never be theirs? Were this the case, this text would already be a significant pre-empting of prevalent nationalist ideology, substituting hunger for idyllic romance. But this would still be to read it as a simple updating of the national image that, regardless of how radical it might appear, would still not go to the very core of nationalistic logic. Yet, throughout, more than just displacing or reversing her model, Lispector actually annuls it.

Any nation, at the same time that it likes to pretend that it has always existed, is also above all concerned with the future. Nations not only imagine themselves, they also invent a destiny, which can be framed out of historical events and cultural norms or embody collective desires. In *A hora da estrela*, this teleology of the nation is represented in the figure of Olímpico, whose ambition to become a politician will be fulfilled—or so the narrator tells us—at the same time that he states that he will not include the future in his narrative (46): 'No futuro, que eu não digo nesta história, não é que ele terminou mesmo deputado?' [In the future, which I don't tell you about in this story, did he not become a politician after all?] Perhaps this refusal to tell the future is what makes

A hora da estrela a radical transformation of the cultural order inherent in nationalism to the point of annulling it, or at least denying it. Macabéa imagines a future, of herself as movie star, and after visiting the fortune-teller she is given a destiny. But she never has a chance to fulfil it, because she is overtaken by another woman's destiny. For it was not Macabéa, but the woman who had just preceded her at the fortune-teller's, who was meant to be run over, as we can learn through the words of the fortune-teller herself (77): 'E sou sempre sincera: por exemplo, acabei de ter a franqueza de dizer para aquela moça que saiu daqui que ela ia ser atropelada, ela até chorou muito, viu os olhos avermelhados dela?' [I'm always honest: for example, I've just been frank enough to tell that girl who just left that she was going to get run over. Actually she couldn't stop crying. Did you see how red her eyes were?]

This denial of any specifity of an individual destiny can also be read as a denial of any collective destiny and thus as an erasure of the teleological conception of the nation. Macabéa's last words, '— Quanto ao futuro.' [—As for the future] (85), are uttered clearly even though none of the onlookers can make them out. That this future is not just suspended but actually halted had already been made clear by Rodrigo at the beginning of the narrative, even though at that early stage its significance might not have been clearly understood. 'As for the Future' is already one of the alternative titles of the narrative, and it comes just after the signature of Clarice Lispector that also serves as one of the titles. The phrase, so the narrator informs us, is one of the 'secrets' that the narrative, apparently so explicit, does contain, and its inclusion between two full stops, we are also told (13), is not a chance whim of the narrator but a necessity.

One can only speculate about exactly what the secret or the reasons for the delimitation of the phrase to be viewed as a necessity might be, but I would like to suggest that if one defining characteristic of any future is its openness, its unpredictable possibilities, by enclosing the phrase between full stops the text is effectively denying such openness and thus denying the possibility of the future at all. Macabéa's death is the death of the narrator as well as her own personal death—'Macabéa me matou' [Macabéa has killed me] (86)—and not least of all the death of (a certain idea of) the nation too. For as we read in the 'author's dedication', the one textual site where Clarice Lispector relinquishes the mask of the male narrator, the very book is incomplete because it lacks 'the answer', as it has been written in a state of emergency (10): 'Esta história acontece em estado de emergência e de calamidade pública' [This story takes place in a state of emergency and public calamity]. Foundational narratives that allegorize the nation always provide answers, first and foremost with regard to the origins and purpose of that nation. By contrast, rather than imagining answers, as Rodrigo remarks, 'Este livro é uma pergunta' [This book is a question] (17).

Notes to Chapter 9

1. 'So long as I have questions to which there are no answers, I shall go on writing.' Clarice Lispector, *A hora da estrela* (Rio de Janeiro: Rocco, 1999), 11. Page nos. elsewhere in this article refer to this edition.

2. Teresa Cristina Montero Ferreira, *Eu sou uma pergunta: Uma biografia de Clarice Lispector* (Rio de Janeiro: Rocco, 1999).

3. Nádia Batella Gotlib, *Clarice: Uma vida que se conta* (São Paulo: Editora Ática, 1995), 52. Although Gotlib does not provide full information on the text she cites, it is identified in Diane E. Marting (ed.), *Clarice Lispector: A Bio-Bibliography* (Westport, CT, and London: Greenwood Press, 1993), 221: 'B50. Callado, Antônio. "O dia em que Clarice desapareceu." *Perto de Clarice*. Program from the Homage to CL, 23–9 Nov. 1987, on the tenth anniversary of her death. RJ: Casa de Cultura Laura Alvim, Oficina Literária Afrânio Coutinho, Fundação Casa de Rui Barbosa, 1987'.

4. Clarice Lispector in a *crônica*, 'Esclarecimentos: Explicação de uma vez por todas', *Jornal do Brasil* (14 Nov. 1970), cited by Gotlib, *Clarice: Uma vida que se conta*, 114.

5. Regina Zilberman, 'A estrela e seus críticos', in *Clarice Lispector: A narração do indizível*, ed. Regina Zilberman et al. (Porto Alegre: Artes e Ofícios, 1998), 7. Claire Varin explored the question of Lispector's relation to Yiddish in *Langues de feu: Essais sur Clarice Lispector* (Québéc: Trois, 1990). See also Nelson H. Vieira, *Jewish Voices in Brazilian Literature: A Prophetic Discourse of Alterity* (Gainesville: University Press of Florida, 1995).

6. Carlos Mendes de Sousa, *Clarice Lispector: Figuras da escrita* (Braga: Universidade do Minho/Centro de Estudos Humanísticos, 2000). Cf. (32, 33): 'O território da língua passara a ser para Clarice Lispector um horizonte de busca nascido da tensão entre o efeito desterritorializador e a instauração de um espaço nos próprios limites da língua a que deseja, de facto, pertencer. Na tensão entre a existência do espaço da confinação geograficamente referencializada e a procura do espaço da potencial amplidão que subsume toda a energia criadora é que ela é estrangeira procurando não o ser e sendo-o, em simultâneo.' [For Clarice Lispector, the territory of language had come to be a sought after horizon arising from the tension between the de-territorialising effect and the establishment of a space within the very limits of the language to which it actually wants to belong. In the tension between the existence of the space confined by geographical references and the search for the potentially wide-open space that subsumes all the creative energy is the fact that she is a foreigner trying not to be one and being one at the same time]. 'Eis o pensamento de Deleuze repetido vezes sem conta: a arte da literatura é ser-se estrangeiro na própria língua.'

[This is Deleuze's endlessly repeated concept: the art of literature is being a foreigner in your own language.]

7. Débora Ferreira, 'O imaginário nacionalístico na obra de Clarice Lispector', *Romance Languages Annual* 9 (1997): 472–3.

8. Thus, in her conclusion (ibid., 473), Ferreira states that 'Lispector, para além de sua alcunha de escritora intimista, revela dispersamente em sua obra um Brasil que exclui as mulheres. Para sobreviver a esta realidade que as objetifica e/ou marginaliza, suas protagonistas escapam para um imaginário acronológico onde estabelecem alternativas à maneira patriarcal de ordenar a sociedade.' [Beyond the categorization of her as an intimate writer, on various occasions in her work Lispector portrays a Brazil which excludes women. To survive this reality that objectifies and/or marginalizes them, her protagonists escape into an achronological imaginary world where they establish alternatives to the patriarchal way of organizing society.]

9. The work being quoted (ibid., 472) is Maria José Barbosa, *Clarice Lispector: Spinning the Webs of Passion* (New Orleans: University Press, 1997), 57.

10. Benedict Anderson, *Imagined Communities: Reflections on the Origin and Spread of Nationalism*, 2nd edn. (London and New York: Verso, 1991; 1st edn. 1983). Two collective works that offer an extensive insight into the scope of studies on nationalism and representations of the nation are Gopal Balakrishnan (ed.), *Mapping the Nation* (London and New York: Verso, 1996); John Hutchinson and Anthony D. Smith (eds.), *Nationalism* (Oxford and New York: Oxford University Press, 1994).

11. The work of Floya Anthias and Nira Yuval-Davis (eds.), *Woman-Nation-State* (New York: St. Martin's Press, 1989), has become well known, and so has that of Sylvia Walby, 'Woman and Nation', *Mapping the Nation*, 235–54. More recently Lois A. West has edited a collection of essays that build on these, and other, seminal studies to develop specific case studies in different parts of the world: Lois A. West (ed.), *Feminist Nationalism* (New York and London: Routledge, 1997).

12. This is how she starts her essay (Ferreira, 'O imaginário nacionalístico', 472): 'Muito já foi dito acerca do esforço da elite intelectual brasileira em construir um imaginário nacionalístico que nos explique as origens e nos esboce um retrato daquilo que constitua o Brasil enquanto uma nação. No entanto, ainda não se aprofundou o suficiente a possibilidade das mulheres expressarem um conceito diferente de brasilidade, talvez até desafiando propostas tradicionalmente concebidas como sendo a norma.' [Much has already been said about the effects of top Brazilian intellectuals to construct an image of the nation which can explain our beginnings and sketch a portrait of what constitutes Brazil in terms of its nationhood. Nevertheless there has not yet been sufficient opportunity for women to express an alternative concept of Brazilianness, maybe even by challenging conventions that are traditionally seen as the norm].

13. Regina Zilberman, *A terra em que nasceste: Imagens do Brasil na literatura* (Porto Alegre: Editora da Universidade Federal do Rio Grande do Sul, 1994), 106.

14. Ibid., 96.

15. The current version of the national anthem was written by Joaquim Osório Duque Estrada, while the words of the first version were by Evaristo da Veiga.

16. From the Introduction to Anthias and Yuval-Davis, *Woman-Nation-State*, 313.

17. In that petition, cited in Ferreira, *Eu sou uma pergunta*, 88–9, we can read: 'Senhor Presidente Getúlio Vargas: Quem lhe escreve é uma jornalista, ex-redatora da Agência Nacional [...]. Uma russa de 21 anos de idade e que está no Brasil há 21 anos menos alguns meses. Que não conhece uma só palavra de russo mas que pensa, fala, escreve e age em português, fazendo disso sua profissão, e nisso pousando todos os projetos do seu futuro [...]. Que deseja casar-se com brasileiro e ter filhos brasileiros. [...] Se trago a V. Exa o resumo dos meus trabalhos jornalísticos não é para pedir-lhe, como recompensa, o direito de ser brasileira. Prestei esses serviços espontânea e naturalmente, e nem poderia deixar de executá-los. Se neles falo é para atestar que já sou brasileira.' [Dear President Getúlio Vargas: This letter to you is from a journalist, an ex-reporter for the Agência Nacional. A Russian, 21 years old who has lived in Brazil for 21 years minus a few months. Who knows not one word of Russian but thinks, speaks, writes and functions in Portuguese, indeed, carves her profession out from it and is depending on it to be able to carry out all her future projects. Who wants to marry a Brazilian man and have Brazilian children. I am not sending you a resumé of my journalistic work with the idea of asking you for something in return: the right to be Brazilian. I have done my duty spontaneously and freely nor could I help doing it. I only mention my work to prove that I already am Brazilian.]

18. Although not explictly formulating these conclusions, Benjamin Abdala Júnior and Samira Youssef Campedelli, 'Vozes da crítica', in the critical edition of *A paixão segundo G.H.* (1964), ed. Benedito Nunes (Florianópolis: Editora da Universidade Federal de Santa Catarina, 1988), 196–209, draw precisely on the correlation between Lispector's writing and Brazilian historical events. They also note (201) how 'A crítica tem ressaltado *A paixão segundo G.H.* como narrativa síntese dos procedimentos enunciativos de Clarice Lispector' [The critics have emphasized that *A paixão segundo G.H.* is a narrative synthesis of Clarice Lispector's enunciative practices]. In reference to *A hora da estrela*, Lúcia Helena, *Nem Musa, nem Medusa: Itinerários da escrita em Clarice Lispector* (Niterói and Rio de Janeiro: Editora da Universidade Federal Fluminense, 1997) states (70; emphasis original): 'Não só a autora concebe que um texto sempre se produz em diálogo com outros textos, existentes ou virtuais, mas ela mesma constitui sua obra através do adensamento de núcleos de força, as *cenas fulgor*, que estão presentes em seu trabalho desde os primeiros livros' [Not only does the author believe that a text can only be produced in dialogue with other texts, real or virtual, but she herself becomes her work through the concentration of nuclei of strength, the *blazing scenes* that are present in her work since the first books].

19. Doris Sommer, *Foundational Fictions: The National Romances of Latin America* (Berkeley: University of California Press, 1991), 40–1.

20. The insertion of Lispector's work within a postmodern frame is, even if not completely explicit, always present and examined in detail by Carlos Mendes de Sousa in *Clarice Lispector: Figuras da escrita*. The specific relationship between *A hora da estrela* and postmodernism is discussed by Américo António Lindeza Diogo, *Cadáver supersónico: Uma leitura de 'A hora da estrela'* (Braga[?]: Cadernos do Povo, 1997).

21. Sommer devotes one chapter of *Foundational Fictions* to discussing both *Iracema* and *O Guarani*.

22. Lispector is too lucid for that, just like her narrator Rodrigo, who comments on his desire to be the other, and who sarcastically deflates the value of social criticism by remarking on the reader's presumed social class and the text's mere function as an escape valve (30): 'Se o leitor possui alguma riqueza e vida bem acomodada, sairá de si para ver como é às vezes o outro. Se é pobre, não estará me lendo porque ler-me é supérfluo para quem tem uma leve fome permanente. Faço aqui o papel de vossa válvula de escape e da vida massacrante da média burguesia.' [If the reader has a certain amount of money and enjoys a comfortable life, he will step outside himself to see what the other is like sometimes. If he is poor, he will not be reading this story because reading me is superfluous for he who feels a vague and permanent hunger. Here, I am acting as a safety-valve for you and the tedious life of the petty bourgeoisie.]

23. Marta Peixoto, *Passionate Fictions: Gender, Narrative, and Violence in Clarice Lispector* (Minneapolis and London: University of Minnesota Press, 1994), 89.

24. First presented in 1949, this is one of the best known of Lacan's essays: 'Le stade du miroir comme formateur de la fonction de Je', *Écrits*, i (Paris: Seuil, 1966).

25. 'She—What shall we talk about then? / He—We could talk about you. / She—Me! / He—Why make such a fuss? You're a person, aren't you? People talk about people. / She—forgive me, but I don't think that I am much of a person.'

26. 'The typist lived in a kind of dizzy limbo, between heaven and hell. She had never thought about "I am me." I reckon she felt she had no right to do so, she was a misfit. A foetus wrapped up in newspaper and thrown in the dustbin. Are there thousands like her? Yes, thousands of misfits.'

27. Anderson, *Imagined Communities*, 46.

28. Eric Hobsbawm, *The Invention of Tradition*, ed. Eric Hobsbawm and Terence Ranger (Cambridge: Cambridge University Press, 1983), cited from the excerpt in *Nationalism*, ed. John Hutchinson and Anthony D. Smith (Oxford and New York: Oxford University Press, 1994), 76.

29. Sommer, *Foundational Fictions*, 165.

PART III

Critical Reception

CHAPTER 10

The Early Dissemination of Clarice Lispector's Literary Works in the United States

Teresa Montero

In order to consider how and why Clarice Lispector's literary works came to be translated and studied in the United States from the late 1960s onwards, my paper provides a concise overview of the ways in which her writing became known to a growing public. The increasing interest in this Brazilian author is considered from two interconnected aspects: the academic sector—with reference to the presence of university lecturers (be they Brazilian or North American) working in American universities in the field of Brazilian studies and the growing number of Luso-Brazilian courses on offer there—and the publishing market. I focus on the so-called 'boom' in Latin American fiction that took place during the 1960s and '70s, when the government of the United States started to invest in research and teaching about Latin America in reaction the political repercussions arising after the Cuban Revolution.

Firstly, I will outline the political, economic and cultural links established between Brazil and the USA during the 1940s so as to give a more complete view of this first stage of the spread of Lispector's works northwards. Such background information is very important because it was this alliance that paved the way for the positive reception of Brazilian studies in North America and the integration of the subject—which included Brazilian literature and, consequently, Lispector—into university departments.[1]

The United States' influence over Brazil's plans for economic and cultural development became visible when Brazil joined World War II

alongside the Allied forces in 1942. This was the date of the imple-
mentation of the so-called 'Good Neighbour' policy, which promoted
the exchange of cultural and material values between the States and the
other countries in the Americas. President Roosevelt's goal was to
'assegurar no plano internacional o alinhamento do Brasil (e da América
Latina) aos Estados Unidos, país que naquele momento procurava
afirmar-se como uma grande potência e centro de um novo sistema de
poder no plano internacional' [to ensure as part of its international plan
the alignment of Brazil (and Latin America) with the policies of the
United States, a country that was at the time doing its best to assert
itself as a great power and as the centre of a new power system on the
international scale].[2]

   The presence of US culture in Brazilian society was remarkable: it
permeated patterns of behaviour, modes of artistic expression and
scientific knowledge. Concurrently, a series of scientific and academic
exchange programmes were set up between the USA and several
Latin-American countries, permitting the definitive introduction of
Luso-Brazilian studies to North America. But it was through artistic
interaction, largely through music and cinema, that the United States
put together its portraits of Latin America. With a strong emphasis on
pan-American co-operation, countless Latino performers became
involved in North-American show-business, with Carmen Miranda
being adopted as the muse of the 'Good Neighbour' policy. From that
time on, her image as an exotic foreigner became synonymous with
all things Latin American. Carmen Miranda's career in the States
clearly shows the process of the assertion of Brazilian national identity
that was applauded by the Estado Novo.

   Brazilian literature was not indifferent to the policy, since 'é marcada
pelo compromisso com a vida nacional no seu conjunto [...], com a
intenção de estar fazendo um pouco da nação ao fazer literatura' [it was
marked by its engagement with national life as a whole, with the
intention of creating a little bit of nationhood by creating literature].[3]
The novels of the time were concerned less with formal innovation
than with social questions, the most common of which were the rural
exodus caused by drought, the misery of the migrating people and their
propensity for mysticism. As Antonio Candido observes of these novels
and of Brazilian literature as a whole, there is a conformism to style in
Brazil that hinders the true development of literary thought, which
begins with the forging of an appropriate expression.[4] And it is this
tendency of Brazilian writers in general to use 'processos já usados'

[tried-and-tested processes] that lies behind the introduction of Brazilian literature into the United States.[5]

Two articles help to contextualize the beginnings of Brazilian studies as an academic discipline and present a general view of the first stage of its development in the States in the 1940s and 50s. In 'Samuel Putnam, Brazilianist' (1964), Harvey Gardiner describes the career of this pioneer of Brazilian studies who devoted himself to discovering and translating Brazilian fiction. His choice owed much to the considerable remuneration that this kind of work offered him, since private bodies (such as the Nelson Rockefeller Foundation) and government agencies gave plenty of grants for translating books. The reports that Putnam wrote recommending Brazilian titles for publication with North-American publishing houses, Alfred Knopf in particular, refer not only to a given book's literary quality, but also show his awareness of its selling potential.[6] *Os sertões* (1902) / *Rebellion in the Backlands* (1944) by Euclides da Cunha (University of Chicago Press), *Terras do sem fim* (1942) / *The Violent Land* (1945) by Jorge Amado, and *Casa grande e senzala* (1933) / *The Masters and the Slaves* (1946) by Gilberto Freyre (both the last published by Knopf) are some of his most important translations. Putnam's choice of titles shows the kind of Brazilian literature that received favourable attention abroad in the form of translations, as do the scant critical studies published during this period. Fred Ellison's *Brazil's New Novel: Four Northeastern Masters* (1954) introduced the works of José Lins do Rego, Jorge Amado, Graciliano Ramos and Rachel de Queiroz to the North-American public. A look at the range of titles mentioned by Ellison, in his acknowledgements thanking the editors for their permission to quote excerpts from the original works—namely *The Negro in Brazil* (1939), by Arthur Ramos; *Brazil: An Interpretation* (1945), by Gilberto Freyre; *The Masters and the Slaves* (1946), by Gilberto Freyre; and *Rebellion in the Backlands* (1944) by Euclides da Cunha—demonstrates that the themes fashionable at the time were the question of race and the assertion of national identity.[7]

In his article 'Contemporary Portuguese Scholarship in North America', Gerald Moser gives an extensive account of the efforts made to promote Luso-Brazilian Studies, which had begun in the late nineteenth century, continuing up to the 1940s, '50s and '60s.[8] It was in the early 1940s, what he calls the 'third phase' of the process, that it becomes possible to identify a combination of more effective measures which contributed towards the subject's growing popularity. Moser narrates the development of this phase stage by stage, focusing on the organization of the earliest colloquia on Luso-Brazilian topics, and lists the first institutes to include courses relating to Brazil. The first was in Nashville, Tennessee, where courses began in 1947, but this, as well as the so-called 'Summer Institutes' that offered intensive Portuguese courses, lasted for a relatively short period because they were located in universities in such scattered places as Wyoming, Vermont, Pennsylvania and North Carolina. Further pioneering efforts included the plans to form a Portuguese section within the Modern Language Association in 1939, the first meeting of that section two years later in Indianapolis, and the transformation of the American Association of Teachers of Spanish into the American Association of Teachers of Spanish and Portuguese in 1944.

When considering the initiatives that took place during the 1950s, Moser highlights the first Brazilian Studies Colloquium, held in Washington, DC, in 1951, the setting up of the Brazilian Studies Institute at New York University (1958), where Brazilian and Portuguese visiting lecturers began to make regular visits, and the establishment of the Luso-Brazilian Centre at the University of Wisconsin in 1959. Another important element in the expansion of Luso-Brazilian studies was the interaction between foreign teachers and writers and their North-American students. Guest lecturers from Brazil such as Cecília Meireles, Gilberto Freyre and Érico Veríssimo were among the first authors to participate in this experience.[9] Not surprisingly, four decades later, some of the universities that hosted these institutes (namely New York University, University of North Carolina, University of Pennsylvania and Vanderbilt University, Nashville) have become key centres for the dissemination of Brazilian literature and the works of Clarice Lispector in particular, proving that the institutes acted as springboards for the founding of what were to become important Spanish and Portuguese departments in the United States.

During the period we are concerned with, the growth of interest in Brazilian literature abroad was heavily reliant on word of mouth, on the enthusiasm of intellectuals with a passion for Brazil or on the friendships that grew up between Brazilians and foreigners in the diplomatic world. Clarice Lispector's situation was typical: she had lived outside Brazil with her diplomat husband since 1944. In the 1940s, friends in the diplomatic service who were also authors, like Paschoal Carlos Magno in England and João Cabral de Melo Neto in

Spain, encouraged her to try to publish her work abroad, offering to find her translators and publishers, but their good intentions were not enough. Only later, thanks to Beata Vettori, who worked for the Itamaraty (Brazilian Diplomatic Service), did she manage to publish a chapter of *A cidade sitiada* (1949) entitled 'Perseu no trem' in the French magazine *Roman* in July 1952, translated by Beata herself.[10] Two years later, the first of her novels to be published in Europe, *Perto do coração selvagem*, also reached the French editor via Vettori.[11]

The situation in the United States was similar. Until *A maçã no escuro* came out as *The Apple in the Dark* in 1967, Lispector had only published three short stories there—'Tentação' (1955), 'Amor' (1957) and 'O crime do professor de matemática' (1961)—without any significant repercussions.[12] A look at the writer's correspondence with Roland Dickey, the editor of the *New Mexico Quarterly*, the University of New Mexico journal that published 'Love', shows how he discovered Clarice. After reading 'Temptation' in the journal *Américas* in 1955, Dickey contacted the Pan American Union, an organization affiliated with the United Nations and based in Washington, which was then headed by the Brazilian writer Érico Veríssimo.[13] As she had been living in Washington since 1953 and was good friends with Veríssimo, it is more than likely that he put her in touch with American magazines and journals that were interested in publishing short stories by Brazilian authors.

Sérgio Miceli's study of the academic relations between Brazil and the United States in the field of the social sciences examines what caused the intensive interest in Luso-Brazilian studies beginning in the 1960s, namely the reorientation of United States foreign policy towards Latin America.[14] He goes on to indicate the combination of political factors that influenced financial and institutional investments in the areas of Latin-American studies:

A Revolução Cubana de 1959 foi o fator determinante de toda uma reorientação da política externa norte-americana para a América Latina, a começar pela Aliança para o Progresso, e tendo prosseguimento através da criação de um programa de bolsas individuais para treinamento avançado em ciências sociais e humanidades (Brasil e América Hispânica) e das iniciativas que culminaram em 1966 na criação da Latin American Studies Association/LASA.[15]

At the time, the setting up of the first undergraduate and postgraduate programmes in Luso-Brazilian departments and Latin-

American centres was supported by the State Department (using government funds and donations from the Rockefeller Foundation) in order to train a team of specialists in the area. This explains the rise of Brazilian studies as a separate sector within the specialist area of Latin-American studies. The expansion of Latin-American studies 'no contexto mais amplo de emergência das chamadas area studies implantadas no sistema acadêmico norte-americano' [in the wider context of the emergence of so-called area studies integrated within the North-American academic system] is, in Miceli's words, in part due to a 'resposta institucional às demandas por aconselhamento e expertise das agências governamentais e privadas no segundo pós-guerra' [institutional reply to the demands for advice and expertise made by private and government agencies after the war].[16]

Earl Fitz, Professor of Portuguese, Spanish and Comparative Literature at Vanderbilt University, speculates that another significant factor in the dissemination of Luso-Brazilian studies was the American Congress's decision to officially designate Portuguese a 'critical language' as a result of the political crisis that arose in Brazil during João Goulart's presidency in 1964. This official measure led to a considerable investment in grants and scholarships. Henceforth, Latin Americanists began to study Brazilian culture, history and literature and also started to specialize in Brazilian studies.[17]

It is my contention that government, commercial and academic activities also helped to stimulate the North-American literary market to invest in works by Spanish-American authors. The fact that French publishing houses had already brought out several works of Latin-American fiction is particularly relevant because 'a tradução francesa é uma instância de internacionalização do escritor latino-americano' [the French translation is proof of a Latin American writer's inter-national status].[18] The number of European literary prizes awarded to Latin-American authors during the 1960s and 70s is proof of this international recognition. For example, the Formentor prize was presented in Paris to Jorge Luis Borges and Samuel Beckett in 1961, and Nobel prizes for literature were won by Miguel Angel Asturias (1967) and Pablo Neruda (1971). In Earl Fitz's opinion, this had a considerable impact on the reception of Spanish-American literature in North-American universities.[19]

At the same time, various endeavours were taking place in Europe as part of an intense renaissance of all things Latin American, which had until then been relegated to the background after the war because of a retraction in investments. The Cuban Revolution was a strong influence on this process, along with the continuous stream of exiled intellectuals and artists, who, expelled by the authoritarian regimes ruling their countries, went to live in Europe, mostly France; so was the popularity of Latin-American fiction and cinema during this period.[20]

Nevertheless, the greater recognition of Brazilian literature abroad was dependent on the link between Brazilian and Spanish-American literary traditions. Earl Fitz comments that Brazilian literature and culture are classified under 'a rúbrica de literatura "latino-americana"' [the heading 'Latin-American literature'], 'categorização notoriamente vaga e freqüentemente usada em referência exclusiva à tradição da América espanhola, pouco apta a fazer jus à realidade brasileira' [a notably vague but frequently-used classification, employed to refer exclusively to the Spanish-American tradition, and hardly suitable to do justice to the Brazilian situation].[21] As Spanish-American literary and cultural traditions are more widely promoted than those of Brazil, Fitz concludes, Brazilian traditions are rendered 'invisível' [invisible] to a readership who should be much better acquainted with them.

As far as the North-American market was concerned, in terms of the scope of Latin-American literature, Brazilian literature (and therefore Lispector's writing) had a very insignificant role. We can draw conclusions about this sidelining of Brazilian literature by taking a look at the career pattern of the most translated Brazilian author of the period, Jorge Amado. We must not forget that the motivation to translate works by Lispector and other Brazilian writers was triggered as a result of the success of Amado's *Gabriela, cravo e canela* (1958), translated in 1962 as *Gabriela, Clove and Cinnamon*.[22] Lawrence Hallewell suggests that the translation of *Gabriela* helped Amado to achieve the feat of becoming the first Latin-American writer to appear in North-American bestseller lists. This provided an incentive for the publisher Alfred Knopf to invest in other Brazilian writers such as Graciliano Ramos, José Lins do Rego, Guimarães Rosa, Antonio Candido, Autran Dourado and Clarice Lispector, bringing out a total of 22 titles before 1969.[23] Piers Armstrong upholds Hallewell's thesis, emphasizing that the publication by Knopf in 1963 of Guimarães Rosa's *The Devil to Pay in the Backlands* (*Grande sertão: Veredas*, 1956) benefited from the wave of enthusiasm for all things Brazilian in the wake of the popularity of *bossa nova* music and the success of *Gabriela, cravo e canela*.[24] It was not by chance, Armstrong suggests, that Amado was chosen to write the introduction to the translation of Rosa's novel.[25] Besides Hallewell's considerations, it seems to me that the fact that Jorge Amado had already been published successfully on the Spanish-American and European markets might also have influenced Alfred Knopf's decision. The Bahian writer had already gained quite a place for himself on the European cultural scene by the early 1960s.

To return to the rise of Brazilian studies in North-American universities, its status as an academic subject in its own right within the specialist area of Latin-American studies throughout the 1960s was strongly influenced by the ways that Hispanic Studies departments are organized. In a linguistic hierarchy, Spanish, Spanish-American and Portuguese literatures hold a position superior to that of Brazilian literature. Indeed, Spanish courses are more popular, owing to the United States' large Hispanic population. This has a negative effect on Portuguese and Brazilian courses, which do not generate enough interest or student numbers to keep them running.

The influence of the demographic factor and Brazilian literature's identity problem determine the profile of the development of Lispector studies in US universities. Of the six doctoral theses on Clarice Lispector submitted between 1971 and 1979, four are comparative studies that contrast her works with those of authors of the new Latin American narrative. The research was carried out in departments of Spanish and Portuguese in states where there was a large concentration of people of Hispanic origin. The first of these theses, entitled *Julio Cortázar, Clarice Lispector e a nova narrativa latino-americana*, was submitted to the University of New Mexico by the Brazilian researcher Teresinha Alves Pereira in 1971.[26] After taking her Master's degree and Ph.D. at the same university, Pereira taught at Tulane University in Louisiana and at Stanford University in California. In other words, she worked at three of the first universities in the country responsible for setting up courses in Latin-American studies and in fact became a key figure in promoting Lispector's works; her research was read by the next generation of Lispector experts such as Earl Fitz and Gregory Rabassa.[27]

The focal point for the dissemination of research into Lispector's works proved to be the Department of Comparative Literature at the City University of New York in the early 1970s. Two of the most important Lispector experts of the time, Earl Fitz and Elizabeth Lowe (who would make valuable contributions to the field in the 1970s and '80s), took a postgraduate course, involving a strong Brazilian and Spanish-American literary element as well as offering a translation module, led by the lecturer and translator Gregory Rabassa. He had translated Lispector's *A maçã no escuro* (1960) for Knopf as *The Apple in the Dark* (1967), and he is one of the most respected translators of landmark novels from the Latin-American boom, such as *Rayuela* (1963) / *Hopscotch* (1966) by Julio Cortázar and *Cien años de soledad* (1967) / *One Hundred Years of Solitude* (1970) by Gabriel García Márquez. Both Fitz and Lowe won scholarships to enrol on the course, and Fitz has informed me that this was a fundamental motivation for his choice of course and university. The majority of Brazilian authors studied were either modernists or North-Eastern novelists, but the course did also cover writers from the 1940s and onwards, including Lispector and Guimarães Rosa.

Fitz first encountered Lispector when he read Rabassa's translation of *A maçã no escuro*, after which he devoted his research to her works and became the first scholar in his country to accumulate a significant corpus of critical works about her.[28] He has played a dual role in the development of Lispector studies both as a lecturer and as a translator, for he translated *Água viva* as *The Stream of Life* in the mid 1970s. His doctoral thesis and four articles about the author published during this period associate her work with the 'lyrical novel'.[29] His initial approach was to establish differences between the type of novel created by Lispector and the social realism of the North-Eastern novels such as Amado's *Terras do sem fim* (1942) and José Lins do Rego's *Menino do engenho* (1932).[30] Fitz drew attention to a new and innovative tendency in the post-war Brazilian novel, as Rabassa had done previously in his introduction to *The Apple in the Dark*. The arrival of Lispector's work in translation in the United States in the 1960s and '70s paved the way for the reception of a new kind of Brazilian narrative that, according to the critics, showed all the technical innovations associated with the *nueva narrativa* [new narrative] identified in Spanish-American boom literature.[31]

Elizabeth Lowe, Fitz's classmate, was more interested in aspects of translation. She had grown up in Brazil, leaving at the age of 18, and thus had a privileged insight into Brazilian culture and the Portuguese language. Gregory Rabassa invited her to take the Comparative Literature course at City University, where she first read Lispector and felt strongly motivated to translate some of the author's short stories, starting with 'A solução' ('The Solution', 1974), 'Tentação' ('Temptation', 1976) and 'Os desastres de Sofia' ('Sofia's Disasters', 1979).[32] At the same time, Fitz collaborated with her on the translation of

Água viva. Both students corresponded with Lispector during this period. Lowe met the author several times in Rio de Janeiro, discussed the translations with her and read some of her unpublished works. Lowe's personal contacts with the writer, with whom she became friends, enabled her to set up an interview in 1976, the only one that Lispector ever gave to a North-American academic journal, entitled 'The Passion according to C.L.'[33] The American scholar's doctoral thesis deals with the urban tradition in Brazilian literature, an aspect that had received little previous critical attention, through an analysis of works by ten writers including Lispector, whom she presented as an author for whom 'social inter-relationships are the very fabric of her fiction'.[34]

At the same time that Lispector criticism was becoming established in the USA, an equally important research centre was developing at the University of Manchester in the UK, where the lecturer and translator Giovanni Pontiero taught Latin-American and Luso-Brazilian literatures from 1966 to 1996. His first translations appeared in 1966, of works mostly by contemporary Latin-American authors including Manuel Bandeira (the subject of his doctoral thesis), Carlos Drummond de Andrade and Lygia Fagundes Telles. Because of his great admiration for Lispector's writing, he went on to translate a considerable number of her works into English, winning the Camões prize in London in 1968 for 'Love'. In an interview in 1985, he explained that a mutual friend had shown his translation of the short story to Clarice, who immediately suggested that Pontiero translate the other stories in the collection *Laços de família*. So he did, and *Family Ties* was duly published by the University of Texas Press in 1972.[35]

By the end of the 1970s he had also translated some sections of 'Fundo de gaveta' [The bottom drawer], the second part of *A legião estrangeira* (1964), which he called 'From the Chronicles of the Foreign Legion' and which were published in *Review* in 1979. By the late 1980s Pontiero had become a key figure in Lispector studies on an international scale, thanks largely to his translations of her works for Carcanet Press in Manchester, later published in North America.[36]

Critical appreciations of Lispector's work began to appear after the publication of the translation *The Apple in the Dark* (1967) and they confirmed the importance of Rabassa's course at CUNY as a landmark in the introduction of Lispector studies to the States. In 1971, a couple of articles appeared in the journal *Studies in Short Fiction*, but they were written by Pontiero and the Brazilian lecturer Massaud Moisés (in English translation), not by North Americans.[37] Both link Lispector to the phenomenological tradition, in the wake of Benedito Nunes' 1966 work *O mundo de Clarice Lispector* (the first book-length study of Lispector's work, published in Brazil), by making reference to the influence of philosophy on her work (a fashionable approach to literature at the time), particularly Kierkegaard, Heidegger, Sartre and Camus.[38] Rabassa himself mentioned Lispector in an article on 'La nueva narrativa en el Brasil' in 1972 and wrote a short entry on her in the *Encyclopedia of World Literature in the Twentieth Century* in 1975.[39] Articles by the Brazilian literary critics Fabio Lucas and Bella Jozef were also published in journals of Latin-American studies, translated into English and Spanish respectively.[40]

From this overview of the critical material published between 1967 and 1979, it is apparent that Brazilian critics working in the States published more or less the same number of articles as North-American scholars. However, during this stage in the development of academic research into Lispector, most work was being done in Brazil because she was not yet very well known outside her own country. Obviously the North-American critics did their best to familiarize themselves with research by Brazilian experts based both in the United States like Teresinha Alves Pereira and in Brazil. It is common to see the same names (usually Benedito Nunes, Assis Brasil and Massaud Moisés) cropping up in bibliographies and referred to within critical texts written at this time.

Our survey shows that research into Lispector's works in the United States had become more established by the end of the 1970s, when the number of articles and dissertations devoted to her increased considerably. However, the promising evidence that her work was becoming popular in academic circles did not stimulate publishers to invest in further translations. In the period between 1967 and 1979 only one novel, *A maçã no escuro* (1967), and one full collection of short stories, *Laços de família* (1972), were translated, as well as part of *A paixão segundo G.H.* (published by Knopf in 1977) and fifteen uncollected short stories.[41]

The US poet Elizabeth Bishop, who lived in Brazil in the 1960s, was one of Lispector's most distinguished translators and her neighbour in Leme. The contents of two letters written by Bishop hint at the importance of her translations in the popularization of Lispector's work. Her description of the Brazilian writer reveals the seductive impact of Lispector's narrative, above all because it refers to Brazil in an unusual way: 'Os contos dela são quase como as histórias que eu sempre achei que alguém devia escrever sobre o Brasil — tchekovianas, ligeiramente sinistras e fantásticas — devo mandar algumas em breve para a *Encounter*. Ela tem um editor em N.Y. que está interessado e talvez eu traduza o livro dela inteiro.'[42] [Her short stories are almost like the stories that I have always thought someone should write about Brazil—Chekovian, slightly sinister and fantastic—I must send some of them to *Encounter* soon. She has a publisher in New York who is interested, and I might translate her whole book.]

The publisher that Bishop refers to must be Alfred Knopf, for in a second letter she writes: 'Traduzi cinco contos da Clarice [...] A *New Yorker* está interessada [...] — e se eles não quiserem, então a *Encounter*, a *Partisan Review* etc. Alfred Knopf também está interessado em ver o livro inteiro.'[43] [I have translated five of Clarice's short stories. *The New Yorker* is interested—and if they don't want them, there is always *Encounter*, *Partisan Review* etc. Alfred Knopf is also interested in seeing a whole book.] Bishop's enthusiasm for the short stories and her own literary prestige were certainly responsible for introducing and circulating Lispector's name on the North-American publishing market. The letters quoted from date from October 1962 and January 1963 respectively, when only two short stories had been translated, so it seems quite likely that Lispector's first North-American publisher was introduced to her work by way of Bishop's translations. We must not forget that in 1963 Lispector visited the University of Texas at Austin to deliver a speech at the 11th International Congress of the Ibero-American Literature Institute. It was on this occasion that she met Gregory Rabassa. The fact that all these things happened during the same year, 1963, shows that her name must already have begun to circulate in the worlds of academia and publishing.

Yet another fact must be taken into consideration in order to identify the moment when Lispector started to attract the attention of critics and publishers. An anthology of modern Brazilian short stories published in 1967 included a translation of 'O crime do professor de matemática' ('The Crime of the Mathematics Professor') from *Laços de família*. In his acknowledgements, the translator William Grossman thanked the diplomat Dora Vasconcelos for her collaboration in helping him to understand some of the short stories better.[44] As Vasconcelos was a friend of Lispector's (the writer was a witness at Vasconcelos's wedding), it is highly probable that she helped to circulate and propagate her friend's work whenever she was on a diplomatic posting to the United States.

Throughout the 1970s, then, a significant bibliography of work was produced that shows the growing recognition of Clarice Lispector's works in North-American universities and attests to a real appreciation of her writing. Nevertheless, the visibility that she attained in the academic field was clearly not matched in the publishing world. Only in the following decades, in the 1980s and 90s, were these two important audiences of her work to reach a balance, and this was because feminist theory was beginning to develop. A theoretical tendency with strong critical and political potential, feminist thought conquered new readers for Lispector studies in areas where she had previously been unknown: English and French language and literature departments, not to mention the women's studies courses being organized at the time.

The integration of Lispector studies in the context of a debate foregrounding the question of alterity is particularly relevant in light of the political and demographic changes that took place during the process leading towards the opening up of North-American society between the 1960s and the 80s. In *O multiculturalismo e novos critérios de valoração cultural*, George Yúdice shows how, starting with multiculturalism and identity politics, the remapping of contemporary North-American culture had repercussions for the Third World and Latin America in particular.[45] When he discusses the changes that marked the very beginning of this trend in the 1960s, he makes specific reference 'ao movimento para a expansão dos direitos civis dos negros estadunidenses que estimulou movimentos de afirmação política e cultural entre outros grupos, sobretudo, feministas, latinos e gays' [to the movement for the expansion of the civil rights for blacks in the United States, which stimulated movements for political and cultural assertion among other groups, especially feminists, latinos and gays].[46] According to Yúdice, identity politics and multiculturalism constitute a dislocation, or even an elimination of geographical, conceptual, institutional and economic boundaries. The dislocation of boundaries and the recognition of difference—racial, ethnic, gender and sexual orientation—'circunscrevem este processo de remapeamento valorativo em um momento muito particularmente estadunidense que tende à absorção globalizante da diversidade de identidades' [circumscribe this process of valorative remapping at a very particular moment in the history of the United States that tends towards the globalizing absorption of the diversity of identities].[47]

On a par with university courses, the publishing market started to invest more and more in works of fiction, theory and criticism written by women. From then on, Clarice Lispector's presence on the international literary scene was not restricted exclusively to the fact that she was a Brazilian and Latin-American writer, as had been the case in the 1970s, but was principally due to the fact that she was a woman writer, which led to the even wider dissemination of her works.

Notes to Chapter 10

1. By this I mean all departments that include Lispector's work in their courses, such as Spanish Languages and Literatures, Romance Languages and Literatures, Comparative Literature. In North-American, as in British universities, Portuguese is normally part of the department of Spanish or Hispanic studies; the exception is Brown University in Providence, Rhode Island, which has a Department of Portuguese and Brazilian Studies.
2. Gerson Moura, *Tio Sam chega ao Brasil: A penetração cultural americana* (São Paulo: Brasiliense, 1985), 12.
3. Antonio Candido, 'Prefácio da segunda edição', *Formação da literatura brasileira*, 6th edn. (Belo Horizonte: Itatiaia, 1981), i. 15–18 at 18.
4. Antonio Candido, 'No raiar de Clarice Lispector', *Vários escritos* (São Paulo: Duas Cidades, 1970), 123–31 at 124.
5. Ibid., 125.
6. C. Harvey Gardiner, 'Samuel Putnam, Brazilianist', *Luso-Brazilian Review* 1/1 (1964), 103–14.
7. Fred P. Ellison, 'Author's preface', *Brazil's New Novel: Four Northeastern Masters* (Berkeley: University of California Press, 1954), pp. xi–xiii at xiii.
8. Gerald M. Moser, 'Contemporary Portuguese Scholarship in North America', *Luso-Brazilian Review* 1/1 (1964), 19–42.
9. Ibid.
10. Claire Varin, *Rencontres brésiliennes* (Quebec: Trois, 1987), 240.
11. Letter from Clarice Lispector to Pierre Lescure (Washington, 20 June 1954), Clarice Lispector Archive, Fundação Casa de Rui Barbosa, Rio de Janeiro (hereafter abbreviated CLA).
12. 'Temptation' appeared in *Américas* in March 1955. 'The Crime of the Mathematics Professor' was first published in *Odyssey Review* 1 (1961), 107–13, trans. William L. Grossman and Vasconcelos Cordeiro, and a second translation by William L. Grossman and José Roberto Vasconcelos appeared in *Modern Brazilian Short Stories* (Berkeley and Los Angeles: University of California Press, 1967), 146–51. 'Love', trans. Clarice Lispector and Standford Bradshaw, was published in *New Mexico Quarterly* 26 (1956–7), 358–68.
13. Letter from Roland Dickey to Clarice Lispector (Albuquerque, 8 Nov. 1956), CLA.
14. Sérgio Miceli, 'Condicionantes do investimento externo no Brasil', *A desilusão americana: Relações acadêmicas entre Brasil e Estados Unidos* (São Paulo: Editora Sumaré; Programa Nacional do Centenário da República e Bi-Centenário da Inconfidência Mineira—MCT/CNPq, 1990), 11–16.

15. 'The Cuban Revolution in 1959 was a determining factor in the whole reorientation of North America's foreign policy towards Latin America, beginning with the Alliance for Progress and continuing with the creation of a programme of individual grants for advanced research in the social sciences and the humanities (Brazil and Spanish America) and other initiatives that resulted in the creation of the Latin American Studies Association in 1966.' Ibid., 13.

16. Ibid., 57.

17. E-mail communication from Earl Fitz to Teresa Montero (Vanderbilt, 30 Nov. 2000).

18. Pierre Rivas, 'Paris como a capital literária da América Latina', *Literatura e história na América Latina*, ed. Lígia Chiappini and Flavio Aguiar (São Paulo: EDUSP, 1993), 99–114 at 101.

19. E-mail communication from Earl Fitz to Teresa Montero (Vanderbilt, 30 Nov. 2000).

20. Miceli, 'Condicionantes do investimento externo no Brasil', 14.

21. Earl E. Fitz, 'Ambigüidade e gênero: Estabelecendo a diferença entre a ficção escrita por mulheres no Brasil e na América Espanhola', *Entre resistir e identificar-se: Para uma teoria da prática narrativa brasileira de autoria feminina*, ed. Peggy Sharpe (Florianópolis: Editora Mulheres; Goiânia: Editora da UFG, 1997), 17–32 at 25.

22. Prior to *Gabriela*, Knopf had published only one other work by Amado, *Terras do sem fim*, trans. Samuel Putnam as *The Violent Land* in 1945. The translation had come about as a result of Blanche Knopf's travels in Latin America, which enabled her to put Amado (then living in exile in Argentina) in touch with the Knopf publishing house back in New York in 1942. This long period without publishing any of Amado's works was due 'ao fator inibidor do marcatismo' [to the inhibiting factor of the state of the market]: Laurence Hallewell, *O livro no Brasil* (São Paulo: T. A. Queiroz; EDUSP, 1990), 420, 424.

23. Ibid. Of all the commercial publishing houses that did publish Brazilian authors, such as Noonday or Farrar, Straus & Giroux, it was Alfred Knopf that invested in the largest number of Brazilian titles. Indeed, Naomi Lindstrom observes that 'Brazilian writers had been faring somewhat better in the English-language market, owing in part to the enthusiastic backing of Alfred A. Knopf': 'The Boom and its Antecedents, 1950–1970', *Twentieth Century Spanish American Fiction* (Austin: University of Texas Press, 1994), 140–96 at 140.

24. Hallewell, *O livro no Brasil*, 424.

25. Piers Armstrong, 'General reception in North American of Guimarães Rosa's translated works', 'João Guimarães Rosa, Jorge Amado and the International Reception of Brazilian Culture', Ph.D. thesis (University of California, Los Angeles, 1995), 132.

26. The other comparative-literature theses were Owen Kellerman, 'Estudios de la voz narrativa en el relato latino-americano' (Arizona State University, 1975); Anna Tavenner, 'Aspectos de conflicto y enajenamiento de la mujer en las novelas de Silvina Bulrich, Beatriz Guido y Clarice Lispector' (Texas Technological University, 1977); Maria Cristina Gauggel, 'El personaje feminino existencial en las novelas de Clarice Lispector y Julio Cortázar' (Louisiana State University, 1979). See respective entries in Diane Marting, *Clarice Lispector: A Bio-bibliography* (Westport, CT: Greenwood Press, 1993), 36, 275, 271.

27. Letter from Teresinha Alves Pereira to Clarice Lispector (Bloomington, 19 May 1972), CLA.
28. Interview with Earl Fitz by Teresa Montero (Vanderbilt, 8 July 1999).
29. Earl E. Fitz, 'Clarice Lispector: the Nature and Form of the Lyrical Novel', Ph.D. thesis (CUNY, 1977); 'Clarice Lispector and the Lyrical Novel: A Re-examination of *A maçã no escuro*', *Luso-Brazilian Review* 14/2 (1977), 153–60; 'The Leitmotif of Darkness in Seven Novels by Clarice Lispector', *Chasqui* 7/2 (1978), 18–28; 'Conflict and Resolution in the Novels of Clarice Lispector: A Structuralist Approach', *Prismal/Cabral* 3–4 (1979), 104–19; 'The New Latin American Novel: Studies in the Prose Fiction of Carlos Fuentes, Juan Carlos Onetti, José Lezama Lima e Clarice Lispector', *Inter-Muse: An Interdisciplinary Journal* 2 (1979), 17–27.
30. Fitz, 'Clarice Lispector and the Lyrical Novel', 153.
31. Fitz, 'Machado, Borges e Clarice'.
32. Interview with Elizabeth Lowe by Teresa Montero (Gainesville, 11 July 1999); Translations by Lowe: 'The Solution', *Fiction* 3 (1974), 24; 'Temptation', *Inter-Muse* 1 (1976), 91–2; 'Sofia's Disasters', *Review: Latin American Literature and Art* 24 (1979), 27–33.
33. Elizabeth Lowe, 'The Temple and the Tomb: The Urban Tradition in Brazilian Literature and the City in Contemporary Brazilian Narrative', Ph.D. thesis (CUNY, 1977); 'The Passion According to C.L.', *Review: Latin American Literature and Art* 24 (1979), 34–7.
34. Ibid.
35. *Family Ties* (Austin: University of Texas Press, 1972); *The Foreign Legion: Stories and Chronicles* (Manchester: Carcanet, 1986); *The Hour of the Star* (Manchester: Carcanet, 1986); *Near to the Wild Heart* (New York: New Directions, 1990): *Discovering the World* (Manchester: Carcanet, 1992); *The Beseiged City* (Manchester: Carcanet, 1997).
36. Patricia Bins, 'Patricia Bins talks to Giovanni Pontiero', trans. Margaret Martinez, in *The Translator's Dialogue: Giovanni Pontiero*, ed. Pilar Orero and Juan Sager (Philadelphia: John Benjamins North America, 1997), 165–72. This interview was first published in the literary supplement of *O Estado de São Paulo* (25 Aug. 1985).
37. Giovanni Pontiero, 'The Drama of Existence in *Laços de Família*'; Massaud Moisés, 'Clarice Lispector: Fiction and Cosmic Vision', trans. Sara McCabe, *Studies in Short Fiction* 8 (1971) (special issue: Contemporary Latin America), 256–67, 268–81.
38. Benedito Nunes, *O mundo de Clarice Lispector* (Manaus: Governo do Estado de Amazonas, 1966).
39. Gregory Rabassa, 'La nueva narrativa en el Brasil', *Nueva narrativa hispano-americana* 2/1 (1972), 145–8; 'Clarice Lispector', *The Encyclopedia of World Literature in the Twentieth Century*, iv (New York: Frederick Ungar and Lina Mainiero, 1975), 220–3; Fábio Lucas, *Contemporary Latin American Literature*, ed. Harvey Johnson and Phillip Taylor (Houston: University of Houston Press, 1973), 64–6.
40. Bella Jozef, 'Clarice Lispector: La transgresión como acto de libertad', *Revista Iberoamericana* 63/98–9 (1977), 225–31; 'Chronology: Clarice Lispector', trans. Elizabeth Lowe, *Review* 24 (1979), 24–6.

41. Part of 'The Passion according to G.H.', trans. Jack E. Tomlins, *The Borzoi Anthology of Latin American Literature: The Twentieth Century, from Borges and Paz to Guimarães Rosa and Donoso*, ed. Emir Rodriguez Monegal with Thomas Colchie (New York: Alfred Knopf, 1977), ii. 780–792. Fifteen short stories were translated and published in journals: three by Elizabeth Bishop (see n. 43 below); three by Elizabeth Lowe (see n. 32); seven by Alexis Levitin: 'Footsteps' and 'The Man who Appeared', *Shantih* 3/3 (1976); 'Better than to burn', *Latin American Literature Today*, ed. Anne Freemantle (New York: New American Library, 1977), 169–71; 'The Body', *The Literary Review* 21/4 (1978); 'The Way of the Cross', *Ohio Journal* 4/3 (1978); 'The Dead Man in the Sea at Urca', *Webster Review* 4/1 (1978); 'That's where I'm Going', *Webster Review* 4/2 (1978); and two by Giovanni Pontiero: 'The Buffalo', *Short Stories of the Americas* (South San Francisco: Compile-A-Text, 1974), 106–15; 'The Imitation of the Rose', *Contemporary Latin American Short Stories* (Greenwich, CT: Fawcett Premier, 1974), 316–37.

42. Letter from Elizabeth Bishop to Ilse and Kit Barker (Rio de Janeiro, 29 Oct. 1962), in *Uma arte: As cartas de Elizabeth Bishop* , trans. Paulo Henriques Britto (São Paulo: Companhia das Letras, 1995), 725. For some reason the letters I quote in this essay are not included in the original edition of Bishop's letters, selected by Robert Giroux.

43. Letter from Elizabeth Bishop to Robert Lowell (Rio de Janeiro, 8 Jan. 1963), ibid., 729. Although Bishop claimed to have translated five of Lispector's short stories, I have only found three: 'The Smallest Woman in the World', 'Marmosets' and 'A Chicken', *Kenyon Review* 26 (1964), 500–11. The first two stories were included in the anthology *The Eye of the Heart: Short Stories from Latin America*, ed. Barbara Howes (New York: Bobbs-Merrill Avon, 1973), 320–5, 326–8.

44. William Grossman, 'Acknowledgements', *Modern Brazilian Short Stories*, trans. William Grossman (Berkeley and Los Angeles: University of California Press, 1967).

45. George Yúdice, 'O multiculturalismo e novos critérios de valoração cultural', *Revista sociedade e estado* 9/1–2 (1994).

46. Ibid.

47. Ibid.

CHAPTER 11

Readers of Clarice, Who Are You?

Nádia Battella Gotlib

Over the last almost sixty years, the reception of Clarice Lispector's texts by Brazilian readers has been marked by many different phases and faces. The history of this body of critical work, this multiplicity of gazes, which today numbers thousands of critical works along with a similar quantity of oral testimonies, can be charted in terms of its exponential increase and a progressive diversification in theoretical and methodological approaches.[1] But there are certain ways of seeing Clarice that are common to the majority of readers, whether they are from the academic world or casual readers who read without any kind of professional responsibility. It is precisely this affinity among readers with diverse intentions from a variety of intellectual backgrounds that I aim to examine in this brief essay, in the hope of discovering some of the distinguishing marks of the experience of reading Clarice throughout the reception of her work in Brazil.

Setting out on such a journey implies perceiving how, from the earliest manifestations of critical interest at the beginning of the 1940s, Brazilian readers reacted to a narrative that departed considerably from the regionalist tradition of the 1930s,[2] with which they were more familiar, as well as from another more intimate type of novel—less widely known but available none the less, from the early 1930s onwards.[3] Against this background, Lispector's first novel, *Perto do coração selvagem*, elicited diverse reactions, but critics were in agreement in feeling that there was something different and new about it, which lay in its inventive handling of literary language, just as had been the case with the revolutionary Modernist works written in the 1920s.[4] But in terms of the literary scene in Brazil at the time, there were simply no narrative parameters within which this novel, whose technical proximity to the work of Joyce and Woolf was noticed by the earliest critics, could be situated.[5] It was not even possible to compare such writing with the equally innovative fiction of Guimarães Rosa, who had not quite made his debut yet. His first book of short stories, *Sagarana*, was to come out in 1946, just two years after *Perto do coração selvagem*.

Benedito Nunes, whose influential readings of Lispector's works since the 1960s have appeared at regular intervals, establishing fundamental themes in Lispector studies, has identified at least three phases of criticism. The first began with the publication of her first novel, when she became known to a small group of critics and writers. In fact, this group of readers was relatively small, since those who wrote critical appreciations came from no further afield than the outskirts of Rio de Janeiro, the city where the book was launched late in 1943.

The second phase started in 1960 with the publication of *Laços de família*, a collection of short stories that won over the academic readership and aroused their interest in the author's other works like *O lustre* (1946) and *A cidade sitiada* (1949) as well as the subsequent *A maçã no escuro* (1961). Some of the stories had already been published in an earlier volume entitled *Alguns contos*, which had been distributed on a very small scale.[6] But four of the stories from *Laços de família* had also already appeared in *Senhor* magazine in 1959. *Senhor* was a popular magazine with a wide circulation at the time, which became responsible for Clarice's works reaching a larger and more diverse audience.

The third phase, according to Nunes, began after Clarice's death, triggered by the particular nature of her last two books: *A hora da estrela* (1977) and *Um sopro de vida* (published posthumously in 1978). These novels enabled the reader, retrospectively almost, to discover certain motifs articulated throughout the writer's oeuvre in a singular process of creation centred on plumbing the depths of the psyche, which had began with her very first work.[7] Furthermore, Nunes considers that the perspective of introspection, as Lispector's last two works show well (emphasis original):

em vez de constituir um foco fixo, detido na exploração dos momentos de vida [...], o ponto de vista introspectivo [...] ofereceria o conduto para a *problematização das formas narrativas tradicionais* em geral e da posição do próprio narrador em suas relações com a linguagem e a realidade, *por meio de um jogo de identidade da ficcionista consigo mesma e com os seus personagens*—jogo aguçado até o paroxismo em *A paixão segundo G.H.*, que contém uma das chaves do desencadeamento desse processo.[8]

This quotation conveys with precision the central tenets around which Nunes's readings of Clarice Lispector have revolved and been refined over the years:[9] the power of language to demystify literature by dismantling the literary code itself. He considers that one of the fundamental ingredients is the game of identity, what he calls 'o naufrágio da introspecção' [the shipwreck of introspection], narrativized through the loss of 'personhood' and the dramatization of various *personae*.

This being the case, in *A hora da estrela*, 'a escritora se inventa ao inventar a personagem. Está diante dela como de si mesma. Em sua escritura errante, autodilacerada, repercute, secretamente e em permanência, a pergunta — *Eu que narro, quem sou?*, numa réplica ao *Cogito* de René Descartes ("Penso, logo sou")'[10] [The writer invents herself when she invents the character. She [the writer, Clarice] is in front of her [the character], as well as in front of herself. One question echoes secretly but constantly through her meandering, self-destructive writing: *I who narrate, who am I?*, in reply to René Descartes' *cogito* ('I think, therefore I am').] This predicament is still predominant in *Um sopro de vida*, in the permanent presence of the meta-novelistic triangular formation, which in this case unfolds into three separate characters (Clarice–She–He). All of them are Authors, but a structure is maintained whereby each reads and rewrites the other, and in which the novelist Clarice Lispector, according to Benedito Nunes, configures herself as a 'personagem de seus personagens, autora e leitora de seu próprio livro, que nele e através dele se recapitula'[11] [a character written by her characters, author and reader of her own book, who recapitulates herself in it and through it.]

But the question inspired by the Cartesian *cogito*, dismantled systematically by Lispector herself in the shape of characters who gradually become fragmented along the course of her texts, has further implications. The writer sets about destabilizing her role until it reaches out towards the reader, who becomes entangled in the process of the dramatizing experience, thus fuelling the game of interchangeable identities. As a result, it seems to me that Lispector's inventiveness in trying to entangle her reader in the well-laid trap of her text is that of shrewdly leading him to wonder, still inspired by her Cartesian anti-*cogito*: I, the reader, who am I?

It may be as a by-product of this aspect of her fiction—grounded in the disarticulation of all possible systems, where even the stability of the 'I' is under threat, through the very system of literary devices she uses—that Clarice's writing has the power to so disturb her readers. And to fuel the kind of criticism that has arisen in the post-modern era, examining the experiences of decentring from various theoretical and methodological viewpoints, including those of anthro-pological, psychoanalytical and feminist criticism to name just a few.

Nevertheless, although Lispector's critical fortune currently consists of abundant material, there still exists what I would call a certain discreet reserve on the part of the readers towards her work. I am not referring to the reader who reacts negatively to the text because he simply 'doesn't want' to read Clarice. I am referring to the reader who 'wants' to get closer to Clarice's texts, but encounters difficulties, which result in a complicated pattern of reactions: the reader 'wants' and 'doesn't want' at the same time. I am referring, then, to the reader who attempts to enter this territory, who finds obstacles there when he approaches the text and then finds himself in the situation of having either to abandon the undertaking or to arm himself with certain strategies, shielding himself when he tries to touch the text, as if it were difficult, or even impossible, to proceed in order to successfully reach the ultimate goal: understanding the work. What may be merely external controversy—between those who read and those who don't—becomes an internal controversy, dwelling within the twists and turns of the reading process. And this throws up questions: what is the reason behind such a posture? Could it be any different? Will any reader be able to free himself of the difficulties, or the strategies and reserve that I have referred to, when encountering this kind of writing?

In my opinion, this contentious scheme is part of Clarice Lispector's process of narrative construction and therefore one of the 'graphemes' scattered throughout her works. It exists as an element in the construction both of her narratives (in their images and structures), and of her biography (through her adoption of certain postures and behaviours, biographemes), thereby inviting a multiplicity of readings. It is present in all the various strands of Clarice's production: novellas, short stories, notes, *crônicas*, pieces for the women's pages of newspapers, interviews she made, interviews she gave, statements, memories, fragments, autobiographical texts, gestures, situations—establishing a multifaceted system of active voices intimately intertwined with explosions of signs both intra- and intertextually, like a minefield strewn with puzzling dismantlings.[12]

And nothing escapes from it, not even the reader, especially not the reader. For the dramatic situation is set up by a narrator who 'contaminates' the reader. The making and the reading of her work are constructed using these relationships between the voices—fusions, confusions, diffusions of 'I's—in both the intimate, personal sphere, and in the possible metaphorical developments that overflow into the institutional domain, involving the social experiences of the *personae* in the dramatic action.

Clarice Lispector herself, in a memorable interview given to Júlio Lerner for the TV programme 'Panorama especial', recorded in the studios of TV Cultura in São Paulo in February 1977,[13] describes her surprise at the disparity in behaviour of the readers of her works:

Lerner — De seus trabalhos qual aquele que você acredita que mais atinja o público jovem?

Clarice — Depende, depende inteiramente. Por exemplo, o meu livro *A paixão segundo G.H.*, um professor de português do d. Pedro II veio lá em casa e disse que leu quatro vezes o livro e não sabe do que se trata. No dia seguinte uma jovem de dezessete anos, universitária, disse que este livro é o livro de cabeceira dela. Quer dizer, não dá para entender...

Lerner — E isso aconteceu em relação a outros de seus trabalhos?

Clarice — Também em relação a outros de meus trabalhos, ou toca ou não toca... Suponho que não entender não é uma questão de inteligência e sim de sentir, de entrar em contato. Tanto que o professor de português e literatura, que deveria ser o mais apto a me entender, não me entendia... E a moça de dezessete anos lia e relia o livro. Parece que eu ganho na releitura, não é? O que é um alívio...[14]

These testimonies, which led the author to take into account two opposite reactions to her writing, are confirmed in a statement later in the same interview, where she puts herself in the role of reader of her own texts. When asked if she considers herself a popular writer, she replies that she is not and explains: 'Clarice — Me chamam até de hermética... Como é que eu posso ser popular sendo hermética? / Lerner — E como você vê esta observação que nós colocamos entre aspas: "hermética"? / Clarice — Eu me compreendo. De modo que não sou hermética para mim. Bom, tem um conto meu que não compreendo muito bem... / Lerner — Que conto? / Clarice — "O ovo e a galinha"' [Clarice—They even call me hermetic... How can I be popular if I'm hermetic? / Lerner—And what do you think about the observation that you are, let's put it in inverted commas, 'hermetic'? / Clarice—I understand myself. So I'm not hermetic as far as I'm concerned. Well, there is one of my stories that I don't really understand... / Lerner—Which one? / Clarice—'The Chicken and the Egg'.]

Curiously, when Lerner asks her, next, which of her wide range of works is her favourite, in other words, the one that she regards 'com maior carinho até hoje' [with the greatest affection so far], Clarice replies: "O ovo e a galinha', que é um mistério para mim' ['The Chicken and the Egg', which is a mystery to me].

This interview, in its sequence of visual images, also visually re-enacts the complex set of interactions that Clarice weaves into her fiction. It is the only 'live' documentary material of Clarice Lispector involving sound and images that exists. In her interventions, the author reiterates the disparity that she observed in her readers: the literature teacher and the young university student. But she does so not only by playing the role of reader of her own texts, claiming that she understands them, yet that she does not understand at least one of them, the very one that is her favourite... She also plays the game in the way in which she uses her body language, surprising her interviewer, bewitching him, and at the same time, making it difficult for him to do his job. The journalist confirms this, in a subsequent statement he made to accompany the transcription of the interview:

A entrevista avança. Seus olhos azuis-oceânicos revelam solidão e tristeza. Quero mergulhar, por vezes consigo... Clarice [...] se deixa agarrar mas logo escapa, e volta, e me pega, e me sugere o longe e o não-dizível, depois se cala... E quando nada mais espero, ela volta a falar...Faço uma antientrevista, pausas, silêncios, Clarice agora está fugindo para uma galáxia inabitada e inatingível, mas volta em seguida e, tolerante, suporta toda a minha limitação. [...] Acho que ela vai se levantar a qualquer instante e me dizer: 'Chega!' [...] Seu corpo exprime receios, ela me afasta mas de novo me atrai, suas pernas se cruzam e se descruzam sem parar e telegrafam que de repente ela poderá se levantar e partir.[15]

If an excerpt from the film shows discomfort and some degree of remoteness on the part of the interviewee, the interviewer's statement reveals that he feels similar emotions when encountering the text that constitutes the person-Clarice there in front of him, as if it were difficult for him to continue a dialogue that he insists on maintaining to its end, in spite of everything.

The interviewer seems to have been caught by his guest going down the 'wrong track', in other words, conducting an interview that comes apart as it is being made. It is the most difficult and uncomfortable track to follow, given the successive and contradictory surprises responsible for his uneasiness in front of this person who appears to be so close one minute and so distant the next, whom he does not really understand very well, but who 'moves' him deeply. Just as Clarice moves the interviewer, she also moves the viewer, who seems to be following the role previously played by the reporter, confronted with the contradictory signals that her image sends out.

This television interview, which shows the difficult dialogue between the writer and a reporter, can be read as another manifestation of a scene that occurs repeatedly in Lispector's works: the complicated interaction between two people. The reactions of the reporter, at once enchanted and uncomfortable, needing to make an effort not to sink amid the sea of provocations in which the interviewee swamps him during their conversation, constitute part of the perverse process that the author cultivates throughout her literary career. The combination of contradictory signals—inhibiting, yet surprising—are all part of one of her constant themes: seduction. This theme is present in her work from the very first short stories dating from the early 1940s to her last texts, the fragments written shortly before her death, some of which are collected in the volume entitled *A bela e a fera*.[16]

If all writing constitutes a form of seduction, since the text only exists through the reader who must be lured into and conquered by it, in Lispector's writing the theme is refined and used with the utmost sophistication. The texts that she produced at the very beginning of her career, when she was 20 years old, show a rare sensitivity to certain concerns, including seduction, which were to remain constants in her work. A simple relationship between two people becomes part of an intricate and complex process of asserting alterity, also manifest in the relationship between text and reader, where sadism and masochism are the main ingredients.

In one of the early short stories, for example, entitled 'História interrompida', which dates from October 1941, throughout the whole process of conquest, the main character tries to defeat her boyfriend (simultaneously her adversary), in the art of love (a war of emotions). She demands marriage, in other words the officialization of a loving union. But her boyfriend catches her out. He refuses to submit to an institutionalized relationship that would smother his strange, rebellious nature—'sua tendência para a destruição' [his tendency for destruction].[17] He anticipates the girl's attack by striking a blow himself, committing suicide. The story is thus interrupted 'com a brusquidão e a falta de lógica de uma bofetada em pleno rosto' [with the bluntness and lack of logic of a slap in the face]. The narrator states that she wrote the story 'para ver se conseguia achar uma resposta a perguntas que me torturam, de quando em quando, perturbando minha paz' [to see if I could manage to find an answer to questions that torture me from time to time, disturbing my peace].[18] If the language has a cathartic effect for her, it does not however manage to alleviate the disturbing effect of the final dilemmas, which linger on to haunt the reader.

This fusion of love and hate, like two sides of a coin, appears frequently in Clarice's narratives of love. The enchanted garden of Eden where the housewife Ana suddenly finds herself when out doing the shopping for a dinner party is also Hell, where she confronts the equally terrifying faces of eroticism and death. At the climax of this story, 'Amor',[19] Ana's sensations and perceptions are heightened upon losing the notion of linear temporality. She undergoes the paradoxical experience of finding herself in the imaginary space of both territories at the same time. The structural scheme of the story 'O búfalo', also from *Laços de família* (1960), conforms to a similar pattern. Here the spotlight falls on hate, while at the same time its opposite, love (in this case desperate love, as the character has been abandoned by the one she loves), hovers in the background. The character tries in vain to find a male creature who can serve as a pretext for her to let out her repressed anger, until her eyes meet those of a buffalo. Then the female human in the brown coat becomes animalized through the gaze of the male animal. In this meeting of gazes, a phallic dagger describes the inevitable murder of one of the partners in the duel of love. The female faints, submissive, her strength sapped away after stretching her instinct for wounded savagery to the limits and accepting the consequences.

And it is the duel—fought largely through the exchange of looks— that outlines the relationship or connection between the dominant and the dominated in the story 'Os desastres de Sofia', from *A legião estrangeira* (1964). But the body language is accompanied closely by elaborate metalanguage, which reaches one of the high points in Lispector's figurative invention in this text. A schoolgirl feels attracted to her teacher and wants to defy him. The teacher, demanding from the girl something that she does not give him, ends up being caught out. The essay that she writes for him is the vehicle of seduction.

The theme is reworked in the later story 'Felicidade clandestina', from the eponymous volume published in 1971. Here a book is the object of a desire that will be satisfied through the act of reading, but in order to better explore that desire, the moment of consummation is postponed. Firstly, the loan of the book is constantly denied by its owner, the rich, well-fed daughter of the bookseller, in a clearly sadistic manner. Later, other means are employed. Once the first obstacle is overcome, when the wealthy girl's mother decides to take charge of the situation and the book reaches the hands of its future reader, it is then the girl-reader who, emotionally involved with the object, delays the moment of reading in a markedly masochistic way.[20]

But maybe it is the story 'A quinta história', from *A legião estrangeira* (1964), that most effectively carries out the plan of creating a universe of cycles of destruction. By means of a recipe for 'how to kill' (cockroaches, in this case), the narrator also becomes embroiled in several cyclical murder plots, seen from different perspectives, but radiating from the same point: the main reason for the story, which is the recipe for how to attract/seduce/kill cockroaches. Each of the stories within the main text (all with different titles that take up the previous one and develop it, inventing an unusual kind of continuity) explores an alternative viewpoint: the 'I' who kills one minute, the object being killed the next, and then the act of killing itself, until the last, incomprehensible and unnameable quintessential, or 'quinta história' [fifth story], which 'seriam mil e uma, se mil e uma noites me dessem' [they could become a thousand and one, were I to be granted a thousand and one nights].[21]

Lispector's first, rather curious version of this particular configuration—that is, a text that revolves around the act of 'killing cockroaches'—had appeared in the women's section ('Entre mulheres' [Between women], written under the pseudonym Teresa Quadros) of the newspaper *Comício*. The short recipe was published on 8 August 1952, with the title 'Meio cômico, mas eficaz...' [A comical but effective means...], which gives a good idea of the narrator's tone, stirring together a narrative whose main ingredients were cheerful humour and a clever and subtle craftiness to accomplish her purpose: to attract female readers.[22] The writer, then working as a journalist, got the mixture just right, whipping up light texts of pure entertainment like recipes for *bolinhos de queijo* [little cheese scones] and dress patterns cut out from other magazines, but interspersing these texts with others like the recipe for how to kill cockroaches, where we can clearly see her bewitching yet lethal process of seduction, in this case the seduction of her 'caríssimas leitoras' [dearest readers].[23]

And the formula is repeated across the whole spectrum of her texts in which we find ourselves, like characters transfigured into cockroaches, being devoured or murdered or seduced by this voracious and determined witch-writer. Indeed, part of the recipe that appears in the story, recycled from the *Comício* article, lays out the instructions for the murder-plot: 'Deixe, todas as noites, nos lugares preferidos por esses bichinhos nojentos, a seguinte receita: açúcar, farinha e gesso, misturados em partes iguais. Essa iguaria atrai as baratas que a comerão radiantes. Passado algum tempo, insidiosamente o gesso endurecerá dentro das mesmas, o que lhes causará morte certa.' [Every night, leave the following recipe in the places these disgusting little bugs like best: sugar, flour and plaster, equal quantities, mixed together. This delicacy will attract the cockroaches who will eat it with gusto. After a while, the plaster will insidiously start to harden inside them, which will mean certain death.]

Apparently inoffensive texts, entertaining pieces appearing in the women's section of a newspaper, turn into deadly poison. It spreads to the readers' very hearts, provoking a radical transformation, leading them to experience the death of what is inside them. And all this happens 'insidiously', in a covert and a diabolically cruel way, for they are not even aware of what is happening until they are already infected with the poison (by reading the text), carefully prepared by the enchantress (the writer) as part of her double-edged plan (to lure in order to kill, transfigure or transform).

In this sinister light, *A paixão segundo G.H.* can be read as yet another rendition of the same process. The sculptress sets out to clean her apartment and finds, in the midst of what ought to be dirty, the sparkling clean universe of the other: Janair, her former maid. Janair is present both as a dark African queen and the cockroach that G.H. finds in the maid's room, the cockroach she faces right up to the final moment of their encounter, when she eats the disgusting white paste that oozes from its broken shell, in the crudeness of live pulsing matter. Throughout such texts, the construction of seduction implies a primitive act of devouring: the absorption of the previously hidden or masked other, in a kind of anthropological ritual. The passion for the image of the self reflected in that other returns suddenly, and is restored to it in a transfigured form.

Following the logic of this narrative of primal impulses, reading is also a way of devouring the other, of exhausting its potential to the maximum, reconstructing oneself through this murderous conquest. In other words, while on one level readers may be reduced to mere cockroaches, on another they simultaneously become endowed with the potential to rebuild themselves after every ritual massacre. This is why the kind of writing practised by Lispector is ambiguous, because of the effects that it provokes in a dead reader brought back to life. Such writing effectively dismantles both solid institutional frameworks and flimsy webs of futility. The writer uses stereotypes and revisits conventions and traditions only to pull them up by their roots. The (pseudo-)values implode into the very material, language, of which her language is made.

On the surface, the climate that governs the later contact between Clarice Lispector, columnist at the *Jornal do Brasil*, and her 'caríssimos leitores', who felt the need to communicate with her, by letter in the majority of cases, is rather different. Instead of the dense writing achieved in her fiction, through the originality of her images and a tense rhythm which allowed the reader no respite, in some of the *crônicas* we find a relaxed and congenial tone of conversation between people who are 'almost friends'. Nevertheless, Clarice used these apparently light and almost ingenuous texts to surprise her dear readers yet again.

I would like begin by analyzing some excerpts from *crônicas* that were not included in the volume *A descoberta do mundo*,[24] such as 'Um fato inusitado e um pedido' ['An unexpected fact and a request'], which appeared in the *Jornal do Brasil* on 21 October 1967, and where Clarice (reading her readers) commented on the letters which she had been sent. She transcribed some of them, like the one she received from a reader who addressed her in a ceremonious and respectful tone, using the almost official term 'Vossa Senhoria'. This assiduous reader, who read all through the night in his job as a night-watchman, asked her for more books, because he did not earn enough to continue such an expensive pastime. Her response was to contact the Instituto Nacional do Livro and ask them to send him some books.[25]

On 25 May 1968 she wrote about 'O carinho de um leitor' ['The kind thoughts of a reader'] who sent her a book, roses and a letter and mentioned her 'olhinhos de lua nova' [enticing new-moon eyes].[26] On 29 June of the same year, in the fragment entitled 'Correspondência' ['Correspondence'], she apologized to her readers:

'não respondi porque não sei onde guardei as cartas: vivo perdendo coisas dentro de casa mesmo. Mas um dia acho e respondo.' [I didn't reply because I don't know where I put your letters: I am always losing things, even at home. But one day I'll find them and reply.][27] In fact, replies to several readers appeared in another fragment published on the same day. The main body of the text consists of a series of replies in the form of brief, chatty notes, almost as if these reminders, recommendations and comments were her way of fulfilling a promise that could be postponed no longer.

The profile of these readers becomes clear in the replies that the columnist wrote to them. One example is an irritatingly nosy lady who commented upon Clarice's personal life, which was difficult at that time because her ex-husband had recently remarried. The columnist's reply addressed the lady rather curtly. Without mincing words, Lispector rejected the pity that her reader felt for her, denying that she had been suffering from depression as a result of her ex-husband's marriage. And furthermore, she told the lady that she could keep her pity 'para si própria, que não tem o que fazer' [for yourself, since you have nothing to do]. She stated that not only did she approve of her ex-husband's marriage, but also that she got along famously with him and his new wife. She refused to explain the real reason for her depression and she ended the crônica on a sarcastic note: 'Está bem, meu benzinho?' [Is that all right with you, my dear?]

Like a selection of faits-divers, the replies followed thick and fast within the crônica entitled 'Correspondência'. She recognized talent in a writer who sent her texts. She apologized for not having been able to attend shows to which she was invited. And she suggested to another reader: 'Não procure adivinhar quem eu sou: eu mesma até hoje não adivinhei' [Don't try to guess who I am: I myself haven't guessed yet]. She acknowledged compliments about the interviews that she was publishing during this period in the magazine Manchete. She turned down an invitation to dinner with a reader because 'seria o começo de um mau hábito' [it would lead me into bad habits].[28]

I should like to highlight one reader's comment about another crônica Clarice had published in the Jornal do Brasil on 9 March 1968, entitled 'O grito' [The scream]:[29] 'Gostei de seu grito, é um grito tão forte que despertei. Não sei se o entendi completamente, mas despertei.' [I liked your scream, it was a scream so loud that it woke me up. I don't know if I understood it completely, but it woke me up.] The action is repeated: the reader asserts that he was awoken, or 'moved', without knowing whether or not he fully understood the text.

The *crônica* he refers to is constructed as a collage of random subjects, just as the set of replies that we have been looking at was put together as a collage of replies to various readers and for various reasons. In 'O grito', however, one element triggers the action, or her act of writing: tiredness, or rather the scream of tiredness. This is the raw material of the text; a text that is a 'scream' and 'não se pode chamar nem de crônica nem de coluna nem de artigo' [cannot be classified as a *crônica*, column or article]. After this metafictional comment, the writer described details of her everyday life: her children, who brought her joy and pain, her godchildren, from whom she receives love. And she confessed her frustrations: 'O mundo falhou para mim, eu falhei para o mundo' [The world has failed me, and I have failed the world]. She also confessed to being tired of so many people liking her and preferring those who consider her unfriendly, with whom she feels an affinity because she too finds herself unpleasant. And she affirms at the end of the *crônica*: 'O que farei de mim? Quase nada. Não vou escrever mais livros. Porque se escrevesse diria minhas verdades tão duras que seriam difíceis de serem suportadas por mim e pelos outros. Há um limite de se ser. Já cheguei a esse limite.' [What am I to do with myself? Not much. I shall give up writing books. For if I write any more, I shall say such harsh things that they will deeply upset me and others. There is a limit to being oneself. And I have reached that limit.]

In fact, in this *crônica* Clarice writes about what she asserts she will not touch upon again in her books: the truths that are too hard for her and for others to bear. And which woke up one of her readers, even though he was not quite sure what was going on. All this is done in her own special way: starting out from these apparently trivial and almost ingenuous texts, Clarice Lispector tries to surprise the other, who cannot escape her fictional manipulations even here, eventually pushing her 'dear' readers to experience limits that become all but unbearable. In other words, in the pages of the *Jornal do Brasil* she stirs sugary sweet entertainment together with poisonous plaster (which is easy to confuse with sugar) to create a concoction to attract and destroy her reader from the inside out.

In the face of such dramatic circumstances, even though they may feel the lure of the object-text, who can blame the readers who resort to strategies of evasion to try to protect themselves from such dangers?

It remains to be seen whether or not these 'caríssimos leitores' really did exist, whether or not Lispector did receive letters, books, roses and spiteful comments, whether or not this was another of her fictions, written for her Saturday readers...

Be this as it may, all readers of Clarice will either have already been through the processes I have described, or may one day have to undergo the enchanted sacrifice of letting themselves be caught out by such a reading, carried to the extremes of the process, letting it consume them totally in the minefield of the interview, the story, the *crônica*, the women's section or any other text by Clarice where the lethal poison of the well-crafted literary invention has spread. The reader, barely surviving, discovers himself culturally denuded, in a hazardous state of not-knowing, close to his own savage perception, in an advanced stage of another 'reader-being', diluted in his own lack of personhood, committing suicide through his reading. And predisposed, in this way, to a beneficial reinvention of himself.

Notes to Chapter 11

1. A look at the bibliographies that list critical works about Clarice Lispector are proof of this diversity. In 1991, Glória Maria Cordovani collected almost 1,220 texts on Lispector's work for her Master's thesis 'Clarice Lispector: Esboço de uma bibliografia', (São Paulo, 1991), building upon important references from the bibliographic work previously done by Earl E. Fitz. For a more recent bibliography, see Diane E. Marting (ed.), *Clarice Lispector: A Bio-Bibliography* (Westport, CT: Greenwood Press, 1993).

2. The regionalist writing of the 1930s is important in terms of its quantity and also of its quality, including key texts in the history of Brazilian literature such as *O quinze* (1930) by Rachel de Queiroz and *Vidas secas* (1938) by Graciliano Ramos. Both these authors highlight the problems of the drought-struck *sertão* area in the North-East of Brazil, a theme which was to be reworked by Lispector in *A hora da estrela*.

3. Here I am referring to the works of e.g. Lúcio Cardoso and Otávio de Faria, who began to produce novels in the late 1930s. Clarice was actually friends with both of them in the 1940s and corresponded with them after moving to Italy with her diplomat husband.

4. Antonio Candido, 'Língua, pensamento, literatura', *Folha da manhã* (25 June 1944); and 'Perto do coração selvagem', *Folha da manhã* (16 July 1944), repr. with alterations as 'No raiar de Clarice Lispector', *Vários escritos* (São Paulo: Duas Cidades, 1970), 123–31.

5. Cf. Álvaro Lins, 'Romance lírico', *Correio da manhã* (11 Feb. 1944), repr. as 'A experiência incompleta', *Os mortos de sobrecasaca: Ensaios e estudos (1940–1960)* (Rio de Janeiro: Civilização Brasileira, 1963), 186–91 at 187–8.

6. *Alguns contos* (Rio de Janeiro: Ministério de Educação e Saúde/Serviço de Documentação, 1952).

7. Benedito Nunes, 'Clarice Lispector ou o naufrágio da introspecção', *Colóquio-Letras* 70 (1970), 13–14. Nunes later included this essay in *O drama da linguagem: Uma leitura de Clarice Lispector* (São Paulo: Ática, 1989) as 'O jogo da identidade', leaving out the first part.

8. 'Rather than constituting a fixed focus, concentrating on the exploration of moments in one's life, the introspective point of view could offer the way towards *the problematization of traditional narrative forms* in general and the position of the narrator himself in his relationships with language and reality, *by means of a game of identity that the writer plays with himself and his characters*—a game stretched to paroxysm in *A paixão segundo G.H.*, which contains one of the keys to the unravelling of this process.' Nunes, 'Clarice Lispector ou o naufrágio da introspecção', 14.

9. I am referring to the critical essays on Clarice Lispector written by Nunes during the 1960s, which were first published in *O mundo de Clarice Lispector* (Manaus: Ed. do Governo do Estado do Amazonas, 1966) and a second publication in Part II, 'O mundo imaginário de Clarice Lispector', which appears in *O dorso do tigre* (São Paulo: Perspectiva, 1970). Next came the essays written in 1972 and collected in *Leitura de Clarice Lispector* (São Paulo: Quíron, 1973), later repr. as *O drama da linguagem*, with the addition of the two last chapters, 'O improviso ficcional' and 'O jogo da identidade'.

10. Nunes, 'O improviso ficcional', *O drama da linguagem*, 156.

11. Nunes, 'O jogo da identidade', ibid., 169.

12. For more on the 'biographemes', see my biography of Lispector, *Clarice: Uma vida que se conta* (São Paulo: Ática, 1995; currently in its 5th edn.).

13. The programme only went on air after Lispector's death, to honour a request the author made of the journalist Júlio Lerner while the programme was being recorded at TV Cultura. The interview was published with an introductory text by Lerner as 'A última entrevista de Clarice Lispector', *Shalom* 296 (1992), 62–9.

14. 'Lerner—Which of your works do you believe has touched the young audience? / Clarice—That depends, it depends entirely. For example, about my book *A paixão segundo G.H.*, a Portuguese teacher at Dom Pedro II school came to my house and said that he has read the book four times and he doesn't know what it's about. The next day a 17-year-old girl, a university student, said that that book is the one she always keeps by her bed. I mean, there is no way of explaining it... / Lerner—And has that happened with any of your other works? / Clarice—It has, with other works, either they move you or they don't... I suppose that not understanding is not a question of intelligence but one of feeling, of entering into contact. So much so that the Portuguese teacher, who teaches language and literature, who should have been the one who was better equipped to understand me, couldn't... And the 17-year-old read and reread the book. It looks like I get better with rereadings, doesn't it? Which is a relief...'

15. 'The interview advances. Her ocean-blue eyes reveal loneliness and sadness. Sometimes I want to dive with you... Clarice lets herself be caught, then escapes, and comes back and grabs me, and suggests to me the far-off and the unsayable, then she is silent... And when I expect nothing more, she starts talking again... I'm doing an anti-interview, pauses, silences, now Clarice is fleeing to an uninhabited, unattainable galaxy, but she comes back right away and, tolerant, bears with all my limitations. I think she is going to stand up at any moment and

say to me 'That's enough!' Her body expresses reserve, she pushes me away then attracts me again, her legs cross and uncross again and again and telegraph that suddenly she can get up and go.'

16. *A bela e a fera*, 2nd edn. (Rio de Janeiro: Nova Fronteira, 1979).
17. Ibid., 15.
18. Ibid., 21.
19. This story was included in the small volume *Alguns contos* (1952) and *Laços de família* (1960).
20. On the theme of reading in the works of Clarice Lispector, see Ricardo Iannace, *A leitora Clarice Lispector* (São Paulo: Edusp, 2001).
21. *A legião estrangeira* (Rio de Janeiro: Editora do Autor, 1964), 91; *The Foreign Legion: Stories and Chronicles*, trans. Giovanni Pontiero (Manchester: Carcanet, 1986), 75.
22. These works of journalism have been analyzed by Aparecida Maria Nunes in two academic studies forthcoming in 2002, to be published in São Paulo by SENAC.
23. Cf. 'A conversa "entre mulheres" and "A dupla feiticeira", Nádia Battella Gotlib, *Clarice: Uma vida que se conta*, 278–83.
24. 120 *crônicas* were left out of *A descoberta do mundo* according to the research done by Célia Maria Ranzolin, who carefully checked and compared the texts published in the newspaper and those that appear in the book in her Master's thesis, 'Clarice Lispector: Cronista no *Jornal do Brasil* (1967–1973)' (Universidade Federal de Santa Caterina, 1985).
25. Ibid., 34–5.
26. Ibid., 38.
27. Ibid., 38–9.
28. Ibid., 39–40.
29. *A descoberta do mundo* (Rio de Janeiro: Nova Fronteira, 1984), 102; *Discovering the World*, trans. Giovanni Pontiero (Carcanet: Manchester, 1992), 110.

CHAPTER 12

The Invention of a
Non-Modern World

William Paulson

Nuestra verdad posible tiene que ser *invención...* [Our possible
truth has to be *invention...*]
JULIO CORTÁZAR, *Rayuela*

Cuidado que a Natureza pensa. [Careful, Nature thinks.]
CLARICE LISPECTOR, *Um sopro de vida*

What does a writer who died twenty-five years ago have to say to the
new century?

The French philosopher Michel Serres claims that literature often
anticipates the work and the discoveries of tomorrow's sciences—that
writers invent articulations that only later will scientists come to
construct through their experimental dialogue with things and
creatures. Lispector, I will argue, is one such anticipatory and inventive
writer. What she discovered, or at least what her texts were working
toward, however, was not a future development in science *per se*, but a
future state of cultural attempts to come to terms with a world largely
revealed by, and increasingly constructed by, natural science. Or, to put
it another way, Lispector was inventing a way of living with the things
and creatures of the world that neither reduces them to their cultural
meanings and interests, nor claims that they transcend cultures and
communities. A way of coming to terms with a world both cultural
and natural, one in which these very categories are not as solid as they
long have seemed.

More specifically, I intend to explore and interrogate the convergence between Lispector's writings and an important philosophical current of the last decade and the beginning of the new century: work in the social and philosophical study of science as cultural practice that suggests that science, far from disenchanting the world and inaugurating modernity by separating nature and culture, instead weaves them ever more intimately together. Rather than saying that we live in a combination of nature and society, writes Bruno Latour, the best-known exponent of this kind of 'science studies', we should say that we live in a *collective of humans and nonhumans*, a world of multiple differences and continuities rather than of great divides. For Latour, this intrication shows that 'we have never been modern': that what are often called modernity and post-modernity are complex but not ontologically differentiated versions of a *non-modern* world that we can never have left behind. Living in such a world requires the invention of a politics—a *cosmopolitics,* in the Belgian philosopher Isabelle Stengers's formulation—enlarged to include nonhumans: the objects, both found and made, and the creatures that act alongside human actors so as to form our collectives.

Latour's non-modern perspective calls into question the categories of subject and object, society and nature: these are not fundamental realities that engage in a dialectic in which they may become synthesized, but are instead the outcomes of the work of becoming modern: it takes a lot of natural science to come up with a non-social nature, a lot of social science to separate out a notion of society without things and techniques, a lot of aesthetic theory and art-world talk, one might add, to constitute the aesthetic as an autonomous category. So to read with Latour, or to attempt a 'non-modern' reading, is to try to understand what texts have to say and how they work if we no longer consider such categories and binaries as fundamental or inevitable.

What first led me to consider Lispector as an inventor of non-modernity was a structural parallel between two sentences, one in Latour's *We Have Never Been Modern,* the other in Lispector's short text 'Tanta mansidão'. Latour, first: 'For its own good, the modern world can no longer extend itself without becoming once again what it has never ceased to be in practice—that is, a non-modern world like all the others.'[1] And now Lispector: 'Não tivesse eu, logo depois de nascer, tomado involuntária e forçadamente o caminho que tomei — e teria sido sempre o que realmente estou sendo: uma camponesa que está num campo onde chove.' [If, straight after I was born, I hadn't taken, involuntarily, by compulsion, the road I took—I would have always been what in fact I really am being: a country girl in a field where it is raining.][2] To be sure, much is different in these sentences; what they crucially have in common is the recognition that a world or a person has remained in a condition thought to have been left behind: that of being a world that has never modernized or a peasant out in the elements. And in both cases, this has happened despite and at the same time as the taking of a developmental path. Such a path is explicit in Lispector's sentence and implicit in Latour's, since the modern world is said to have become modern by developing in specific ways that other societies, which modernity tolerantly relegates to the status of premodern, have not. In both cases, the path has been toward an exceptional destiny, and the retrospective insight is that one never ceased to be something fundamental and common. Lispector evokes the feeling of belonging to the world outside of windows, outside of cities, outside of class privileges: of still being part of a fundamental and material mode of life, of never having really left it, even while looking out at it from a window. Of course the narrator of this text and Lori in *Uma aprendizagem ou o livro dos prazeres* have taken the other path and become something else, but they still are what they always would have been; that 'something else' is not a substitution, as modern stories of development and progress would have it, but an addition.

   This sentence is not the only example of this temporal configuration in Lispector's writing. At the beginning of the third chapter of *A paixão segundo G.H.*, for example, G.H. states that she likes tidying up, making order (*arrumar*); in fact, it is her 'única vocação verdadeira' [only true calling].[3] But her material well-being and social position have taken her away from this vocation (PGH 29): 'não pertencesse eu por dinheiro e por cultura à classe a que pertenço, e teria normalmente tido o emprego de arrumadeira numa grande casa de ricos' [if I hadn't belonged to the class that I do for reasons of both money and culture, I would normally have had a domestic's job tidying up in a great big house belonging to someone rich]. Confronting the maid's task and the maid's room, G.H. realizes that she cannot go on living in her comfortable, middle-class, artistic world: arguably a *modern* world in which the natural and the cultural have been successfully separated, and in which humans become free by progressively replacing natural givens by a humanly constructed environment.

Such a rejection of the modern is often called *postmodern*. But to do so is to assume that we transformed and disenchanted the world and then became disenchanted with its disenchantment, thereby casting ourselves into a limbo of irony and simulacra. What Latour suggests, in contrast, based on the lessons of anthropologists who have studied science, is that since not even science separated nature and culture absolutely, modernity—in the strongest philosophical sense, at any rate—can never have happened. The literate, introspective, indoor subject has never become essentially different from the peasant woman in a field; the well-off artist still feels the call to tidy up. As Lispector's formulations suggest, this is not a negation of a negation but a fundamental continuity.

Lispector at times states this contrast between double negation and affirmative continuity with great conceptual clarity. Consider this passage, also from *A paixão* (65–6):

certamente o que me havia salvo até aquele momento da vida sentimentizada de que eu vivia, é que o inhumano é o melhor nosso, é a coisa, a parte coisa da gente. Só por isso é que, como pessoa falsa, eu não havia até então soçobrado sob a construção sentimentária e utilitária: meus sentimentos humanos eram utilitários, mas eu não tinha soçobrado porque a parte coisa, matéria de Deus, era forte demais e esperava para me reivindicar. O grande castigo neutro da vida geral é que ela de repente pode solapar uma vida; se não lhe for dada a força dela mesma, então ela rebenta como um dique rebenta — e vem pura, sem mistura nenhuma: puramente neutra. Aí estava o grande perigo: quando essa parte neutra de coisa não embebe uma vida pessoal, a vida vem toda puramente neutra.[4]

Once again, a modern, seemingly purified condition ('a construção sentimentária e utilitária') is revealed to have never really come into its own, but instead to have been always accompanied by its supposed opposite. Continuity and mixture with animality and thingness are described as entirely positive, the better and saving part of a person; what is destructive and dehumanizing is the negation of their negation, the return of a repressed corporeality that explodes and dominates after having been excluded from participation. There is, in other words, a mode of integrative continuity between matter and meaning, but there is also the possibility of losing this continuity in a dialectic of extremes.

Lispector's works have a thematic as well as conceptual affinity for non-modern collectives of humans and nonhumans. Scientific and technological references and metaphors are frequent in her writing, though they are rarely as prominent as at the beginning of *A hora da estrela*: 'Tudo no mundo começou com um sim. Uma molécula disse sim a outra molécula e nasceu a vida.' [Everything in the world began with a yes. One molecule said yes to another molecule and life was born.][5] This statement could be described as extravagantly anthropomorphic, but if 'said yes' is read figuratively, it could imply an extension of the agency of the subject into the domain of things, or a sense that information ('a difference that makes a difference', as Gregory Bateson defined it)[6] is in fact present in many processes that we think of as primarily material rather than symbolic. The beginning of *A hora* is characteristic of Lispector's evocations of the processes and objects of science and technology, in that she often describes them as comparable to or compatible with rather than opposed to the world of human actors and actions. The 'Autor' in *Um sopro de vida* speculatively compares his character Ângela to an electronic computer, a test-tube baby or—more archaically—a machine of springs and screws.[7]

Science is also crucially present in *A paixão segundo G.H.* In escaping from, or at least testing the boundaries of, a civilization that suffuses the world with human meaning, G.H. sees herself as an unauthorized, clandestine, female version of the scientist or priest, two figures whose specialized function it is to be emissaries to the infra-human or supra-human worlds (59). The comparison to the priest surely seems more in resonance with the novel as a whole, with its extensive echoes of both Christ's Passion and the Black Mass of a witches' sabbath. Yet the comparison to the scientist is in some ways even more important, given that, in the modern, secular world in which G.H. thought she lived, science is more influential than the Church in defining the parameters of reality and in producing knowledge in which people can be compelled to believe. She calls the room she has entered a 'laboratório de inferno' [hellish laboratory] (PGH 55).

Of course G.H. is no more a scientist than a priest; what she tries to tell her reader is what it feels like for a non-scientist to encounter the non-human world as deeply as a scientist does, and yet in an experiential rather than an experimental way, with no protocols or instruments to protect her. This itself is a refusal of modernity's nature/culture divide: what if the material world that we expect science to be surprised by, and to tell about, were suddenly something we had to live with, something that interrupts our sense of living in a social and cultural world? Of course we have always been living in it, since we could never have stopped doing so, but that is something rarely recognized or acknowledged.

The title character G.H. resorts to descriptive figures of material transformations in describing an experience of unknown character. She feels compelled to talk about an experience that falls outside normal perception and thought, a departure from the safe high ground of human categories. All that can safely be said about the putative experience is its lack of human form, and so to tell about it G.H. tries to abandon herself to a self-organizing process of indeterminate outcome (PGH 10–11):

Quem sabe me aconteceu apenas uma lenta e grande dissolução? E que minha luta contra essa disintegração está sendo esta: a de tentar agora dar-lhe uma forma? [...] que pelo menos eu tenha a coragem de deixar que essa forma se forme sozinha como uma crosta que por si mesma endurece, a nebulosa de fogo que se esfria em terra.[8]

G.H. also uses material communications devices and the sounds of language to describe metaphorically her project of telling and writing (PGH 18): 'Os sinais de telégrafo. O mundo eriçado de antenas, e eu captando o sinal. Só poderei fazer a transcrição fonética.' [The telegraph signals. The world bristling with antennas, and me receiving the signal. I'll be able to do only a phonetic transcription.] Such figures place her cognitive relation to the world on the cusp or frontier of matter and information, of objects and meanings.

The novel contains multiple images and allegories of a renunciation of human words and thought in favour of inhuman forms and processes. Through these rhetorical figures, the reader is invited to experience how such a giving up of significant marks of difference might proceed. The central figure is that of narrowing intervals and dilution of contrasts; its most obvious and striking example is the relation between the names of the author and the narrator. A prefatory note 'a possíveis leitores' [to potential readers] is signed not Clarice Lispector, but C.L. This reduction to initials is already a step toward reduced differentiation, and it invites comparison of the author to the narrator, identified only by her initials. If we look at the set of letters in the alphabet delimited by C and L, and then move inward from each end, we reach G and H, the minimal interval at the centre of the set with which we began:

C d e f G H i j k L

G.H. is a less differentiated version of C.L., the name under which the writing of C.L. can seek the neutral and the silent.

The encounter with the cockroach is a slow abandonment of taste for insipidity. Staring into the insect's eyes, G.H. recalls the eyes of a former lover, the salt of his tears that she once tasted. Yet salt, she realizes, is a *human* taste. The eyes of the cockroach can only be insipid; its flesh cannot recall the most expressive of human tissues or fluids, tears, but only the most neutral: blood, semen, milk, placenta, protoplasm (PGH 82): 'E seus olhos eram insossos, não salgados como eu quereria: sal seria o sentimento e a palavra e o gosto.' [And its eyes were tasteless, not salty as I would have liked them to be: salt would be the feeling, and the word, and the taste.] Like the replacement of C.L. by G.H., the giving up of salt for insipidity is part of a general narrowing of intervals and differences (PGH 94): 'Vou agora te contar como entrei no inexpressivo [...] naquilo que existe entre o número um e o número dois, de como vi a linha de mistério e fogo, e que é linha sub-reptícia. Entre duas notas de música existe uma nota, entre dois fatos existe um fato... existe um sentir que é entre o sentir...' [Now I'm going to tell you about how I went into the inexpressive, into what exists between the number one and the number two, about how I saw the mysterious, fiery line, about how it is a surreptitious line. Between two musical notes, another note exists; between two facts another fact exists... a way of feeling exists between feeling...] This reduction of intervals, this exploration of the in-between, appears to be a central strategy of C.L./G.H. for moving from human language with its sharp differentiations towards the more insipid variation and less difference-making differences found among things.

The many references to saltiness and insipidity culminate in a statement about language (PGH 156): 'Falar com as coisas, é mudo. Eu sei que isso te soa triste, e a mim também, pois ando viciada pelo condimento da palavra.' [Speaking to things is mute. I know that that sounds sad to you, and to me as well, for I am still addicted ·to the condiment of the word.] Like salt, words heighten and sharpen variety into differences and oppositions. Through language, humans live in vast systems of organized differences, an environment constantly producing information, distinctions, differentiations. The cockroach with its saltless eyes makes do with less, being 'sem nome de dor ou de amor. Sua única diferenciação de vida é que ela devia ser macho ou fêmea' [without love or pain to its name. Its only differentiation in life is that it has to be either male or female] (PGH 89).

Through G.H., Lispector never claims to abolish differentiation so as to arrive at pure presence; she merely reduces it, narrows the intervals, shows us differences less articulated and complex than those of human language. The universe is organized matter, information through and through. Seeking contact with what is outside of culture and humanity does not require a mysterious leap outside language or a transcendence of the semiotic; instead it requires the patient elaboration and extension of new networks of differences. This is arguably one of the strongest instances of Lispector's invention of a world comparable to that of scientific research as understood by today's science studies.[9]

This comparability does not exclude the social and temporal dimensions of *A paixão*. For Latour, the claim that modern science has objective access to nature, or that nature and culture can be cleanly separated, underwrites two disturbing political myths: that of Western superiority (on the basis of science) and that of objective knowledge of nature as an antidote to the subjective passions of the *demos* and thus to mob rule. Lispector does not make a conceptual argument of this kind, but G.H.'s loss of subjective boundaries and her encounter with a world simultaneously human and nonhuman have strong social implications. She can be taken to be a representative figure not only of literary and artistic culture, but more generally of the service-sector or 'new class' bourgeoisie: she lives her life primarily in the symbolic and social orders. Her life situation appears to be a typical end-product of a process of social and economic modernization. Her discovery that she herself and her experience are what we can now call non-modern thus would appear to apply to the social modernity she embodies. In her Passion, she will encounter not only a cockroach, the most concentrated symbol of her belonging to a materiality she had once ignored or rejected as unclean and now must learn to accept, but also human subordinates (her former maid, Janair), practical infrastructure (the back of her apartment building), and the time of geological and human evolution as well as that of human history and her own biography. The sight of the *barata* brings back visions of the bedbugs of her childhood poverty; relating this episode, she notes (PGH 44): 'A lembrança de minha pobreza em criança, com percevejos, goteiras, baratas e ratos, era de como um meu passado pré-histórico, eu já havia vivido com os primeiros bichos da terra' [The memory of my childhood poverty, with bedbugs, leaky roofs, cockroaches and mice was like a version of my prehistoric past;

I had already lived alongside the first creatures on earth]. Her fully humanized, socialized and economically privileged life turns out to be inseparable from its economic, material and animal others. Indeed, the present moment of her life and experience reveals itself to be not the most advanced moment of history but instead to be structured by many other times. G.H. stops experiencing a coherent present that has put the past behind it; instead, her narrative is filled with moments in which she identifies her own existence with different scales of historical, archaeological, and geological time: 'Há dois séculos que não vou' (PGH 124); 'há quinze séculos eu não lutava' (49); 'Há três mil anos desvairei-me' (18); 'O mesmo que no segundo milênio antes de Cristo' (102) [I have not been for two centuries ... for fifteen centuries I hadn't fought ... Three thousand years ago I went mad ... Just like what happened in the second millennium before Christ]. The present of human history and culture thus seems but a coincidental moment in a nested concatenation of self-similar structures and time-frames.

I have focused on *A paixão segundo G.H.* both because of its centrality in the canon of Lispector's works and because it is an exemplary case of the literary invention and exploration of a non-modern, human/nonhuman collective. But it is by no means unique. An equally pertinent instance of Lispector's non-modern inventiveness is provided by the sustained treatment of objects (and relations with them) in the first part of *Um sopro de vida*'s 'Livro de Ângela'. The character Ângela's fictional creator, the fictional (and male) 'Autor', describes and criticizes her plan to write a novel about things and objects; meanwhile, Ângela's own writings appear to be sketches or preliminary commentaries for this possible work. In these fragments, things become quasi-humanly active, and the materiality of human beings makes them describable as things (SV 102, 106):

a vida [...] é uma trágica ópera em que num balé fantástico se cruzam ovos, relógios, telefones, patinadores de gelo e o retrato de um desconhecido morto no ano de 1920.[10]

Eu sou um objeto que vê outros objetos. Uns são meus irmãos e outros inimigos. Há também objeto que não diz nada. Eu sou um objeto que me sirvo de outros objetos, que os usufrui ou os rejeita.[11]

The 'Autor', to be sure, accuses Ângela of 'humanizing' things, of being caught between contradictory desires to observe things in their naked thingness and to lend them human qualities; he also claims that she throws around fashionable words and is downright crazy. But these characteristically 'modern' accusations are, of course, but one voice in the text, and one that is obviously struggling to control (or perhaps accept) Ângela's mobility. Even if the 'Autor', like Ângela, is in some sense a projection of aspects or possibilities of Lispector herself, there is no reason to give him the last word when he frets that his character is crazy to warn that nature thinks. Much of the power of Lispector's works comes from her on the one hand having the intuition that there are mind-like processes in nonhuman nature and on the other hand acknowledging that to say and think such things can only amount to craziness within most 'normal' intellectual perspectives of her era.

The kind of reading proposed here runs the risk of anachronistically enrolling Lispector in an intellectual cause of our own time, one she might well have neither understood nor approved of. One recently popular way of getting around such a risk would be to recall that what matters are not Lispector's inaccessible thoughts or wishes but simply her texts, and that the meaning of those texts should rightfully be decided by today's interpretive communities. That is not, however, an appropriate argument in this case, because such textualism and constructionism is itself called into question by the 'science studies' perspective with which Lispector's work seems to have affinities. By what right does one assume a position of superiority that reduces the statements of others to impersonal cultural or textual processes? The Belgian philosopher of science Isabelle Stengers has laid down the provocative challenge of what she calls 'overcoming tolerance', of ceasing to suppose that I or we have *knowledge* while you or they have only *beliefs*: beliefs that we shall then tolerate out of our condescending liberality. In her view, far too many of the human sciences are predicated on reducing those they study to holders of belief, worthy of interest and tolerance but not of the respect accorded to one's peers in the making of knowledge. And she is not just questioning the tactics of empirical social scientists armed with questionnaires. In a remark that cuts close to home for many of us, she writes: 'what would be implied and required by the ethical challenge that, in dealing with people, and even with dead or absent authors, we should be able to present ourselves to them, to explain directly how we intend to deal with them, and the reasons why they should accept that we do so?'[12]

Stengers's approach to the ethics, validity, and political legitimacy of knowledge in the human sciences has a literary parallel in Doris

Sommer's recent *Proceed with Caution, when Engaged by Minority Writing in the Americas*. Sommer's basic point is that texts sometimes resist our reading and appropriation of them, not in the deconstructive sense of having the absences and deferrals characteristic of textuality rather than the plenitude allegedly borne by consciousness, but rather in the social sense in which members of minority or communities often speak among themselves in ways that exclude or confuse majoritarian listeners. Arguing from this insight, she wonders—in a formulation similar to the question from Stengers quoted above—whether 'we should hesitate before dismissing the ghost of the admittedly absent author'.[13]

In the spirit of Sommer's and Stengers's work, it is important to consider whether to speak of Lispector's 'non-modernity' is to produce badly-formed knowledge or to treat Lispector's textual delegates with a lack of collegiality or consideration. It is nevertheless right not to worry about 'what the author would have said', since by publishing her works Lispector accepted making them part of future cultural processes that she could neither master nor imagine. The challenge is instead to invent something like political relations of respect with the text, both accepting its textuality and yet acknowledging that it is the delegate of a person with a mind, and thus that it participates in mind-like powers on a par with our own. The problem cannot be completely solved, because there are asymmetries: Clarice Lispector is dead, and in any case the textual delegates that she sent out in the world to encounter us cannot respond actively to what we do with them.

It is thus important to acknowledge differences and resistances even as we look for similarities. The field of science studies, after all, is not concerned with intensely personal and corporeal encounters with the nonhuman. Nor do its practitioners believe in the pure inhumanity of things: forms of matter revealed by science are always part of the human world, because only through the human activity of science can they come to our attention and thus become part of the collectives of humans and nonhumans in which we live. Science studies are concerned with the ways in which scientific knowledge is made; Lispector and her characters are more concerned with how one lives in the world than with how one knows it, though clearly living and knowing are connected. Hence the psychologically intense, even searing character of texts such as *A paixão* and *Um sopro de vida*, or certain similarly intense (if more benign) moments of *Uma aprendizagem* and *Água viva*.

More important is the need to acknowledge that Lispector's approach to the relation of human to nonhuman is by no means always as monistic or as graduated as in the passages I have chosen to discuss here. There is also considerable evidence of dualism and polarization in her texts. Much of *A paixão* presents the encounter of human subject with matter in dualistic, dramatic terms that have very little kinship to the philosophy of the new science studies. It seems clear that Lispector has both a traumatic, dualistic and extremist mode of trying to overcome the separation of mind and matter, most obviously employed in *A paixão*, and also a more benign, monistic way, most purely expressed in 'Tanta mansidão' and also to a considerable degree in *Uma aprendizagem* (and in many moments of *A paixão* as well). It is as though Lispector at times imagined escape from subject/object dualism as only possible through violence, negation and antithesis, and at other times saw how it could occur in a milder mode, one of blending and association.

One way of interpreting this would be to assert that Lispector had something like an intuition of a completely nondualistic philosophy, one for which 'mind' and 'matter' or 'subject' and 'object' would be in no way fundamental, but that, restrained by the conceptual vocabulary of her time and the need to use conventional words and concepts to reach her readers, she often had to describe the path to a nondualistic belonging in the world in terms of a drama of antitheses.

Lispector has often been characterized as an Existentialist writer and the episodes of intense contact with materiality in her writings compared to Sartrean nausea. But Existentialism is very much a philosophy of the separateness of mind and things: of human subjects struggling to create themselves in a world of objects that is alien and disconcerting in its non-humanity. And this is, at best, one very partial aspect of Lispector's articulation of subject and object, person and thing. Nausea there is, to be sure—for instance in the moment of contact with the cockroach's flesh—but to concentrate on such a moment of contact between extremes is to neglect the paths by which G.H. reaches that moment and returns from it. Existentialism essentializes existence, turning it into an -ism. Lispector's texts are far more subtle; they exceed any attempt to describe them in terms of a philosophy, no matter how resonant or influential it may have been in her time.

The advantage of looking at the affinities between her writings and a subsequent philosophical current is not that we can prove her to have been more advanced than we thought. Nor is it to affirm the rightness of a non-modern, science-studies perspective by showing how it accounts for her texts. Rather the advantage of showing how Lispector can be construed as non-modern lies in freeing her thoughts and works from reduction to the intellectual languages of her own time. To my mind, the risk of misreading Lispector by provisionally enrolling her in a later intellectual project and context (that of science studies) is outweighed by the potential gain stemming from reading her outside of conceptual categories available to her: categories she could not avoid using but from which she may have been trying to escape, perhaps in ways that my 'anachronistic' reading has highlighted.

Yet it is also important to acknowledge the antithetical modes of encountering the nonhuman in Lispector's writings. Their presence can be read as a mark of great complexity. Lispector, on this view, articulates a protest against any attempt to bring off an easy, low-risk reconciliation of the human and nonhuman worlds, even while passionately desiring such a reconciliation and believing it to be ultimately possible. The price of the encounter of these worlds, in *A paixão*, is paid in abjection, disgust and—in a crucial sense—error: it is not with cockroaches that humans truly have to encounter their embodied materiality. Lispector, then, would be telling the story of how hard it is to give up the extremes, the polarities, to which we are accustomed: humanization and its abject opposite. What makes this novel a novel, after all, and not a brief treatise or meditation or even a short story, is the slowness and difficulty of the approach, the enormous effort to tell something that seems to call for few words: 'Ah, mas para se chegar à mudez, que grande esforço da voz' [Oh, but to achieve silence, what a huge effort of voice] (PGH 171). Lispector is the teller and thinker of the pain and difficulty, but also of the great promise, of giving up crucial features of a cultural and conceptual order that is revealed to be inadequate to experience. (The core of Latour's thesis on modernity is that its dualistic conceptual order is inadequate to the actual experience of what has been done by those who considered themselves modern: the official story of science is inadequate to account for what science has achieved.)

It may be, then, that Lispector articulates both the desire for and the resistance to a non-modern construction of the world as an alternative to modernity and postmodernity. By including both desire and resistance, her texts add theoretical richness to the science-studies problematic in whose context I have tried to read them. And in this sense, surely, Clarice Lispector is one of the inventors of a twenty-first century trying to free itself from the conceptual psychodramas of modernity and its discontents.

Notes to Chapter 12

1. Bruno Latour, *We Have Never Been Modern*, trans. Catherine Porter (Cambridge, MA: Harvard University Press, 1993), 135.
2. 'Tanta mansidão', *Onde estivestes de noite*, 3rd edn. (Rio de Janeiro: Nova Fronteira, 1980), 116. An almost identical passage, but transposed to the third person, figures in *Uma aprendizagem ou o livro dos prazeres*, 19th edn. (Rio de Janeiro: Francisco Alves, 1993), 166–7.
3. *A paixão segundo G.H.*, 12th edn. (Rio de Janeiro: Nova Fronteira, 1986), 29. Hereafter abbreviated PGH, with page references in the text.
4. 'Without doubt, what had saved me up to that point in the sentimentalized life that I was living was the fact that the inhuman is the best we have to offer, is the thing, the thing part of people. It was only because of this that I, as a false person, had not by then crumbled under my sentimental and utilitarian constitution: my human sentiments were utilitarian, but I had not crumbled because the thing part, God-matter, was too strong and was waiting to reclaim me. The great neutral punishment of life in general is that it can suddenly undermine a life; if it is not given strength of its own, then it bursts like a dike bursts—and becomes pure, not mixed with anything; purely neutral. That was where the great danger lay: when that neutral thing part does not soak into a personal life, all that life becomes purely neutral.'
5. *A hora da estrela*, 25th edn. (Rio de Janeiro: Francisco Alves, 1997), 25.
6. Gregory Bateson, 'Form, Substance, and Difference', in his *Steps to an Ecology of Mind* (New York: Ballantine, 1972), 453.
7. *Um sopro de vida*, 6th edn. (Rio de Janeiro: Nova Fronteira, 1985). Hereafter abbreviated SV, with page references in the text.
8. 'Who knows, maybe I have merely undergone a great, slow disintegration. And my struggle against that disintegration is just this: is it just trying, now, to give it a form? At least let me have the courage to let that form form by itself, like a crust that hardens by itself, a fiery nebula that cools into earth.'
9. On the nature of linguistic reference, or the ways 'by which the world is loaded into discourse', see Bruno Latour, 'Circulating Reference', in his *Pandora's Hope: Essays on the Reality of Science Studies* (Cambridge, MA: Harvard University Press, 1999), 24–79. I discuss the literary implications of 'circulating reference' in 'For a Cosmopolitical Philology: Lessons from Science Studies', *Substance* 96 (2001): 101–19.
10. 'life is a tragic opera in which, in a fantastic ballet, eggs, clocks, telephones, ice-skaters and the portrait of an unknown person who died in 1920 all cross paths.'
11. 'I am an object that sees other objects. Some are my brothers and others my enemies. There are also objects that say nothing. I am an object that uses other objects, that enjoys them or rejects them.'
12. Isabelle Stengers, 'La guerre des sciences: Et la paix?', in *Impostures scientifiques: Les malentendus de l'affaire Sokal*, ed. Baudoin Jurdant (Paris: La Découverte;

Alliage, 1998), 289; trans. eadem (unpubl. typescript); see eadem, *Pour en finir avec la tolérance: Cosmopolitiques 7* (Paris: La Découverte, 1997).

13. Doris Sommer, *Proceed with Caution, when Engaged by Minority Writing in the Americas* (Cambridge, MA: Harvard University Press, 1999), 27.

BIBLIOGRAPHY

I. Primary Sources

I.1 Works by Clarice Lispector

(Only first editions are listed here. Where contributors have used later editions, full details are given in the endnotes of individual articles.)

Perto do coração selvagem (Rio de Janeiro: A Noite, 1944).
O lustre (Rio de Janeiro: Agir, 1946).
A cidade sitiada (Rio de Janeiro: A Noite, 1949).
Alguns contos (Rio de Janeiro: Ministério de Educação e Saúde, 1952).
Laços de família (Rio de Janeiro: Francisco Alves, 1960).
A maçã no escuro (Rio de Janeiro: Francisco Alves, 1961).
A legião estrangeira (Rio de Janeiro: Ed. do Autor, 1964).
A paixão segundo G.H. (Rio de Janeiro: Ed. do Autor, 1964).
O mistério do coelho pensante (Rio de Janeiro: José Alvaro, 1967).
Uma aprendizagem ou o livro dos prazeres (Rio de Janeiro: Sabiá, 1969).
A mulher que matou os peixes (Rio de Janeiro: Sabiá, 1969).
Felicidade clandestina (Rio de Janeiro: Sabiá, 1971).
Água viva (Rio de Janeiro: Artenova, 1973).
Onde estivestes de noite (Rio de Janeiro: Artenova, 1974).
A via crucis do corpo (Rio de Janeiro: Artenova, 1974).
A vida íntima de Laura (Rio de Janeiro: José Olympio, 1974).
Visão do esplendor: Impressões leves (Rio de Janeiro: Francisco Alves, 1975).
A hora da estrela (Rio de Janeiro: Francisco Alves, 1977).
Um sopro de vida (Pulsações) (Rio de Janeiro: Nova Fronteira, 1978).
A bela e a fera (Rio de Janeiro: Nova Fronteira, 1979).
Para não esquecer (São Paulo: Ática, 1979).
A descoberta do mundo (Rio de Janeiro: Nova Fronteira, 1984).

I.2. Translations into English of Works by Clarice Lispector

[*Perto do coração selvagem*] *Near to the Wild Heart*, trans. Giovanni Pontiero (New York: New Directions, 1990).
[*A cidade sitiada*] *The Beseiged City*, trans. Giovanni Pontiero (Manchester: Carcanet, 1997).

[*Laços de família*] *Family Ties*, trans. Giovanni Pontiero (Austin: University of Texas Press, 1972).

[*A maçã no escuro*] *The Apple in the Dark*, trans. Gregory Rabassa (New York: A. Knopf, 1967).

[*A legião estrangeira*] *The Foreign Legion: Stories and Chronicles*, trans. Giovanni Pontiero (Manchester: Carcanet, 1986).

[*A paixão segundo G.H.*] *The Passion according to G.H.*, trans. Ronald W. Souza (Minneapolis: University of Minnesota Press, 1988).

[*Uma aprendizagem ou o livro dos prazeres*] *An Apprenticeship, or The Book of Delights*, trans. Richard A. Mazzara and Lorri A. Parris (Austin: University of Texas Press, 1986).

[*Água viva*] *The Stream of Life*, trans. Elizabeth Lowe and Earl Fitz (Minneapolis: Univ. of Minnesota Press, 1989).

[*Onde estivestes de noite* and *A via crucis do corpo*] *Soulstorm*, trans. Alexis Levitin (New York: New Directions, 1989).

[*A hora da estrela*] *The Hour of the Star*, trans. Giovanni Pontiero (Manchester: Carcanet, 1986).

[*A descoberta do mundo*] *Discovering the World*, trans. Giovanni Pontiero (Manchester: Carcanet, 1992).

I.3. Miscellaneous Writings by Clarice Lispector

'Desespero e desenlace às três da tarde', *Colóquio-Letras* 25 (1975), 50–3.

Miscellaneous *crônicas*, interviews and articles published in Brazilian newspapers (such as *Jornal do Brasil*), correspondence and other unpublished material (such as the manuscript 'Objeto gritante') are collected in the Clarice Lispector Archive at the Fundação Casa Rui Barbosa. For a full description of the contents of the Archive, please refer to:

VASCONCELLOS, ELIANE (ed.), *Inventário do arquivo 5: Clarice Lispector* (Rio de Janeiro: Ministério da Cultura and Fundação Casa de Rui Barbosa, 1994).

II. Secondary Sources

(Only material published during the period 1990–2001 is listed here)

II.1 Published Material

ABÓS, ALVARO, 'Una extranjera en la tierra', *La Nación (Suplemento cultura)* (18 Jan. 1998), 6.

AGUALUSA, JOSÉ EDUARDO, 'Do outro lado do espelho', *Público (Leituras)* (10 July 1999), 3.

ALBUQUERQUE, SEVERINO J., 'Reading Translation Queerly: Lispector's Translation of *The Picture of Dorian Gray*', *Bulletin of Hispanic Studies* [Glasgow] 76 (1999), 691–702.

—— 'Fictions of the Impossible: Clarice Lispector, Lúcio Cardoso, and "Impossibilidade"', in *Lusosex: Gender and Sexuality in the Portuguese-speaking World*, ed. Susan Canty Quinlan and Fernando Arenas (Minneapolis: University of Minnesota Press, forthcoming).

ALMEIDA, CARLOS HELÍ DE, 'Mistérios de Clarice', *O Globo, segundo caderno* (11 Mar. 1998), 1–2.

ALMEIDA, MARIA INÊS DE, 'Clarice e a estrela', *Revista tempo brasileiro* 104 (1991), 43–8.

ALMEIDA, SANDRA REGINA GOULART, 'The Madness of Lispector's Writing', in *Brazilian Feminisms*, ed. Solange Ribeiro de Oliveira and Judith Still (University of Nottingham Monographs in the Humanities; Nottingham: University of Nottingham Press, 1999), 101–15.

ALONSO, CLÁUDIA PAZOS, 'Do centro e da periferia: Uma re-leitura de *Laços de família*', *Veredas* 3 (2000), 287–99.

ALVARINO, MADELYN L., 'La fragmentación como constante en *A hora da estrela*', *Anuario de cine y literatura en español: An International Journal on Film and Literature* [Villanova, PA] 3 (1997), 25–31.

ALVES, JÚNIA DE CASTRO MAGALHÃES, 'Talvez o esboço de retratos: Lillian Hellman e Clarice Lispector', *Boletim do CESP* 16/20 (1996), 181–6.

ALVES, MARIA ANGÉLICA, 'Uma mulher de coração doce', *Seminário Nacional Mulher e Literatura: Anais 6* (Rio de Janeiro: NIELM, 1996), 174–81.

AMORIM, BEATRIZ DE CASTRO, 'Between Heaven and Hell: A (Re)evaluation of Generic Problems in Lispector's *A maçã no escuro* and "Perdoando Deus"', *Brasil/Brazil* 5/8 (1992), 29–51.

ANDRADE, ANA LUIZA, 'Entre o ruão e a donzela: A mulher, do sexo à linguagem', *Travessia* 22/1 (1991), 143–60.

—— 'In the Inter(t)sex(t) of Clarice Lispector and Nelson Rodrigues: From Drama to Language', in *Tropical Paths: Essays on Modern Brazilian Literature*, ed. Randal Johnson (New York and London: Garland, 1993), 133–52.

—— 'El Cuerpo-texto caníbal en Clarice Lispector', *Revista de estúdios hispánicos* 22 (1995), 205–15.

ARAÚJO, ANA, 'Os múltiplos aspectos da palavra em *Água viva* e *Perto do coração selvagem*', *Romance Languages Annual* 2 (1990), 310–12.

ARCHER, DEBORAH J., 'Receiving the Other: The Feminine Economy of Clarice Lispector's *The Hour of the Star*', in *Anxious Power: Reading, Writing and Ambivalence in Narrative by Women*, ed. Carol J. Singley and Susan Elizabeth Sweeney (Albany: State University of New York Press, 1993), 253–63.

ARÊAS, VILMA, 'O sexo dos clowns', *Revista tempo brasileiro* 104 (1991), 145–54.

—— 'Em torno de Teolinda Gersão e Clarice Lispector', in *Cleonice, clara em sua geração*, ed. Gilda Santos, Jorge Fernandes da Silveira and Teresa Cristina Cerdeira da Silva (Rio de Janeiro: UFRJ, 1995), 664–70.

—— 'Con la punta de los dedos', *Clarice Lispector: La escritura del cuerpo y el silencio: Anthropos extra* 2 (1997), 68–72.

ARÊAS, VILMA, 'Narrativas de la experencia (aproximación a *A hora da estrela, O motor da luz, A doença, uma experiência* y *Resumo de Ana*)', *Revista de filologia: Anejos* 2 (2001), 11–48.

ARENAS, FERNANDO, 'Being Here with Vergílio Ferreira and Clarice Lispector: At the Limits of Language and Subjectivity', *Portuguese Studies* 14 (1998), 181–94.

ARROJO, ROSEMARY, 'Interpretation as Possessive Love: Hélène Cixous, Clarice Lispector and the Ambivalence of Fidelity', in *Post-Colonial Translation: Theory and Practice*, ed. Susan Bassnett and Harish Trivedi (London: Routledge, 1999), 141–61.

BAPTISTA, ABEL BARROS, 'Aprender a paixão', *Expresso (Cartaz)* (17 Aug. 1999), 30.

—— 'A hora de Clarice?', *Expresso (Cartaz)* (1 Aug. 2000), 36.

BARBOSA, MARIA JOSÉ SOMERLATE, 'The Transgression of Literary and Ontological Boundaries According to Clarice Lispector', *Romance Languages Annual* 2 (1990), 327–9.

—— '*A hora da estrela* and *Um sopro de vida*: Parodies of Narrative Power', *Chasqui* 20/2 (1991), 116–21.

—— 'Brás's Delirium and G.H.'s Rêverie: The Quest for the Origin of Time', *Luso-Brazilian Review* 29/1 (1992), 19–27.

—— 'Critical Categories of Clarice Lispector's Texts: An Annotated Bibliography', *Inter-American Review of Bibliography* [Washington, DC] 43/4 (1993), 523–70.

—— *Clarice Lispector: Spinning the Webs of Passion* (New Orleans: University Press of the South, 1997).

—— *Clarice Lispector: Mutações faiscantes/Sparkling Mutations* (Belo Horizonte: GAM, 1998).

BARBOSA, SÓNIA MONNERAT, 'Escutas e escritas do feminino em Lispector e Cixous', *Revista tempo brasileiro* 128 (1997), 53–62.

BEDASEE, RAIMUNDA, 'A crônica e o romance clariceano: Um encontro com a grande deusa', *Seminário Nacional Mulher e Literatura: Anais 6* (Rio de Janeiro: NIELM, 1996), 153–8.

—— *Violência e ideologia feminista na obra de Clarice Lispector* (Salvador: EDUFBA, 1999).

BERG, WALTER BRUNO, 'La otredad del sexo: Escritura femenina en Gorodischer and Lispector', in *Boca de dama: La narrativa de Angelica Gorodischer*, comp. and intr. Miriam Balboa Echeverria (Buenos Aires: Feminaria, 1995), 53–68

BESSE, MARIA GRACIETE, 'Clarice Lispector: L'éclosion d'une écriture et la célébration de l'instant', *Actes du Colloque International 'La création des femmes en Amérique Latine'* (Paris, 1996).

—— '*Água viva* de Clarice Lispector: Une écriture rhizomatique', *Intercâmbio* [Porto] 8 (1997), 39–50.

BIRMAN, JOEL, 'A escrita feminina e a psicanálise', *Jornal do Brasil, Caderno B: Clarice Lispector* (9 Dec. 1997), 5.

BIRON, REBECCA E., 'Crime and Punishment Reconsidered: Clarice Lispector's *A maçã no escuro*', in her *Murder and Masculinity: Violent Fictions of Twentieth Century Latin America* (Nashville, TN: Vanderbilt University Press, 2000), 67–89.

BORELLI, OLGA, 'Imagen de Clarice Lispector', *Clarice Lispector: La escritura del cuerpo y el silencio: Anthropos extra* 2 (1997), 30–2.

BRANCO, LÚCIA CASTELLO, 'Todos os sopros, o sopro', *Revista tempo brasileiro* 104 (1991), 65–72.

BRANDÃO, RUTH SILVIANO, 'Feminina mãe imperfeita', *Revista tempo brasileiro* 104 (1991), 101–10.

BRITTIN, ALICE A. and LÓPEZ, KIMBERLE SCHUMOCK, 'The Body Written: L'écriture féminine in Two Brazilian Novels: *A hora da estrela* and *As mulheres de Tijucopapo*', *Lucero: A Journal of Iberian and Latin-American Studies* [Berkeley, CA] 1 (1990), 48–55.

BROWER, KEITH H., 'The Narratee in Clarice Lispector's *Água viva*', *Romance Notes* [Chapel Hill, NC] 32/2 (1991), 111–18.

CALEIRO, MARIA DA CONCEIÇÃO, 'Clarice: Celebremos a aparição de *Uma aprendizagem ou o livro dos prazeres*', *Público (Leituras)* (10 July 1999), 1–2.

CALEIRO-PEREIRA, ANDREÏA, 'Clarice Lispector et Grace Paley: L'art dans l'exil ou la construction de l'auto-dérision', in *Armées d'humour: Rires au féminin*, ed. Judith Stora-Sandor and Elisabeth Pillet (Montpellier: Humoresques, 2000).

CARRERA, ELENA, 'Heterophagous Passion: Eating the Other, Vomiting the Self', in *Inequality and Difference in Hispanic and Latin American Cultures*, ed. Bernard McGuirk and Mark Millington (Lampeter: Edwin Mellen, 1995), 127–39.

—— 'The Reception of Clarice Lispector via Hélène Cixous: Reading from the Whale's Belly', in *Brazilian Feminisms*, ed. Solange Ribeiro de Oliveira and Judith Still (University of Nottingham Monographs in the Humanities; Nottingham: University of Nottingham Press, 1999), 85–100.

CASTILLO, DEBRA A., *Talking Back: Toward a Latin American Feminist Literary Criticism* (Ithaca, NY: Cornell University Press, 1992).

CASTRO, PERCIO B. DE, JR, '*Um sopro de vida*: El ultimo suspiro como realidad narrativa en Clarice Lispector', *Textos: Works and Criticism* [Columbia, SC] 5/2 (1997), 35–8.

CAVALIERI, RUTH VILLELA, 'A plenitude na perda: Uma paixão', *Minas Gerais, Suplemento literário* (21 May 1986), 1024.

CHIAPPINI, LÍGIA, 'Mulheres e galinhas sem mendigos: Leitura de "Imitação da rosa" de Clarice Lispector', *Brasil/Brazil* 16 (1996), 57–63.

CHIARA, ANA CRISTINA DE RESENDE, 'Clarice: Essa grande e inumana galinha...', *Limites: Anais do 3° congresso ABRALIC, Niterói, 1992* (São Paulo: EDUSP/ ABRALIC, 1994), 65–8.

CHINDLER, DANIELA, 'Clarice Lispector sem mistérios ou enigmas', *O Globo* (9 Oct. 1999).

CIXOUS, HÉLÈNE, 'Clarice Lispector; Marina Tsvetaieva: Portraits', *Femmes, Frauen, Women*, ed. Françoise van Rossum-Guyon (Arts et littératures au XXᵉ siècle, 4; Amsterdam: Rodopi, 1990), 147–55.

—— *Reading with Clarice Lispector*, ed. and trans. Verena Andermatt Conley (London: Harvester, 1990).

—— *'Coming to Writing' and Other Essays*, ed. Deborah Jenson (Cambridge, MA: Harvard University Press, 1991).

—— '"Mamãe, disse ele", or Joyce's Second Hand', *Poetics Today* 17/3 (1996), 339–66.

—— 'Voir à ne pas savoir', *Clarice Lispector: La escritura del cuerpo y el silencio: Anthropos extra* 2 (1997), 40–6.

CLARK, MARÍA, 'Facing the Other in Clarice Lispector's Short Story "Amor"', *Letras femeninas* 16/1–2 (1990), 13–20.

COELHO, EDUARDO PRADO, 'A delicadeza infinita da alegria', *Público (Leituras)* (10 July 1999), 8.

COLL, DORELEY, 'Postmodern Discourse: Subversive Re-Writing in Clarice Lispector', in *Latin American Postmodernisms*, ed. Richard A. Young (Postmodern Studies, 22; Amsterdam, Atlanta: Rodopi, 1997), 258–70.

—— 'Clarice Lispector y la economia androgina de *Água viva*', *Revista canadiense de estudios hispánicos* 26 (2001), 199–210.

COLLETTE, MARIANELLA, 'El reconocimiento de la identidade corporal femenina en *La pasión según G.H.*, de Clarice Lispector', *Revista canadiense de estudios hispánicos* 26 (2001), 211–25.

COOK, MANUELA, '"Dá-me a tua mão": A busca da essência do ser na obra de Clarice Lispector', *Actas do quinto congresso, Associação Internacional de Lusitanistas* (Coimbra: Lidel, 1998), 577–81.

—— 'Deus, vida e morte em *A paixão segundo G.H.* de Clarice Lispector', *Boletim do CESP* 19/24 (1999), 169–80.

CORLETT, WILLIAM, 'Lispector Haunting Marxism', *Strategies: A Journal of Theory, Culture and Politics* 9–10 (1996), 69–93.

COSTA, CRISTIANE, 'Crônica de uma escritora', *Jornal do Brasil* (8 May 1999).

CRÓQUER PEDRÓN, ELEONORA, *El gesto de Antigona o la escritura como responsabilidad (Clarice Lispector, Diamela Eltit y Carmen Boullosa)* (Santiago: Cuarto Propio, 2002).

CURI, SIMONE RIBEIRO DA COSTA, *A escritura nômade em Clarice Lispector* (Chapecó, SC: Argos, 2001).

DAIDONE, LISA CASALI, with CLIFFORD, JOHN, 'Clarice Lispector: Anticipating the Postmodern', in *Multicultural Literatures through Feminist/Poststructuralist Lenses*, ed. Barbara Frey Waxman (Knoxville: University of Tennessee Press, 1994), 190–201.

DALCASTAGNÉ, REGINA, 'Contas a prestar: O intelectual e a massa em *A hora da estrela*, de Clarice Lispector', *Revista de crítica literaria latinoamericana* 26/51 (2000), 83–98.

DECIA, PATRÍCIA, 'Os originais de Lispector: Paradeiro é mistério para pesquisadores', *Folha de São Paulo* (18 July 1998).

D'ELIA, LILIANA, 'Una construcción de la femineidad en el discurso literário brasileño de Clarice Lispector', *Celehis: Revista del Centro de Letras Hispanoamericanas* [La Plata] 5/6–8 (1996), 269–74.

DINIZ, JÚLIO, 'O olhar (do) estrangeiro: Uma possível leitura de Clarice Lispector', *Revista tempo brasileiro* 101 (1990), 29–50.

DIOGO, AMÉRICO ANTÓNIO LINDEZA, *Da vida das baratas: Uma leitura d''A paixão segundo G.H.' de Clarice Lispector* (Braga: Angelus Novus, 1993).

—— *Cadáver supersónico: Uma leitura de 'A hora da estrela'* (n.p.: Associação Portuguesa de Pais e Amigos do Cidadão Deficiente Mental, 1997).

—— 'Do valor da literatura em *A hora da estrela*', in *Literatura brasileira em questão: Actas do II congresso português de literatura brasileira, Porto, 8–10 de Maio de 1997*, ed. Arnaldo Saraiva (Porto: Faculdade de Letras, 2000), 135–44.

DOMINGUEZ DE RODRIGUEZ PASQUES, MIGNON, 'La transparencia interior en cuentos de Clarice Lispector y Julio Cortázar', in *II Coloquio Internacional de Literatura Comparada: 'El cuento'*, ed. Martha Vanbiesem de Burbridge (Buenos Aires: Fundacion Maria Teresa Maiorana, 1995), 39–44.

—— 'Clarice Lispector: La transgresión en "La bella y la fiera o la herida demasiado grande"', *Alba de América: Revista literária* [Westminster, CA] 14/26–7 (1996), 381–8.

DOUGLASS, ELLEN J., 'Female Quest toward "Agua pura" in Clarice Lispector's *Perto do coração selvagem*', *Brasil/Brazil* 3/3 (1990), 44–64.

DUMAS, CATHERINE, 'L'émergence du sujet féminin dans le roman à la première personne: *A paixão segundo G.H.*', in *A mulher escritora em África e na América Latina*, ed. Ana Maria Mão-de-Ferro Martinho (Évora: NUM, 1999), 123–49.

—— 'Le personnage féminin et la perception du monde dans *A paixão segundo G.H.* de Clarice Lispector et *A paixão segundo Constança H.* de Maria Teresa Horta', in *Ser mujer y tomar la palabra en América Latina: pensar y escribir, obrar y reaccionar*, ed. Juan Andreo and Roland Forgues (Murcia and Pau: Red ALFA Tupac Amaru, 1999), 119–21.

ESTEVEZ, BERTHA, 'Clarice Lispector, Catherine Clément y la vivencia de la síncope', *Romance Languages Annual* 9 (1998), 460–6.

FELINTO, MARILENE, 'Sentimentos de perplexidade', *Folha de São Paulo (Mais!)* (7 Dec. 1997), 13.

—— 'Um surto lésbico-literário', *Folha de São Paulo* (5 Sept. 1999).

FERREIRA, DÉBORA, 'O imaginário nacionalístico na obra de Clarice Lispector', *Romance Languages Annual* 9 (1998), 472–3.

FERREIRA, TERESA CRISTINA MONTERO, *Eu sou uma pergunta: Uma biografia de Clarice Lispector* (Rio de Janeiro: Rocco, 1999).
—— 'Imagens de Clarice Lispector no Brasil e no exterior', in *Fronteiras da literatura: Discursos transculturais*, ed. Luiza Lobo (Rio de Janeiro: UFRJ; Relume-Dumará, 1999), ii. 61–6.
—— *See also* MONTERO, TERESA CRISTINA FERREIRA.
FILIPOUSKI, ANA MARIZA RIBEIRO, 'Um espaço de hesitação da narrativa infantil: O narrador em busca de diálogo com o leitor', in Zilberman et al. (eds.), *Clarice Lispector*, 129–44.
FISCHMAN, SARA, 'Que opção escolher? Como em "Por onde comecar?" de Roland Barthes: Uma leitura de "A quinta história" de Clarice Lispector', *Reflejos: Revista del Departamento de Estudios Españoles y Latinoamericanos* [Jerusalem] 4 (1995), 18–20.
FITZ, EARL E., 'Hélène Cixous' Debt to Clarice Lispector: The Case of *Vivre l'orange* and "l'écriture féminine"', *Romance de littérature comparée*, 64/1 (1990), 235–49.
—— '"A pecadora queimada e os anjos harmoniosos:" Clarice Lispector as Dramatist', *Luso-Brazilian Review* 34/2 (1997), 25–39.
—— 'Eroticizing the Sign: Sexuality and Being in the Narrative World of Clarice Lispector', *Romance Languages Annual* 9 (1998), 478–85.
—— 'Reading Clarice in the Context of Modern Latin American Narrative: A Comparative Assessment', *Brasil/Brazil* 20 (1998), 43–66.
—— *Sexuality and Being in the Poststructuralist Universe of Clarice Lispector* (Austin: University of Texas Press, 2001)
—— *See also* PAYNE and FITZ (1993).
FRANCO, CARLOS, 'Clarice nas nervuras da arte', *Jornal do Brasil, Caderno B: Clarice Lispector* (9 Dec. 1997), 6.
—— 'O olhar da menina impossível', ibid., 7.
—— 'O retrato da artista por Scliar', ibid., 4.
FREITAS, IACYR ANDERSON, '"A menor mulher do mundo" e outros laços', *Minas Gerais, Suplemento literário* (3 Mar. 1990), 6–7.
FREIXAS, LAURA, *Clarice Lispector* (Barcelona: Omega, 2001).
FRIAS, JOANA MATOS, '*Um sopro de vida* de Clarice Lispector: A auto-destruição criadora do sujeito moderno', *Línguas e literaturas* [Porto] 15 (1998), 121–47.
FRONKOWIAK, ANGELA, 'O ato de narrar em *A paixão segundo G.H.*', in Zilberman et al. (eds.), *Clarice Lispector*, 65–74.
FUKELMAN, CLARISSE, 'Gritos e susurros: aspectos românticos na obra de Clarice Lispector', *Seminário Nacional Mulher e Literatura: Anais 4* (Niterói: NIELM, 1991), 167–77.
GALVÃO, WALNICE NOGUEIRA, 'Entre o silêncio e a vertigem', introduction to *Os melhores contos: Clarice Lispector* (São Paulo: Global, 1996), 7–11.

—— 'Clarice Lispector: Uma leitura', *Revista de crítica literaria latinoamericana* 24/47 (1998), 67–75.

GALVEZ-BRETON, MARA, 'Post-feminist Discourse in Clarice Lispector's *The Hour of the Star*', in *Splintering Darkness: Latin American Women Writers in Search of Themselves*, ed. Lucia Guerra-Cunningham (Pittsburgh, PA: Latin American Literary Review Press, 1990), 63–78.

GARABANO, SANDRA, 'Textualidad femenina e historicidad en *A paixão segundo G. H.* de Clarice Lispector', *Feminaria literaria* 5/9 (1995), 6–8.

GIRARDI, ANGELA MARIA OLIVA, '*A hora da estrela*: (in)competência da linguagem', in *Tudo no feminino: A mulher e a narrativa brasileira contemporânea*, ed. Elódia Xavier (Rio de Janeiro: Francisco Alves, 1991), 131–49.

GOMES, RENATO CORDEIRO, 'Processo de viver/processo de escrever em Clarice Lispector', *Revista tempo brasileiro* 128 (1997), 27–35.

GONÇALVES, GLAUCIA RENATE, 'Náusea e epifania em Clarice Lispector e Agostinho Neto: A literatura do 'colonizado' sob a luz do existencialismo', *Torre de papel* [Iowa City] 2/1 (1992), 40–7.

GORGULHO, FERNANDO JESUS SANTOS, '*Laços de família* de Clarice Lispector: Uma forma de pensar o que nos une de verdade', *Lusorama* 19 (1992), 41–51.

GOTLIB, NÁDIA BATTELLA, 'Las mujeres y "el Otro": Tres narradoras brasileñas', *Escritura* 16/31–2 (1991), 123–36.

—— *Clarice: Uma vida que se conta*, 2nd edn. (São Paulo: Ática, 1995).

—— 'Retratos de Clarice', *Seminário Nacional Mulher e Literatura: Anais 6* (Rio de Janeiro: NIELM, 1996), 67–74.

—— 'Eça de Clarice (Devaneios)', *150 anos com Eça de Queirós: III Encontro Internacional de Queirosianos, São Paulo, 1995* (São Paulo: USP, Centro de Estudos Portugueses, 1997), 446–53.

—— 'Tres casos sobre Clarice', *Clarice Lispector: La escritura del cuerpo y el silencio: Anthropos extra* 2 (1997), 84–8.

—— 'Ser ou não ser autobiográfica (a propósito de Clarice Lispector)', in *Navegar é preciso, viver: Escritos para Silviano Santiago*, ed. Eneida Maria de Souza and Wander Melo Miranda (Belo Horizonte: Ed. UFMG; Salvador: EDUFBA; Niterói: EDUFF, 1997), 314–22.

GRAÇA, EDUARDO, 'Aracy no mundo da escritora', *Jornal do Brasil, Caderno B: Clarice Lispector* (9 Dec. 1997), 4.

GRAF, MARGA, 'A ficção suprapessoal: O mundo íntimo de Autran Dourado e Clarice Lispector; Aspectos da *nova literatura* no Brasil dos anos sessenta', in *Actas do Quarto Congresso da Associação Internacional de Lusitanistas, Hamburg, 1993*, ed. M. Fátima Viegas Brauer-Figueiredo, Fernando Clara and Alexandra Pinho (Lisbon: Lidel, 1995), 529–35.

GRECO, SIMONE, '*A paixão segundo G. H.* de Clarice Lispector: Do discurso crítico à busca espiritual', *Lusorama* 24 (1994), 40–5.

GUELBENZU, JOSÉ MARÍA, 'Viaje al fondo del abismo', *El País: Supl. Babelia* (27 Nov. 1999).

GUIDIN, MÁRCIA LÍGIA, *Roteiro de leitura: 'A hora da estrela', Clarice Lispector* (São Paulo: Ática, 1994).

—— 'Feminino e morte em *A hora da estrela*, de Clarice Lispector', *Seminário Nacional Mulher e Literatura: Anais 6* (Rio de Janeiro: NIELM, 1996), 214–18.

GUZIK, ALBERTO, 'Duas Clarices se revezam no mesmo palco', *Jornal da tarde* (8 Sept. 2000).

HART, STEPHEN M., 'On the Threshold: Cixous, Lispector, Tusquets', in *Feminist Readings on Spanish and Latin American Literature*, ed. Lisa P. Condé and Stephen M. Hart (Lewiston, ME; Queenstown; Lampeter: Edwin Mellen, 1991), 91–101.

—— 'Clarice Lispector: *Perto do coração selvagem*', in his *White Ink: Essays on Twentieth-Century Feminine Fiction in Spain and Latin America* (London: Támesis, 1993) 28–35. .

HEDRICK, TACE, 'Mother, Blessed be You Among Cockroaches: Essentialism, Fecundity, and Death in Clarice Lispector', *Luso-Brazilian Review* 34/2 (1997), 41–57.

HELENA, LÚCIA, 'Genre and Gender in Clarice Lispector's "The Imitation of the Rose"', *Style* 24/2 (1990), 215–27.

—— 'A literatura segundo Lispector', *Revista tempo brasileiro* 104 (1991), 25–42.

—— 'A problematização da narrativa em Clarice Lispector', *Hispania* 75 (1992), 1164–73.

—— 'Um texto fugitivo em *Água viva*: Sujeito, escrita e cultura em Clarice Lispector', *Brasil/Brazil* 12/7 (1994), 9–28.

—— 'Hélène e Clarice: Mão invertida no fluxo de influências', *Seminário Nacional Mulher e Literatura: Anais 6* (Rio de Janeiro: NIELM, 1996), 75–83.

—— 'Lispector e Llansol: Um encontro de corpos de escrita', *Revista tempo brasileiro* 128 (1997), 19–26.

—— *Nem musa, nem medusa: Itinerários da escrita em Clarice Lispector* (Niterói: EDUFF, 1997).

—— *See also* VIANNA, LUCIA HELENA.

HERRERO, ALEJANDRO, 'The Filming of a Novel: An Analysis of Lispector's *The Hour of the Star* and Amaral's Adaptation', *Aleph* [University Park, PA] 5 (1990), 4–11.

HILL, AMARILES G., 'Referencias cristianas y judaicas en *A maçã no escuro* y *A paixão segundo G.H.*', *Clarice Lispector: La escritura del cuerpo y el silencio: Anthropos extra 2* (1997), 72–6.

IANNACE, RICARDO, *A leitora Clarice Lispector* (Ensaios de Cultura, 18; São Paulo: EDUSP; FAPESP, 2001).

JOZEF, BELLA, 'Clarice Lispector, ser por la palabra', *Clarice Lispector: La escritura del cuerpo y el silencio: Anthropos extra 2* (1997), 81–4.

KLOBUCKA, ANNA, 'Hélène Cixous and the Hour of Clarice Lispector', *SubStance* 73 (1994), 41–62.

—— 'In Different Voices: Gender and Dialogue in Clarice Lispector's Metafiction', in *Women, Literature and Culture in the Portuguese-Speaking World*, ed. Cláudia Pazos Alonso (Lampeter: Edwin Mellen, 1996), 155–72.

—— 'Quest and Romance in Lispector's *Uma aprendizagem ou o livro dos prazeres*', *Luso-Brazilian Review* 36/1 (1999), 123–30.

KRABBENHOFT, KENNETH, 'From Mysticism to Sacrament in *A paixão segundo G. H.*', *Luso-Brazilian Review* 32/1 (1995), 51–60.

LATORRE, CAROLINA, 'El Cuerpo como espacio de aprendizaje: Transcendencia de lo corporal en "Colheita" de Nélida Piñon y *Uma aprendizagem ou o livro dos prazeres* de Clarice Lispector', *Romance Languages Annual* 9 (1998), 555–60.

LERNER, JÚLIO, 'A última entrevista de Clarice Lispector', *Shalom* 27 (1992), 62–9.

LINDSTROM, NAOMI, 'The Pattern of Allusions in Clarice Lispector', *Luso-Brazilian Review* 36/1 (1999), 111–21.

LOKENSGARD, MARK A., 'Clarice, "Eu" e Borges: Interpretando os textos borgianos de Clarice Lispector', *Seminário Nacional Mulher e Literatura: Anais* 5 (Natal: UFRN; NIELM, 1993), 219–25.

LOSADA SOLER, ELENA, 'Clarice Lispector: La palabra rigorosa', *Mujeres y literatura*, ed. Àngels Carabí and Marta Segarra (Barcelona: PPU, 1994), 123–36.

—— 'Tres imágenes (con espejos) en la obra de Clarice Lispector: Lóri, Glória y Macabéa', *Clarice Lispector: La escritura del cuerpo y el silencio: Anthropos extra* 2 (1997), 55–9.

LOWE, ELIZABETH, 'Liberating the Rose: Clarice Lispector's *Água viva* (*The Stream of Life*) as a Political Statement', in *Splintering Darkness: Latin American Women Writers in Search of Themselves*, ed. Lucia Guerra-Cunningham (Pittsburgh, PA: Latin American Literary Review Press, 1990), 79–84.

LUCCHESI, IVO, 'A paixão do corpo entre os fantasmas e as fantasias do desejo', introduction to Clarice Lispector *A via crucis do corpo*, 4th edn. (Rio de Janeiro: Francisco Alves, 1991), 3–15.

MCAVEY, M. SHEILA, '"The Smallest Woman in the World": Refractions of Identity in Elizabeth Bishop's Translation of Clarice Lispector's Tale', in *'In Worcester, Massachussetts': Essays on Elizabeth Bishop from the 1997 Elizabeth Bishop Conference at WPI*, ed. Laura Jehn Menides and Angela G. Dorenkamp (New York: Peter Lang, 1999), 279–86.

MCBRIDE, KARA, '*No caso a outra*: A Look at the Role of the Male Narrator in Clarice Lispector's *A hora da estrela*', *Romance Languages Annual* 9 (1998), 609–12.

MAGALHÃES, BELMIRA, 'Representação de gênero em *Uma aprendizagem ou o livro dos prazeres*, de Clarice Lispector', *Seminário Nacional Mulher e Literatura: Anais* 6 (Rio de Janeiro: NIELM, 1996), 226–51.

MALARD, LETÍCIA, 'Comer esta coisa: uma barata', *Estado de Minas* (30 Mar. 1998).

MALDONADO, FÁTIMA, 'Álgebra da vida: *Perto do coração selvagem*', *Expresso (Cartaz)* (1 July 2000), 37.

MANZO, LÍCIA, *Era uma vez: Eu; A não-ficção na obra de Clarice Lispector* (Curitiba: Governo do Estado de Paraná; Secretaria de Estado da Cultura; Xerox do Brasil, 1998).

MARGARIDO, ALFREDO, 'A relação animais-Bíblia na obra de Clarice Lispector', *Colóquio-Letras* 125–6 (1992), 239–45.

MARTIN, ANNABEL, '*The Hour of the Star*: Poverty, Feminism and Realist Narrative', *Selecta: Journal of the Pacific Northwest Council on Foreign Languages* [Pocatello, ID] 12 (1991), 37–40.

MARTIN, SUSAN, 'A paixão segundo Peixoto: Uma leitura da violência em Clarice Lispector', *Revista de crítica literaria latinoamericana* 21/442 (1995), 241–6.

MARTING, DIANE E., 'The Brazilian Writer Clarice Lispector: "I never set foot in the Ukraine"', *Journal of Interdisciplinary Literary Studies* [Lincoln, NE] 6/1 (1994), 87–101.

—— 'Clarice Lispector's (Post)Modernity and the Adolescence of the Girl-Colt', *Modern Language Notes* 113 (1998), 433–44.

—— *The Sexual Woman in Latin American Literature: Dangerous Desires* (Gainesville: University Press of Florida, 2001).

—— (ed.), *Clarice Lispector: A Bio-Bibliography* (Westport, CT: Greenwood Press, 1993).

MATHIE, BARBARA, 'Feminism, Language or Existentialism: The Search for the Self in the Works of Clarice Lispector', in *Subjectivity and Literature from the Romantics to the Present Day*, ed. Philip Shaw and Peter Stockwell (London: Pinter, 1991), 121–35.

MATTOS, CÉLIA REGINA DE BARROS, 'Sombra/luz, o Contraponto da revelação', *Revista tempo brasileiro* 128 (1997), 75–84.

MAURA, ANTONIO, 'Presentación', *Clarice Lispector: La escritura del cuerpo y el silencio: Anthropos extra* 2 (1997), 36–40.

—— 'Resonancias hebraicas en la obra de Clarice Lispector', ibid., 77–81.

MAYA, IVONE, 'Os subúrbios existenciais', *Revista tempo brasileiro* 128 (1997), 37–40.

MEDEIROS, ALEXANDRE, 'Um abismo entre duas Clarices', *Jornal do Brasil, Caderno B: Clarice Lispector* (9 Dec. 1997), 1–4.

—— 'Cartas falam de sonhos', ibid., 6.

MERTEN, LUIZ CARLOS, 'Clarice Lispector é obsessão de diretora', *estadao.com.br* (21 Dec. 2000).

MIRANDA, ANA, *Clarice Lispector: O tesouro da minha cidade* (Perfis do Rio, 3; Rio de Janeiro: Relume-Dumará; Prefeitura, 1996).

MONIZ, NAOMI HOKI, 'A menor mulher do mundo: O ovo ou a maçã no escuro', *Revista de crítica literaria latinoamericana*, 20/40 (1994), 53–60.

MONTENEGRO, JOÃO ALFREDO DE SOUSA, *História e ontologia em 'A hora da estrela' de Clarice Lispector* (Rio de Janeiro: Tempo Brasileiro, 2001).

MÜLLER, HANS-JOACHIM, '*A paixão segundo G.H.* von Clarice Lispector oder Spinoza im zersprochenen Spiegel des Narziss', in *Canticum ibericum*, ed. Erna Pfeiffer and Heinz Kubarth (Frankfurt am Main: Peter Lang, 1991), 264–82.

MULLER, INGRID R., 'The Problematics of the Body in Clarice Lispector's *Family Ties*', *Chasqui* 20/1 (1991), 34/42.

NAME, DANIELA, 'A política da boca do cofre', *O Globo* (12 Mar. 1997), Segundo caderno, 1–4.

—— and PIRES, PAULO ROBERTO, 'Vestígios de Clarice', *O Globo* (7 Dec. 1997), Segundo caderno, 1–2.

NASCIMENTO, EVANDO, 'Clarice: Literatura e pensamento', *Revista tempo brasileiro* 128 (1997), 47–52.

NEGRON, MARA, 'A gênese de um pensar-sentir mulher em *A maçã no escuro*', *Revista tempo brasileiro* 104 (1991), 73–82.

—— *Une Genèse au 'féminin': Étude de 'La pomme dans le noir' de Clarice Lispector* (Amsterdam: Rodopi, 1997).

NINA, CLÁUDIA, 'Muita amplitude, pouca profundidade', *Jornal do Brasil* (20 Mar. 1999), Caderno B.

NOLASCO, EDGAR CÉZAR, *Clarice Lispector: Nas estrelinhas da escritura* (São Paulo: Annablume, 2001).

NOVAES, WAGNER, 'Bibliocronología de Clarice Lispector', *Clarice Lispector: La escritura del cuerpo y el silencio: Anthropos extra* 2 (1997), 32–4.

NUNES, APARECIDA MARIA, 'Clarice Lispector jornalista: Primeiros textos, páginas femininas e entrevistas', *Limites: Anais do 3º Congresso ABRALIC, Niterói, 1992* (São Paulo: EDUSP/ABRALIC, 1994), i. 167–72.

—— 'Diálogos possíveis: Entrevistas de Clarice Lispector na revista *Manchete*', *Seminário Nacional Mulher e Literatura: Anais* 6 (Rio de Janeiro: NIELM, 1996), 159–62.

NUNES, BENEDITO, 'La pasión de Clarice Lispector', *Clarice Lispector: La escritura del cuerpo y el silencio: Anthropos extra* 2 (1997), 46–54.

—— 'Os destroços da introspecção', in Zilberman et al. (eds.), *Clarice Lispector*, 35–48.

ODBER DE BAUBETA, PATRICIA ANNE, 'Another Kind of Comparativism: *A hora da estrela* and *The Hour of the Star*', *Cadernos de tradução* [UFSC] 2 (1997), 249–85.

OLIVEIRA, MARLY, 'Un perfil de Clarice', *Clarice Lispector: La escritura del cuerpo y el silencio: Anthropos extra* 2 (1997), 88–90.

OLIVEIRA, REJANE PIVETTA DE, 'Brincadeira de narrar', in Zilberman et al. (eds.), *Clarice Lispector*, 105–28.

OLIVEIRA, SOLANGE RIBEIRO DE, *Literatura e artes plásticas: O Kunstlerroman na ficção contemporânea* (Ouro Preto: UFOP, 1993).

OLIVEIRA, SOLANGE RIBEIRO DE, 'A paixão segundo G.H.: Uma lectura ideológica de Clarice Lispector', *Clarice Lispector: La escritura del cuerpo y el silencio: Anthropos extra* 2 (1997), 59–67.

—— 'The Dry and the Wet: Cultural Configurations in Clarice Lispector's Novels', in *Brazilian Feminisms*, ed. Solange Ribeiro de Oliveira and Judith Still (University of Nottingham Monographs in the Humanities; Nottingham: University of Nottingham Press, 1999), 116–32.

OWEN, HILARY, 'Clarice Lispector beyond Cixous: Ecofeminism and Zen in *A paixão segundo G.H.*', in *Gender, Ethnicity and Class in Modern Portuguese-Speaking Culture*, ed. Hilary Owen (Lampeter: Edwin Mellen, 1996), 161–84.

—— 'Giovanni Pontiero's Translation of Clarice Lispector's *Discovering the World*', in *The Translator's Dialogue: Giovanni Pontiero*, ed. Pilar Orero and Juan C. Sager (Amsterdam; Philadelphia: John Benjamins, 1997), 135–44.

—— 'Masculine Impostures and Feminine Ripostes: Onetti and Clarice Lispector', in *Onetti and Others: Comparative Essays on a Major Figure in Latin American Literature*, ed. Gustavo San Román (Albany: State University of New York Press, 1999), 133–43.

—— 'Clarice Lispector: Re-Joycing in "The Dead"', in *Fiction in the Portuguese-Speaking World: Essays in Memory of Alexandre Pinheiro Torres*, ed. Charles M. Kelley (Cardiff: University of Wales Press, 2000), 176–93.

PAIXÃO, SYLVIA, 'Um sopro de vida na hora da estrela: Uma leitura das crônicas de Clarice Lispector', *Revista tempo brasileiro* 104 (1991), 111–20.

PALERMO, PATRICIA, 'Self Discovery and Re-Creation in Clarice Lispector's *The Apple in the Dark*', *South Eastern Latin Americanist* 38/2 (1994), 19–25.

PATAI, DAPHNE, 'El esencialismo de Clarice Lispector', *Nuevo texto crítico* 3/1 (1990), 21–35.

PAYNE, JUDITH A., 'The Heroic Journey: A Feminine Model in Clarice Lispector's *Perto do coração selvagem* and *Água viva*', *Romance Languages Annual* 3 (1991), 554–60.

—— 'Being-unto-Birth: *Água Viva* as a Feminine Transformation of the Heideggerian Model', *Romance Languages Annual* 10 (1998), 767–71.

—— and FITZ, EARL E. (eds.), *Ambiguity and Gender in the New Novel of Brazil and Spanish America: A Comparative Assessment* (Iowa City: University of Iowa Press, 1993).

PEIXOTO, MARTA, 'Rape and Textual Violence in Clarice Lispector', in *Rape and Representation*, ed. Lynn A. Higgins and Brenda R. Silver (New York: Columbia University Press, 1991), 182–203; repr. in *Remate de males* 12 (1992), 101–14.

—— *Passionate Fictions: Gender, Narrative and Violence in Clarice Lispector* (Minneapolis: University of Minnesota Press, 1994).

PERES, DÉLIA CONCEIÇÃO, et al., 'A hora da estrela: Uma conversa com Clarice Lispector e Suzana Amaral', *Revista tempo brasileiro* 128 (1997), 85–92.

PERRONE-MOISÉS, LEYLA, 'Clarice Lispector', *La quinzaine littéraire* (1–15 Sept. 1993), 21–2.

PIÑON, NÉLIDA, 'El rostro de Clarice', *Clarice Lispector: La escritura del cuerpo y el silencio*: Anthropos extra 2 (1997), 29–30.

PINTO, CRISTINA FERREIRA, '*Perto do coração selvagem*: Romance de formação, romance de transformação', in *O Bildungsroman feminino: Quatro exemplos brasileiros*, ed. Cristina Ferreira Pinto (São Paulo: Perspectiva, 1990), 77–108.

PIRES, ANTÓNIO DONIZETI, 'Uma barata cheia de espinhos: Leitura intertextual de *A metamorfose*, de Franz Kafka, e *A paixão segundo G. H.*, de Clarice Lispector', *Itinerários: Revista de literatura* [Araraquara] 12 (1998), 165–75.

PLATT, KAMALA, 'Race and Gender Representations in Clarice Lispector's "A menor mulher do mundo" and Carolina Maria de Jesus' *Quarto de despejo*', *Afro-Hispanic Review* 9/1–3 (1992), 51–7.

PONTIERI, REGINA, *Clarice Lispector: Uma política do olhar* (São Paulo: Ateliê, 1999).

PONTIERO, GIOVANNI, 'Clarice Lispector and *The Hour of the Star*', in *Feminist Readings on Spanish and Latin American Literature*, ed. Lisa P. Condé and Stephen M. Hart (Lewiston, ME; Queenstown; Lampeter: Edwin Mellen, 1991), 161–72.

—— 'Clarice Lispector: Dreams of Language', in *A Dream of Light and Shadow: Portraits of Latin American Women Writers*, ed. Marjorie Agosín (Albuquerque: University of New Mexico Press, 1995), 271–89.

PORTO, MARIA BERNADETTE VELLOSO, 'Fazendo o gênero diabólico: Feitiços, desvios e a reinvenção do quotidiano em *Les enfants du sabbat* (Anne Hébert) e *Onde estivestes de noite* (Clarice Lispector)', *Seminário Nacional Mulher e Literatura: Anais* 6 (Rio de Janeiro: NIELM, 1996), 278–87.

QUEIROZ, VERA, 'Tríptico para Clarice', *Revista tempo brasileiro* 104 (1991), 121–44.

—— 'O olhar das mulheres', *Travessia* 25 (1992), 40–50.

—— 'Clarice em questão: 20 anos sem Clarice; Apresentação', *Revista tempo brasileiro* 128 (1997), 5–6.

—— 'Clarice, o cânone e a crítica cultural', *Revista tempo brasileiro* 128 (1997), 41–6.

RASHKIN, ELISSA, 'Swearing the Body: Female Violence and Revolt in 'O corpo' and *Mar de rosas*', *Torre de papel* [Iowa City] 4/1 (1994), 27–41.

REZENDE, NEIDE LUZIA DE, 'A problematização da alteridade em "A menor mulher do mundo" de Clarice Lispector', *Quaderni ibero-americani* 81–2 (1997), 51–8.

RIBEIRO, FRANCISCO AURÉLIO, *A literatura infanto-juvenil de Clarice Lispector* (Vitória: Nemar, 1993)

RICHE, ROSA MARIA CUBA, 'Mme de Ségur e Clarice Lispector: O olhar da e para a criança; Um contraponto', *Revista tempo brasileiro* 128 (1997), 63–74.

RODRIGUES, SELMA CALASANS, 'A paródia sacrílega e as máscaras da ficcionalidade em *A paixão segundo G.H.*, de Clarice Lispector', *Seminário Nacional Mulher e Literatura: Anais 6* (Rio de Janeiro: NIELM, 1996), 163–73.

—— 'Alguns aspectos da recepção da obra de Clarice Lispector pela Psicanálise', in *Literatura brasileira em questão: Actas do II congresso português de literatura brasileira, Porto, 8–10 de Maio de 1997*, ed. Arnaldo Saraiva (Porto: Faculdade de Letras, 2000), 411–22.

RONCADOR, SONIA, 'Autobiógrafo como toureiro: A anti-autobiografia de Clarice Lispector', *Cerrados* 5 (1996), 37–44.

—— 'Some Considerations on the Genealogy of Clarice Lispector's *Água viva*', *Romance Notes* 38/3 (1998), 271–9.

—— 'Clarice Lispector Hides a Screaming Object: Notes on an Abandoned Project', *Brasil/Brazil* 14/25 (2001), 69–86.

—— *Poéticas do empobrecimento: A escrita derradeira de Clarice* (São Paulo: Annablume, 2002).

ROSAROSSA, MARIA ALEJANDRA, 'La imagen religiosa en Flannery O'Connor y Clarice Lispector', in *II Coloquio Internacional de Literatura Comparada: 'El cuento'*, ed. Martha Vanbiesem de Burbridge (Buenos Aires: Fundacion Maria Teresa Maiorana, 1995), 98–102.

ROSENBAUM, YUDITH, *Metamorfoses do mal: Uma leitura de Clarice Lispector* (Ensaios de Cultura, 18; São Paulo: EDUSP; FAPESP, 1999).

ROSENSTEIN, ROY, 'Re(dis)covering Wilde for Latin America: Martí, Darío, Borges, Lispector', in *Rediscovering Oscar Wilde*, ed. C. George Sandulescu (Gerrards Cross: Colin Smythe, 1994), 348–61.

RUSSOTTO, MÁRGARA, 'Pequeña diacronia: La heroína melodramática', *Escritura* 16/31–2 (1991), 231–45.

—— 'Encantamiento y compasión: Un estudio de 'El huevo y la gallina'', *Inti: Revista de Literatura Hispánica* [Cranston, RI] 43–4 (1996), 167–75.

SÁ, OLGA DE, *Clarice Lispector: A travessia do oposto* (São Paulo: Annablume, 1993).

SABINE, MARK, 'Giovanni Pontiero's Translation of Clarice Lispector's *Laços de família*', in *The Translator's Dialogue: Giovanni Pontiero*, ed. Pilar Orero and Juan C. Sager (Amsterdam; Philadelphia: John Benjamins, 1997), 145–53.

SABINO, FERNANDO, *Cartas perto do coração* (Rio de Janeiro: Record, 2001).

SADLIER, DARLENE J., 'The Text and the Palimpsest: Clarice Lispector's "A bela e a fera, ou A ferida grande demais"', *Travessia* 21 (1990), 105–19; repr. in *Hispanófila* [Chapel Hill, NC] 35/2 [104] (1992), 77–88.

SÁENZ DE TEJADA, CRISTINA, 'El Espejo, símbolo de la escritura de Clarice Lispector', *Romance Notes* 33/1 (1992), 61–9.

—— 'The Eternal Non-Difference: Clarice Lispector's Concept of Androgyny', *Luso-Brazilian Review* 31/1 (1994), 39–56.

—— 'Ecologist and Ecofeminist Awareness in *Água viva*: A Brazilian Woman Rereading Nature', *Brasil/Brazil* 18 (1997), 39–57.

SANTIAGO, SILVIANO, 'A aula inaugural de Clarice', *Folha de São Paulo, mais!* (9 Dec. 1997), 12–14.

SANTOS, JEANA LAURA DA CUNHA, *A estética da melancolia em Clarice Lispector* (Florianópolis: Editora da UFSC, 2000).

SANTOS, LIDIA, *Kitsch tropical: Los medios en la literatura y el arte en América Latina* (Nexos y diferencias, 2; Madrid: Iberoamericana; Frankfurt am Main: Vervuert, 2001), 'Clarice Lispector: La clases obrera nova al paraíso', 186–96.

SANTOS, ROBERTO CORRÊA DOS, 'Discurso feminino, corpo, arte gestual, as margens recentes', *Revista tempo brasileiro* 104 (1991), 49–64.

—— 'Artes de fiandeira', Introduction to Clarice Lispector, *Laços de família*, 25th edn. (Rio de Janeiro: Francisco Alves, 1993), 5–14.

—— 'Percepção e sistemas cognitivos construtos de "Menino a bico de pena"', *Revista tempo brasileiro* 128 (1997), 93–101.

SCHIMINOVICH, FLORA H., 'Two Modes of Writing the Female Self: Isabel Allende's *The House of the Spirits* and Clarice Lispector's *The Stream of Life*', in *Gender and Genre in Literature: Redefining Autobiography in Twentieth Century Women's Fiction*, ed. Janice Morgan and Colette T. Hall (Garland Reference Library of the Humanities, 3; New York and London: Garland, 1991), 103–16.

SCHLAFMAN, LÉO, 'Clarice e a crise da palavra', *Jornal do Brasil* (9 Dec. 1997), Caderno B: 'Clarice Lispector', 5.

SCHMIDT, RITA TEREZINHA, 'Pelos caminhos do coração selvagem, sob o signo do desejo', *Revista tempo brasileiro* 104 (1991), 83–100.

SCHMITZ, HEIKE, *Von Sturm- und Geisteswut : Mystische Spuren und das Kleid der Kunst bei Ingeborg Bachmann und Clarice Lispector* (Königstein im Taunus: Helmer, 1998).

SEREZA, HAROLDO CERAVOLO, 'O desafio de entender as muitas Clarices', *O Estado de São Paulo* (21 Apr. 2001), *Caderno 2*.

SIGANOS, ANDRÉ, 'La Solitude du violent: Trois moments-clefs chez Dostoievski, Le Clézio et Lispector', in *Solitudes: Écriture et représentation*, ed. André Siganos (Grenoble: ELLUG, 1995), 123–30.

SOARES, ANTHONY, 'A Return Passage to Non-Intelligence in Clarice Lispector's *A paixão segundo G.H.*', *Gender, Ethnicity and Class in Modern Portuguese-Speaking Culture*, ed. Hilary Owen (Lampeter: Edwin Mellen, 1996), 225–35.

SOUSA, CARLOS MENDES DE, 'Tão escura quanto é a noite enquanto se dorme: Uma leitura de Clarice Lispector', in *Actas do Quarto Congresso da Associação Internacional de Lusitanistas (1993)*, ed. M. Fátima Viegas Brauer-Figueiredo, Fernando Clara and Alexandra Pinho (Lisbon: Lidel, 1995), 675–81.

—— 'A assinatura, o nome, a coisa: Lispector', *Diacrítica* [Braga] 11 (1996), 167–74.

—— *Clarice Lispector: Figuras da escrita* (Braga: Universidade do Minho; Centro de Estudos Humanísticos, 2000).

SOUSA, CARLOS MENDES DE, 'A escrita autobiográfica de Clarice Lispector', in *Literatura brasileira em questão: Actas do II congresso português de literatura brasileira, Porto, 8–10 de Maio de 1997*, ed. Arnaldo Saraiva (Porto: Faculdade de Letras, 2000), 489–95.

SOUZA, ENEIDA MARIA DE, 'Apresentação: O brilho no escuro', Introduction to Clarice Lispector, *A cidade sitiada*, 7th edn. (Rio de Janeiro: Francisco Alves, 1992), 1–4.

SPERBER, SUZI FRANKL, 'Clarice Lispector: Uma judia no Brasil', *Lusorama* 16 (1991), 96–109.

STAVANS, ILAN (ed.), *Mutual Impressions: Writers from the Americas Reading One Another* (Durham, NC: Duke University Press, 1999).

SWANSON, PHILIP, 'Clarice Lispector and *A hora da estrela*: "Féminité" or "Réalité"?', *Romance Quarterly* 42/3 (1995), 143–53.

TIAGO-JONES, HAYDN, 'The Quest in Lispector's *A paixão segundo G.H.* and *A hora da estrela*', *Romance Languages Annual* 4 (1992), 615–19.

TRAVASSOS, JACINEIDE, '*Ut pictura poesis* na obra de Clarice Lispector: Um flerte entre as artes', *Encontro: Revista do Gabinete Português de Leitura de Pernambuco* 15 (1999), 225–9.

UTEZA, FRANCIS, 'Clarice Lispector, *As águas do mundo*: Une allégorie du grand oeuvre', *Les langues néo-latines* 4 (2001), 169–96.

VIANNA, LÚCIA HELENA, 'A problematização da narrativa em Clarice Lispector', *Hispania* 75 (1992), 1164–73.

—— 'O figurativo inominável: Os quadros de Clarice (ou restos de ficção)', in Zilberman et al. (eds.), *Clarice Lispector*, 49–64.

—— See also HELENA, LÚCIA.

VIEIRA, NELSON H., *Ser judeu e escritor: Três casos brasileiros: Samuel Rawet, Clarice Lispector, Moacyr Scliar* (Papéis avulsos, 25; Rio de Janeiro: Centro Interdisciplinar de Estudos Contemporâneos, 1990).

——, 'Bruxaria (Witchcraft) and Espiritismo (Spiritism): Popular Culture and Popular Religion in Contemporary Brazilian Fiction', *Studies in Latin-American Popular Culture* [Tucson, AZ] 15 (1996), 175–88.

—— 'Uma mulher de espírito', in Zilberman et al. (eds.), *Clarice Lispector*, 17–34.

—— 'Clarice Lispector's Jewish Universe: Passion in Search of Narrative Identity', in *Passion, Memory, Identity*, ed. Marjorie Agosín (Albuquerque: University of New Mexico Press, 1999), 85–113.

VIEIRA, TELMA MARIA, *Clarice Lispector: Uma leitura instigante* (São Paulo: Annablume, 1998).

WALDEMAR, THOMAS P., 'Life Eating Life: Food, Drink, and Catharsis in *A hora da estrela*', *Romance Notes* 36/1 (1995), 63–8.

WALDMAN, BERTA, '"Não matarás": Um esboço da figuração do crime em Clarice Lispector', *Remate de males* 12 (1992), 95–100.

—— 'A retórica do silêncio em Clarice Lispector', *Revista tempo brasileiro* 128 (1997), 7–18.

—— 'O estrangeiro em Clarice Lispector: Uma leitura de *A hora da estrela*', in Zilberman et al. (eds.), *Clarice Lispector*, 93–104; also in *Revista de crítica literaria latinoamericana* 24/47 (1998), 95–104.

WASSERMAN, RENATA, 'Trabalho de mulher: Dois contos infantis de Clarice Lispector', *Revista de crítica literaria latinoamericana* 20/40 (1994), 43–52.

—— 'Clarice Lispector tradutora, em *A paixão segundo G.H.*', in Zilberman et al. (eds.), *Clarice Lispector*, 75–92.

WENDE, WALTRAUD (ed.), *Nora verlässt ihr Puppenheim: Autorinnen des zwanzigsten Jahrhunderts und ihr Beitrag zur ästhetischen Innovation* (Stuttgart: J. B. Metzler, 2000).

WILLIAMS, CLAIRE, 'Which Came First? The Question of Maternity in Clarice Lispector's "O ovo e a galinha"', in *Women, Literature and Culture in the Portuguese-Speaking World*, ed. Cláudia Pazos Alonso (Lampeter: Edwin Mellen, 1996), 135–53.

—— 'More Than Meets the Eye, or A Tree House of Her Own: A New Look at a Short Story by Clarice Lispector', *Portuguese Studies* 14 (1998), 170–80.

—— '"Decifra-me ou te devoro": Dimensões da gastronomia ou do gustativo em Clarice Lispector', *Terceira margem* [Revista do Centro de Estudos Brasileiros, Faculdade de Letras da Universidade do Porto] 2 (1999), 29–35.

ZAGO, MIRTA ELSA, '*La manzana en la oscuridad*, de Clarice Lispector frente a *La complicidad*, de Jorgelina Loubet', in *Primeras Jornadas Internacionales de Literatura Argentina/Comparística: Actas*, ed. Teresita Frugoni de Fritzsche (Buenos Aires: Facultad de Filosofía y Letras, Universidad de Buenos Aires, 1996), 465–70.

ZILBERMAN, REGINA, 'A estrela e seus críticos', in Zilberman et al. (eds.), *Clarice Lispector*, 7–16.

—— et al. (eds.), *Clarice Lispector: A narração do indizível* (Porto Alegre: Artes e Ofícios; EDIPUC; Instituto Cultural Judaico Marc Chagall, 1998).

II.2. Unpublished Master's and Doctoral Theses

ALMEIDA, SANDRA REGINA GOULART, 'Writing from the Place of the O(o)ther: the Poetic Discourse of Transgression in the Works of Virginia Woolf, Clarice Lispector and Teolinda Gersão', Ph.D. thesis (University of North Carolina, Chapel Hill, 1994).

AMPARO, SÓNIA OLIVEIRA DO, 'Enunciados modais: Um processo de ficcionalidade em Clarice Lispector', Ph.D. thesis (Universidade Federal do Rio de Janeiro, 1997).

ARENAS, FERNANDO, 'A Breath at the Edge of the Earth: The Limits of Language and Subjectivity in Vergílio Ferreira and Clarice Lispector', Ph.D. thesis (University of California, Berkeley, 1994).

ARRUDA, MARIA EUNICE FURTADO, 'A revolução tranqüila de Gabrielle Roy e Clarice Lispector', Ph.D. thesis (Universidade de São Paulo, 1997).

BAKER, CYNTHIA DENISE, 'Clarice Lispector: Noise and Silence', Master's thesis (University of Texas, Austin, 1994).

BARBOSA, MARIA JOSÉ SOMERLATE, 'Whose Voice is it Anyway? Literary Self-Consciousness in Sterne, Machado, Lispector, and Barth', Ph.D. thesis (University of North Carolina, Chapel Hill, 1990).

BARONI, SILVANA, 'A consciência narrativa em Clarice Lispector e Ingeborg Bachmann', Master's thesis (Universidade de São Paulo, 1997).

BARRIÈRE, MARIE CLAUDE, 'Minuit immense, suivi de Clarice Lispector, ou La voix du parfum: Lecture d'Agua viva', Master's thesis (Université de Sherbrooke, 1993).

BEDASEE, RAIMUNDA MARIA DA SILVA, 'Feminismo e violência: Representação da mulher na obra de Clarice Lispector e Marie-Claire Blais', Ph. thesis (Universidade de São Paulo, 1998).

BEDRAN, ANGELA MARIA, 'Nacos do real: A Paixão escrita entre Lúcio Cardoso e Clarice Lispector', Master's thesis (Universidade Federal de Minas Gerais, 2000).

BIRON, REBECCA E., 'Murder: Narrative Experiments in Subjectivity', Master's thesis (University of Iowa, 1993).

—— 'Murder and Masculinity: Violent Fictions of Twentieth-Century Latin America', Ph.D. thesis (University of Nashville, 2000).

BRACK, CRISTINA GEHRING, 'Experiência-limite e estrutura narrativa: Um estudo da relação entre ambos em Perto do coração selvagem de Clarice Lispector', Master's thesis (Universidade de São Paulo, 1991).

BRAGA-PINTO, CÉSAR A., 'An Other of One's Own: Clarice Lispector and American Audiences', Master's thesis (San Francisco State University, 1993).

CHRISTOPH, NANCY KUNZ, 'Body Matters: The Female Grotesque in Contemporary Latin American Narrative', Ph.D. thesis (Cornell University, 1995).

COLLETTE, MARIANELLA, 'La refiguración metafórica del cuerpo de la mujer en cuatro novelas latinoamericanas', Ph.D. thesis (University of Toronto, 1998).

COLLINS, GINA MICHELLE, 'Writing the Feminine: Maurice Blanchot and Clarice Lispector', Ph.D. thesis (State University of New York, Binghamton, 1990).

COMITTI, LEOPOLDO, 'O trapézio e a vertigem literária: Utopia e identidade cultural', Master's thesis (Universidade Federal de Minas Gerais, 1993).

CORDOVANI, GLORIA MARIA, 'Clarice Lispector: Esboço de uma bibliografia', Master's thesis (Universidade de São Paulo, 1991).

CUNHA, JOÃO MANUEL DOS SANTOS, 'A hora da estrela, do livro ao filme: A intersecção de duas narrativas', Master's thesis (Universidade Federal de Rio Grande do Sul, Porto Alegre, 1991).

DAIDONE, LISA CASALI, 'An Analysis of Clarice Lispector's The Foreign Legion:

A procura de mim mesmo', Master's thesis (University of North Carolina, Wilmington, 1991).

DAS, ASHMITA, 'Jouissance and Divinity: Reading Lispector and Lawrence through Irigaray', Ph.D. thesis (Bowling Green State University, 1994).

DOUGLASS, ELLEN HEATHER, 'Myth as Muteness, Myth as Voice: Feminism, Quest, and Imperialism', Ph.D. thesis (Brown University, 1994).

DOUSSANG, PASCALE, 'La nostalgie de l'archaique chez Clarice Lispector', mémoire de DEA (Université de Bordeaux III, 2001).

FERACHO, LESLEY GRACE, 'The Stylistics of the Reformulation of Identity: Explorations of Feminine Writing as the Interaction of Marginality and Centrality in Four Texts by Carolina Maria de Jesus, Clarice Lispector, Julieta Campos and Zora Neale Hurston', Ph.D. thesis (Duke University, 1997).

FERREIRA, LETANIA PATRÍCIO, 'O conflito interno nas personagens femininas de Clarice Lispector e Leilah Assunção', Master's thesis, (University of Georgia, 2000).

FRANCO JUNIOR, ARNALDO, '*Kitsch* na obra de Clarice Lispector', Master's thesis (Universidade de São Paulo, 1993).

—— 'Mau gosto e *kitsch* nas obras de Clarice Lispector e Dalton Trevisan', Ph.D. thesis (Universidade de São Paulo, 1999).

FUNKHOUSER, KATHRYN JEANNINE, 'The Sick Heart of the House Explodes: Quantum Anarchy in Three Novels by Latin American Women', Ph.D. thesis (University of New Mexico, 1996).

GALHARTE, JÚLIO AUGUSTO XAVIER, 'A palavra extinta: A escrita de silêncios em "O ovo e a galinha", de Clarice Lispector, e "Worstward Ho", de Samuel Beckett', Master's thesis (Universidade de São Paulo, 2000).

GIERING, MARIA EDUARDA, 'Proposta de análise pre-pedagógica de dois textos narrativos literários', Master's thesis (Pontifícia Universidade Católica, Rio Grande do Sul, 1990).

GOMEZ, CONSTANZA, 'Feminine Writing as Jazz in the Works of Clarice Lispector and Marguerite Duras', Master's thesis (University of North Carolina, Chapel Hill, 1994).

GUIMARÃES, ADRIANA SALDANHA, 'Passeio literário pelo território das escrituras de mim: As cartas de Clarice Lispector e Lúcio Cardoso', Master's thesis (Pontifícia Universidade Católica, Rio de Janeiro, 1998).

GURGEL, GABRIELA LÍRIO, 'A procura da palavra no escuro: Uma análise da criação de uma linguagem na obra de Clarice Lispector', Master's thesis (Pontifícia Universidade Católica, Rio de Janeiro, 1999).

HAHN, SANDRA, 'O texto concreto: A reescrita dos textos em Clarice Lispector', Master's thesis (Universidade Federal de Santa Catarina, 1995).

HEDRICK, TACE MEGAN SUTTER, 'The Art of Having: Hunger and Appropriation in the Works of Marilynne Robinson, César Vallejo, and Clarice Lispector', Ph.D. thesis (University of Iowa, 1992).

HOFMANN-ORTEGA LLERAS, GABRIELA, 'Die produktive Rezeption von Thomas Manns *Doktor Faustus*: Einzeltextanalysen zu João Guimarães Rosa, Clarice Lispector, Michel Tournier und Danièle Sallenave', Ph.D. thesis (Universität Nürnberg, 1992).

IANNACE, RICARDO, 'Leituras e leitores no obra de Clarice Lispector', Master's thesis (Universidade de São Paulo, 1998).

JACINTHO, VALÉRIA FRANCO, 'Cartas a Clarice Lispector: correspondência passiva da escritora na Fundação Casa de Rui Barbosa', Master's thesis (Universidade de São Paulo, 1997).

KAHN, DANIELA MERCEDES, 'A via crucis do outro: Aspectos da identidade e da alteridade na obra de Clarice Lispector', Master's thesis (Universidade de São Paulo, 2000).

LEÃO, LÚCIA CLÁUDIA C. DE SOUZA, 'Pletóricos e fugitivos: Os instantes, Clarice Lispector e William Faulkner', Master's thesis (Universidade Federal de Rio de Janeiro, 1992).

LEHNEN, LEILA, 'The Apollinian and the Dionysian According to Clarice Lispector', Master's thesis (University of Washington, 1997).

LOPES, CÁSSIA DOLORES COSTA, 'Nas dobras do vestido: Uma poética da repetição', Master's thesis (Universidade Federal de Bahia, 1995).

MAGALHÃES, LUIZ ANTÓNIO MOUSINHO, 'Uma escuridão em movimento', Master's thesis (Universidade Federal de Paraiba, 1997).

MANZO, LÍCIA MARIA PEDREIRA, 'Era uma vez: Eu — a não ficção na obra de Clarice Lispector', Master's thesis (Pontifícia Universidade Católica, Rio de Janeiro, 1997).

MARRERO NEGRON, MARA, 'Savoir féminin, deux exemples: George Sand, folklore-féminité/Clarice Lispector, au-delà du savoir', Ph.D. thesis (Université de Paris VIII, 1990).

MARTIN, SUSAN DOROTHY, 'Significant M(o)thers: The Politics of Embodiment in the Works of Clarice Lispector and José Maria Arguedas', Ph.D. thesis (University of California, Berkeley, 1998).

MEDEIROS, VERA LÚCIA CARDOSO, 'O direito ao avesso: Uma leitura de *A legião estrangeira*, de Clarice Lispector', Master's thesis (Universidade Federal do Rio Grande do Sul, Porto Alegre, 1995).

MENDONÇA, ELIANE LIMA DE, 'A bela e a fera: Uma abordagem junguiana de *O búfalo*', Master's thesis (Pontifícia Universidade Católica, Rio de Janeiro, 1990).

—— 'Clarice e Cabral: Conjunções e disjunções no imaginário', Ph.D. thesis (Universidade Federal do Rio de Janeiro, 1999).

MONTERO, TERESA CRISTINA FERREIRA, 'Eu sou uma pergunta: Uma biografia de Clarice Lispector', Master's thesis (Pontifícia Universidade Católica, Rio de Janeiro, 1999).

—— 'Yes, nós temos Clarice: A divulgação da obra de Clarice Lispector nos Estados Unidos', Ph.D. thesis (Pontifícia Universidade Católica, Rio de Janeiro, 2001).

—— *See also* FERREIRA, TERESA CRISTINA MONTERO.

MUCHER SERRA, WALTER JOHN, 'Re-Temporalizing the Self: Ontological Fictions of Space-Time', Ph.D. thesis (State University of New York, Stony Brook, 1996).

MURASHIMA, MARY KIMIKO GUIMARÃES, 'A imagem e a miragem: Uma leitura do projeto arqueológico e genealógico de Michel Foucault em direção a Clarice Lispector', Master's thesis (Pontifícia Universidade Católica, Rio de Janeiro, 1994).

NOLASCO, EDGAR CEZAR, 'Clarice Lispector: Nas entrelinhas da escritura; Uma leitura (des)construtora dos processos de criação das escrituras de *Uma aprendizagem ou o livro de prazeres* e *Água Viva*', Master's thesis (Universidade Federal de Minas Gerais, 1997).

NUNES, APARECIDA MARIA, 'Clarice Lispector Jornalista', Master's thesis (Universidade de São Paulo, 1991).

—— 'Páginas femininas de Clarice Lispector', Ph.D. thesis (Universidade de São Paulo, 1997).

OLIVEIRA, MARCOS SANTOS DE, 'A presença e a simbologia dos animais na obra de Clarice Lispector', Master's thesis (Pontifícia Universidade Católica, Minas Gerais, 1997).

OLIVEIRA, MARIA ELISA DE, 'O instante-tempo nos romances de Clarice Lispector', Master's thesis (Pontifícia Universidade Católica, São Paulo, 1991).

OLIVEIRA, ROSA DE SOUZA, 'Olhares epifânicos: A epifania nos contos "Amor" de Clarice Lispector e "À sexta-feira" de Luandino Vieira', Master's thesis (Universidade de São Paulo, 2000).

PENNA, JOÃO CAMILLO, 'Clarice Lispector and the "Thing": The Question of Difference', Ph.D. thesis (University of California, Berkeley, 1993).

PIRES, ANTÓNIO DONIZETTI, 'Uma barata cheia de espinhos: Leitura intertextual de *A metamorfose*, de Franz Kafka, e *A paixão segundo G.H.*, de Clarice Lispector', Master's thesis (Universidade de São Paulo, Araraquara, 1996).

PIRES, LÚCIA REBOUÇAS, 'A trajetória da heroína na obra de Clarice Lispector', Master's thesis (Pontifícia Universidade Católica, Rio de Janeiro, 1996).

PIRES, MIRIAN DA SILVA, 'Clarice Lispector: A descoberta do óbvio', Master's thesis (Universidade Federal do Rio de Janeiro, 1990).

QUIROGA, C. CLÁUDIA, 'Conversa entre seres: Uma aproximação ao bestiário literário latino-americano; Clarice Lispector, Júlio Cortázar, Manoel de Barros', Master's thesis (Universidade de Brasília, 1996).

RANZOLIN, CÉLIA MARIA, 'Clarice Lispector: Cronista no *Jornal do Brasil* (1967–1973)', Master's thesis (Universidade Federal de Santa Catarina, Florianópolis, 1985).

REGO, ADELITA VIEIRA, 'A via crucis do narrador clariceano', Master's thesis (Pontifícia Universidade Católica, Rio Grande do Sul, 1990).

REIS, C. LEVILSON, 'Transnational Feminist Cross-Identifications: The Cases of Teresa de la Parra and Dona Marina, Hélène Cixous and Clarice Lispector', Ph.D. thesis (Florida State University, 1999).

RIBEIRO, EDDA BRANDI, 'A retórica ou ação pela linguagem em *A hora da estrela* de Clarice Lispector', Master's thesis (Universidade de Brasília, 1993).

ROCHA, SOCORRO DE MARIA VALE DA, 'O trágico em Clarice Lispector', Master's thesis (Universidade de Brasília, 1993).

RONCADOR, SONIA, 'A Poetics of Impoverishment: Clarice Lispector's Narrative of the 1970s', Ph.D. thesis (New York University, 1999).

RUGGERO, NIUBE, 'O olhar feminino nas crônicas de Maria Judite de Carvalho e Clarice Lispector', Master's thesis (Universidade de São Paulo, 2000).

SANTOS, JEANA LAURA DA CUNHA, 'A dialetica de Saturno: Os extremos melancólicos em Clarice Lispector', Master's thesis (Universidade Federal de Santa Catarina, Florianópolis, 1997).

SCHAROLD, IRMGARD, 'Epiphanie, Tierbild, Metamorphose, Passion und Eucharistie: Zur Kodierung des "Anderen" in den Werken von Robert Musil, Clarice Lispector und J. M. G. Le Clézio', Ph.D. thesis (Universität Nürnberg, 1999).

SILVA, PATRÍCIA DE SOUZA CAMPOS, 'O texto e a nutrição: Corpos que (se) comem em Clarice Lispector', Master's thesis (Universidade Federal de Santa Catarina, Florianópolis, 1997).

SILVA, SUSANA SOUTO, 'Diálogos possíveis: Primeiros críticos de Clarice Lispector', Master's thesis (Universidade de São Paulo, 1999).

SIMON, CATIA CASTILHO, 'A poética da suspeita: Uma leitura de Clarice Lispector', Master's thesis (Universidade Federal do Rio Grande do Sul, Porto Alegre, 1997).

SLAVINSKY, BARBARA ANNE, 'Clarice Lispector's Fiction: A Dialogic Study toward an Aesthetic and Ethical Exegesis', Ph.D. thesis (Stanford University, 1993).

SLOANE, CYNTHIA ANN, 'Clarice Lispector: Alternate Feminist Readings', Ph.D. thesis (University of Nashville, 1995).

SOBRAL, PATRICIA ISABEL SANTOS, 'Belonging "and" Displacement: Cultural Interspaces in Brazilian Literature', Ph.D. thesis (Brown University, 1997).

SOUSA, CARLOS MENDES DE, 'Clarice Lispector: Figuras da escrita', Ph.D. thesis (Universidade de Minho, 1999).

SOUZA JUNIOR, JOSE LUIZ FOUREAUX, 'Exercício de contemporaneidade: Regionalismo, romance intimista e identidade cultural', Master's thesis (Universidade Federal de Minas Gerais, 1994).

SPIELMANN, ELLEN, 'Brasilianische Fiktionen: Gegenwart als Pastiche', Ph.D. thesis (Alexander-Humboldt-Universität Berlin, 1993).

STEPHENSON, MARCIA C., 'Unveiling the Self-Conscious Narrator: A Study of Two Works by Sylvia Molloy and Clarice Lispector', Ph.D. thesis (Indiana University, 1990).

STRACKE, VERA INÊS, 'Uma aprendizagem com Clarice Lispector', Master's thesis (Universidade Federal do Rio Grande do Sul, Porto Alegre, 1996).

TAVARES, VILMA COSTA, 'Eros na poetica da cidade: Aprendendo o amor e outras artes', Master's thesis (Pontifícia Universidade Católica, Rio de Janeiro, 1997).

TEIXEIRA, ANA MARIA LIMA, 'O encontro do professor e do aluno na leitura de "Os desastres de Sofia", de Clarice Lispector', Master's thesis (Universidade de São Paulo, 1999).

TOMPKINS, CYNTHIA MARGARITA, 'The Spiral Quest in Selected Inter-American Female Fictions: Gabrielle Roy's *La Route d'Altamont*, Marta Lynch's *La señora Ordóñez*, Erica Jong's *Fear of Flying*, Margaret Atwood's *Surfacing*, and Clarice Lispector's *Água viva*', Ph.D. thesis (Pennsylvania State University, 1989).

VALDEZ, CHARLI BUONO DE, *The Apple in the Dark*, trans. and adapted from *A maça no escuro*, Master's thesis (Brown University, 2000).

VIEIRA, ESTELA JOÃO, 'Alternating Focalization: A Comparison of Contrast in "El protector de tempestades" by Luisa Valenzuela and "A partida do trem" by Clarice Lispector', Master's thesis (University of Virginia, 2001).

WILLIAMS, CLAIRE, 'Coming to Terms with the Other: Encounter, Creation, Consumption and Destruction in the Works of Clarice Lispector', Ph.D. thesis (University of Cambridge, 1998).

INDEX